Popular Culture as Pedagogy

TRANSGRESSIONS: CULTURAL STUDIES AND EDUCATION

Series Editor

Shirley R. Steinberg, *University of Calgary; Director of Institute of Youth and Community Studies, University of the West of Scotland*

Founding Editor

Joe L. Kincheloe (1950-2008) *The Paulo and Nita Freire International Project for Critical Pedagogy*

Editorial Board

Rochelle Brock, *Indiana University Northwest, USA*
Rhonda Hammer, *UCLA, USA*
Luis Huerta-Charles, *New Mexico State University, USA*
Christine Quail, *McMaster University, Canada*
Jackie Seidel, *University of Calgary, Canada*
Mark Vicars, *Victoria University, Queensland, Australia*

This book series is dedicated to the radical love and actions of Paulo Freire, Jesus "Pato" Gomez, and Joe L. Kincheloe.

TRANSGRESSIONS: CULTURAL STUDIES AND EDUCATION

Cultural studies provides an analytical toolbox for both making sense of educational practice and extending the insights of educational professionals into their labors. In this context *Transgressions: Cultural Studies and Education* provides a collection of books in the domain that specify this assertion. Crafted for an audience of teachers, teacher educators, scholars and students of cultural studies and others interested in cultural studies and pedagogy, the series documents both the possibilities of and the controversies surrounding the intersection of cultural studies and education. The editors and the authors of this series do not assume that the interaction of cultural studies and education devalues other types of knowledge and analytical forms. Rather the intersection of these knowledge disciplines offers a rejuvenating, optimistic, and positive perspective on education and educational institutions. Some might describe its contribution as democratic, emancipatory, and transformative. The editors and authors maintain that cultural studies helps free educators from sterile, monolithic analyses that have for too long undermined efforts to think of educational practices by providing other words, new languages, and fresh metaphors. Operating in an interdisciplinary cosmos, *Transgressions: Cultural Studies and Education* is dedicated to exploring the ways cultural studies enhances the study and practice of education. With this in mind the series focuses in a non-exclusive way on popular culture as well as other dimensions of cultural studies including social theory, social justice and positionality, cultural dimensions of technological innovation, new media and media literacy, new forms of oppression emerging in an electronic hyperreality, and postcolonial global concerns. With these concerns in mind cultural studies scholars often argue that the realm of popular culture is the most powerful educational force in contemporary culture. Indeed, in the twenty-first century this pedagogical dynamic is sweeping through the entire world. Educators, they believe, must understand these emerging realities in order to gain an important voice in the pedagogical conversation.

Without an understanding of cultural pedagogy's (education that takes place outside of formal schooling) role in the shaping of individual identity – youth identity in particular – the role educators play in the lives of their students will continue to fade. Why do so many of our students feel that life is incomprehensible and devoid of meaning? What does it mean, teachers wonder, when young people are unable to describe their moods, their affective affiliation to the society around them. Meanings provided young people by mainstream institutions often do little to help them deal with their affective complexity, their difficulty negotiating the rift between meaning and affect. School knowledge and educational expectations seem as anachronistic as a ditto machine, not that learning ways of rational thought and making sense of the world are unimportant.

But school knowledge and educational expectations often have little to offer students about making sense of the way they feel, the way their affective lives are shaped. In no way do we argue that analysis of the production of youth in an electronic mediated world demands some "touchy-feely" educational superficiality. What is needed in this context is a rigorous analysis of the interrelationship between pedagogy, popular culture, meaning making, and youth subjectivity. In an era marked by youth depression, violence, and suicide such insights become extremely important, even life saving. Pessimism about the future is the common sense of many contemporary youth with its concomitant feeling that no one can make a difference.

If affective production can be shaped to reflect these perspectives, then it can be reshaped to lay the groundwork for optimism, passionate commitment, and transformative educational and political activity. In these ways cultural studies adds a dimension to the work of education unfilled by any other sub-discipline. This is what *Transgressions: Cultural Studies and Education* seeks to produce – literature on these issues that makes a difference. It seeks to publish studies that help those who work with young people, those individuals involved in the disciplines that study children and youth, and young people themselves improve their lives in these bizarre times.

Popular Culture as Pedagogy

Research in the Field of Adult Education

Edited by

Kaela Jubas
University of Calgary, Canada

Nancy Taber
Brock University, Canada

and

Tony Brown
University of Canberra, Australia

SENSE PUBLISHERS
ROTTERDAM/BOSTON/TAIPEI

A C.I.P. record for this book is available from the Library of Congress.

ISBN: 978-94-6300-272-1 (paperback)
ISBN: 978-94-6300-273-8 (hardback)
ISBN: 978-94-6300-274-5 (e-book)

Published by: Sense Publishers,
P.O. Box 21858,
3001 AW Rotterdam,
The Netherlands
https://www.sensepublishers.com/

All chapters in this book have undergone peer review.

Printed on acid-free paper

All Rights Reserved © 2015 Sense Publishers

No part of this work may be reproduced, stored in a retrieval system, or transmitted in any form or by any means, electronic, mechanical, photocopying, microfilming, recording or otherwise, without written permission from the Publisher, with the exception of any material supplied specifically for the purpose of being entered and executed on a computer system, for exclusive use by the purchaser of the work.

TABLE OF CONTENTS

1. Introduction: Approaching Popular Culture as Pedagogy ... 1
   Kaela Jubas, Nancy Taber and Tony Brown

2. *Doctor Who* Fandom, Critical Engagement, and Transmedia Storytelling: The Public Pedagogy of the Doctor ... 11
   Robin Redmon Wright and Gary L. Wright

3. Learning How to Build Community without Following the Instructions: Finding Pieces of Resistance in *The Lego Movie* ... 31
   Elissa Odgren

4. Teachers on Film: Changing Representations of Teaching in Popular Cinema from Mr. Chips to Jamie Fitzpatrick ... 49
   Tony Brown

5. Discourse Analysis of Adult and Workplace Learning in *Nurse Jackie*: Exploring Learning Processes within a Knowledge Culture ... 67
   Pamela Timanson and Theresa J. Schindel

6. Giving Substance to Ghostly Figures: How Female Nursing Students Respond to a Cultural Portrayal of "Women's Work" in Health Care ... 83
   Kaela Jubas

7. Narratives of Illness in South African Cinema: What Can Popular Culture Teach Us about HIV? ... 103
   Astrid Treffry-Goatley

8. Pedagogies of Gender in a Disney Mash-up: Princesses, Queens, Beasts, Pirates, Lost Boys, and Witches ... 119
   Nancy Taber

9. How to be a Woman: Models of Masochism and Sacrifice in Young Adult Fiction ... 135
   Christine Jarvis

Contributors ... 151

Name Index ... 155

Subject Index ... 157

KAELA JUBAS, NANCY TABER AND TONY BROWN

1. INTRODUCTION

Approaching Popular Culture as Pedagogy

This is a text about stories, about stories that are made, conveyed, and brought to life through film and television. Of course, the characters in fictional stories are not really living in the way that we are. Still, the movies, television shows, music, magazines, novels, and comic books that audience members enjoy become part of our lives as we relate to them and care about the characters that they present. As we come to relate and care about them, we also learn about ourselves and how we might respond in new situations. We learn about how other people live, the dilemmas that they encounter, and the choices that they make. We might learn something about what is problematic or missing in our lives, and about the lives that we might lead.

Those ideas are consistent with scholarship that emerged in adult education decades ago and have become central in the field of cultural studies (see Williams, 1980). As many scholars now recognize, adults are not passive consumers of media; instead, we (re)make our own meanings as we accept, resist, and challenge cultural representations (Guy, 2007; Sandlin, Wright, & Clark, 2013). Furthermore, popular culture and media can be powerful and persuasive vehicles for helping us look at the world in new and different ways and thus can be used by educators to engage students and problematize societal issues (Brown, 2011; Jarvis & Burr, 2010; Tisdell, 2008).

Along with the other contributors to this collection, we as co-editors bring that sensibility to our chapters, and use various texts, concepts, and approaches to explore how, for its viewers, readers, and listeners – its "consumers" – pop culture both reflects and informs real-life. Often, this notion is referred to in scholarly literature as "public pedagogy," a term popularized in educational studies by Carmen Luke (1996) and Henry Giroux (2003, 2010). We use the phrase "popular culture as pedagogy" instead of public pedagogy for two reasons. First, public pedagogy has become associated with Giroux's writing, and not all of the authors in this collection draw on his work directly. Second, public pedagogy encompasses pop culture as well as other cultural plat/forms – including museums and galleries, social media, and culture jamming (see Sandlin, 2007). Our focus here is limited to filmic and televisual texts, which have been pivotal in cultural life throughout the 20th century and continue to occupy attention, in spite of changes accompanying the development of new social media and cultural technologies and practices.[1]

Research and analysis are themselves a kind of storytelling process, as scholars stitch together bits of data and ideas into a coherent narrative. They tell new stories about the topics being discussed. As a collection, the chapters in this book use exemplars from pop culture and build on more conceptually-oriented scholarship to tell stories about how cultural texts, each of which is well-known in mainstream culture, operates pedagogically with and for their adult audiences. This book, then, is a text about stories and a series of stories about texts.

ONCE UPON A TIME...: THE STORY BEHIND THIS TEXT

Like any story, the chapters in this book say as much about their authors as they do about pop culture as pedagogy. In thinking about this book as story, we would like to introduce not just the book, but also ourselves as its editors. In particular, we think it might be helpful to say a bit about how we came to this project. We three are all based in the field of adult education, but are located in different places and have different backgrounds.

When she was hired into the specialization of Workplace and Adult Learning (later renamed Adult Learning) at the University of Calgary in 2008, Kaela Jubas wanted to attach her interest in public pedagogy to her workplace. She began to incorporate film, novels, and examples of "culture jamming" – the disruption of mainstream messages – into her graduate courses. The shows *Grey's Anatomy* and *Scrubs*, both focused on experiences of interns, were unique in highlighting work-related teaching and learning, and quickly became the centre of a proposal. The story of how she came to investigate public pedagogy goes back before that, though, to her doctoral study of critical shopping as a source of learning about identity, globalization, and social change (Jubas, 2010). Before that, she explored a radio contest to ground an analysis of citizenship as a gendered construct, and a novel to ground an analysis of globalization (Jubas, 2005, 2006). Having returned to academe after working in the not-for-profit sector for some 15 years, she brought an interest in adult learning outside the classroom, and stumbled into the territory of culture and consumption. Initially feeling rather lonely in having that focus, she was heartened when she began to meet others who were attracted to the area – Jennifer Sandlin, Robin Redmon Wright, Libby Tisdell, and Christine Jarvis. At the 2013 conference of the Canadian Association for the Study of Adult Education (CASAE), she approached Nancy about the possibility of collaborating on this book. For Kaela, this project was about sharing and celebrating a burgeoning, world-wide community of adult education scholars who embrace questions about pop culture as pedagogy energetically and thoughtfully.

Nancy Taber's (2007) dissertation work explored how mothering intersects with ruling relations in the Canadian military. She built on her own military experiences in her analysis of military policies and regulations. In so doing, she discovered children's books written for and about Canadian military families. Nancy analyzed these books within the larger context of military popular culture representations (see also Taber, 2009). This analysis quite unexpectedly led her into a research agenda with a growing focus on popular culture as pedagogy. She has completed textual analyses of diary cartoon novels, award-winning books, blockbuster movies, and television programs/films based on fairy tales. Additionally, she has co-conducted several reading circles and media discussion groups with girls and women. In these groups, she has drawn on films (such as *Dark Knight Rises*, *Salt*, *Snow White and the Huntsman*, *Sydney White*, and *The Hunger Games*) and television programs (such as *Lost Girl* and *Revenge*) to engage participants in a societal gendered analysis (see Taber, Woloshyn, Munn, & Lane, 2014). As an Associate Professor at Brock University, Nancy also incorporates popular culture into her teaching, both in her classroom pedagogy and in student assignments, to highlight the importance of examining popular culture through a learning lens. For Nancy, editing this collection was an opportunity to highlight the ways in which scholars acknowledge and problematize adults' learning in daily life as they interact with popular culture.

Tony Brown joined the Centre for Popular Education at the University of Technology, Sydney (UTS) in 2003 and one of the first projects he worked on was a Community Leadership development program in Mt. Druitt, a working class and ethnically diverse area in Sydney's western suburbs. One of the strategies was to work with local groups to write their own stories and histories. Storytelling was already something intrinsic to the local Indigenous people and this approach was also developed using PhotoVoice to create a public exhibition of "Women of the West." The power of storytelling for building social connection and confidence as well as a resource for teaching and learning was an eye-opener. In 2005, a new postgraduate subject (or course), "Using Films for Critical Pedagogy," was introduced to the Masters of Adult Education program. It enabled a different way of teaching about difficult contemporary issues, such as unemployment, racism, HIV, privatization, and work. Films that encouraged students to examine common "truths" against actual social conditions, and probed beneath that accepted or prevailing wisdom, were chosen to develop critical understanding or ideology critique and facilitate a dialogic approach to understanding changes taking place in different parts of the world. The approach of using popular media and culture was then adapted for use in a subject on "Contemporary Work," so that photos of work, and popular songs became central resources for developing critical awareness. This was further developed with the introduction of another new subject, "Narrative and Storymaking in Education and Change," which focused much more closely on how narrative was used in an educative way in social change campaigns and the variety of media, images and frames that were part of those campaigns.

Together, the three of us started to map ideas for a collection of scholarly pieces that would help contributors and readers alike journey through some of the territory of popular culture as pedagogy.

EMBARKING ON A JOURNEY

We set out to develop a collection that was unique in four key ways. First, although there are other books in this area that include scholars based in the field of adult education, they tend to be based in educational studies more broadly or in cultural studies. This book is positioned centrally within the field of adult education and emphasises popular culture as a form of pedagogy among adult audience members, connecting the research discussed in its chapters to theories and concepts of adult learning. Despite widespread interest in public pedagogy, this anthology responds to a noted paucity of relevant scholarship in the field of adult education, and to calls for greater attention to this topic among adult educators (Sandlin, Schultz, & Burdick, 2010; Sandlin, Wright, & Clark, 2013; Tisdell, 2008; Tisdell & Thompson, 2007). Despite its grounding in adult education, we believe that this book can be a valuable resource for scholars and students based in other fields, including cultural, media, film, and television studies or in other parts of educational studies.

Second, this book moves beyond conceptual and theoretical approaches to pop culture as pedagogy. We acknowledge the importance of more conceptually-oriented collections (see Burdick, Sandlin, & O'Malley, 2014; Sandlin, Schultz, & Burdick, 2010), which undoubtedly propelled our work forward. At the same time, we and the other contributors to this collection have taken a decidedly different focus, bringing a research orientation to our pieces. Each chapter includes a discussion of methodological questions and decisions involved in using pop culture texts as data.

Third, unlike other anthologies that delve into public pedagogy, this collection focuses on television and film. As we noted above, public pedagogy is a vast sub-field in cultural and educational studies, and scholarly articles explore a range of con/texts. At a time when gaze often seems to turn away from "older" cultural forms toward new social media and online texts, we believe that television and film continue to hold meaning and sway for their audiences. The concerted effort of contributors to this volume to concentrate on televisual and/or filmic texts confirms that point.

Fourth, although we were limited from the outset by our linguistic constraints and needed to restrict this collection to English-language manuscripts, we were committed to including pieces from various parts of the world. There are contributors from Canada, Australia, the United States, England, and South Africa.

In these four ways, this book provides a compelling glimpse at the complexity, politics, and multidimensionality of both adult teaching/learning and cultural consumption as they are being taken up by scholars world-wide.

ENCOUNTERS ALONG THE WAY

Soon after we began this book project, a paradox became evident to us: Although one of our priorities was to develop an international collection about public pedagogy grounded in the field of adult education – something that we saw as distinctive about our then-imagined book – we realized that most of the contributors were dealing with texts produced in the United States. That fact illustrates how contemporary globalization involves the concentration of media production and the spread of popular culture, even as notions of national culture persist. Films and television shows reflect something about the cultural norms and values of the place where they originate (Armstrong, 2008). These norms and values infuse televisual and filmic texts so that they can be seen as taking on a national quality. People talk, for example, about Hollywood films, or French cinema, or British television; these monikers convey something about aesthetic preferences and directorial style, but also thematic preoccupations and representations of everyday practices and settings in particular countries. As they move from place to place, popular culture texts might be received somewhat differently, because adult audiences juxtapose them with somewhat different understandings. Of course, even within one place, individual audience members might take up a cultural text in diverse and unexpected ways.

At the same time as they cross national borders and develop an international audience, televisual and filmic texts produced in one place – often by studios based in the US – inform how values and norms are both represented and understood in other places. In short, place influences both production and reception, and consumption influences place. This is, we believe, an important conceptual point, because it suggests how globalization processes are affecting cultural production, as well as adults' encounters with one another, whether as audience members or scholars, and with popular culture texts.

Conceptual points are about more than words and arguments, though. They are also about decisions and practices. Taking seriously our commitment to developing an international anthology, we were faced with questions beyond how to gather scholarly voices from different countries, especially given our constraint to contributions written in English. As we received and began to review submissions, we saw some subtle technical differences between them. As editors, we looked over the publisher's instructions, and noted the expectation that chapters use American Psychological Association (APA) formatting for citations and references.[2] In other areas, though, we needed more latitude. For example, instructions indicated that we could choose British or American conventions. We realized that variations in such technical matters extend beyond the UK and the US; Canadian English uses some British conventions and other American conventions. For Nancy and Kaela, it is rather common to use a "z" rather than an "s" in some words – "realized" rather than "realised." And, this book includes submissions from Australia and South Africa as well. As a reader, you might notice these technical variations as you read from chapter to chapter; we want to assure you that these variations are not accidental or haphazard, but say something about how we might maintain a critical, collaborative approach to content, to process, and to one another. We needed to ensure both that the book was developed purposefully and logically, and that we were not applying standards in a way that seemed disrespectful of precisely the national and cultural breadth that we were trying to bring to this anthology.

THEMES OF LEARNING

The chapters stand alone as analytical discussions of particular pop culture texts, and stand together as examples of how television series and movies can be researched for their pedagogical importance among adult fans. In the next few paragraphs, we outline some of the themes that are most apparent across these chapters. *Doing Research* is an umbrella theme that encompasses the entire book. The others (*Living in/Thinking about Contemporary Globalization, Health(y) Work(ers)*, and *Social Identity*) arguably overlap.

Doing Research

Part of what we wanted to accomplish in this collection is to develop a resource that moved beyond conceptualization, to suggest how adult education research in this area can be and is being conducted. The chapters included in this collection draw on methodologies and methods from adult education as well as cultural studies, women's and gender studies, and cultural sociology, indicating the inherent interdisciplinarity of public pedagogy scholarship. Critical and feminist textual analysis and discourse analysis are prominent throughout the collection. These methodologies are gaining in currency and use, even as they continue to be developed alongside changing understandings of "the text" and its reception. Shades of other methodological approaches, including ethnography and case study, are invoked in some chapters. In her chapter, Kaela Jubas additionally echoes feminist sociologist Currie's (1999) caution that cultural texts are not stand-ins for people's lived understandings of and experiences with texts, and discusses her combination of textual analysis and qualitative case study. Every chapter devotes some space to a discussion of how the research question and central text were approached and investigated, so that what we as authors have learned as public pedagogy *researchers* is articulated.

Living in/Thinking about Contemporary Globalization

The book begins with Robin Redmon Wright and Gary L. Wright's chapter, "Doctor Who Fandom, Critical Engagement, and Transmedia Storytelling: The Public Pedagogy of the Doctor." They describe the social advocacy of the Doctor as he travels in his Time and Relative Dimensions in Space, or TARDIS, craft. They argue that the show disrupts hegemonic neoliberal, discriminatory ideologies, and suggest how adult educators can use it to engage students in critical learning about globalization, corporatization, and colonialism. Their chapter is followed by Elissa Odgren's "Learning How to Build Community without Following the Instructions: Finding Pieces of Resistance in *The Lego Movie*." She explores the film's satirical edge as a gateway to considering the power and potential of two concepts taken up by many adult educators – communities of practice and transformative learning – in a critique of global capitalism. These two chapters demonstrate the ways in which

Western films and television shows are infused with both promotion and critique of contemporary globalization.

Health(y) Work(ers)

The next series of chapters plays on the ideas of good or "healthy" workers and health care workers. Tony Brown's chapter, "Teachers on Film: Changing Representations of Teaching in Popular Cinema from Mr. Chips to Jamie Fitzpatrick," maintains a focus in the previous two chapters on corporate globalization, and explores how images of and beliefs about teaching and teachers are being overtaken by neoliberal corporate agendas. The next chapter, Pamela Timanson and Theresa J. Schindel's "Discourse Analysis of Adult and Workplace Learning in *Nurse Jackie*: Exploring Learning Processes within a Knowledge Culture" moves to a show about the nursing profession. It examines how that show portrays teaching and learning through clinical practice, as well as encounters with nursing's knowledge culture. Kaela Jubas' chapter, "Giving Substance to Ghostly Figures: How Female Nursing Students Respond to a Cultural Portrayal of 'Women's Work' in Health Care" explores the problematic gendered representation of nursing in *Grey's Anatomy*. Her analysis of conversations with participants illuminates how work-related learning occurs not just in professional education programs and placements, but also through cultural consumption. These chapters explore how work and the workplace is a sphere of important learning about contemporary trends and older questions of how to fit into a profession. Additionally, the chapters illustrate how audience members are set up to understand workplace issues such as scope of practice, workers' rights (especially as juxtaposed with consumers' rights), and the ongoing influence of gender.

Social Identity

As much as it deals with work-related learning and learners, Kaela Jubas' chapter takes up the theme of social identity, particularly gender. Under this theme, race, gender, class, and nationality surface prominently. In her chapter on "Narratives of Illness in South African Cinema: What Can Popular Culture Teach Us about HIV?", Astrid Treffry-Goatley examines the pedagogical elements of African post-apartheid films about HIV, and dwells especially on impacts of poverty and gender. In her chapter, "Pedagogies of Gender in a Disney Mash-up: Princesses, Queens, Beasts, Pirates, Lost Boys, and Witches," Nancy Taber explores how gender is learned and portrayed in *Once Upon a Time*, a television program based on Disney fairy tales. Christine Jarvis, in her chapter, "How to Be a Woman: Models of Masochism and Sacrifice in Young Adult Fiction," examines how constructs of womanhood are portrayed in *Twilight* and *Buffy the Vampire Slayer*. In these television programs or movies, there are many female protagonists who are strong women; however, they are also constrained by heteronormative storylines that direct women into roles as mothers, lovers, and invisible caregivers, with racial, class and other stereotypes and relational effects also continually present. These chapters point to the importance of problematizing gendered and racialized representations in popular culture, and to how the ways in which gender and race relations are performed onscreen intersect with how they are performed and experienced in daily life.

CONCLUDING THOUGHTS

In the televised story of *Doctor Who*, the twelve iterations of the Doctor travel through space and time in the TARDIS. They visit other dimensions, explore unfamiliar worlds, and encounter diverse people. When we began to write this introductory chapter, it occurred to us that this book is a learning TARDIS of sorts. On its pages – through the genres of animation, documentary, edutainment, fantasy, realism, science fiction, the medical drama, and the supernatural – stories of witches intersect with Lego figurines, nurses with vampires, teachers with HIV patients, Time Lords with medical staff. The book as a whole demonstrates that television and film reflects, complicates, and challenges social positioning. Doctor Who (*Doctor Who*) has been described as a social activist. Buffy (*Buffy the Vampire Slayer*) establishes the need for strength, connection and compassion. Emmet (*The Lego Movie*) defends citizenship from corporations but lives in a world that privileges men. Bella (*Twilight* series) is an unfortunate model of self-sacrifice who suffers domestic abuse, as does Belle (*Once upon a Time*). Meredith and other female characters (*Grey's Anatomy*) devalue nursing because it is seen as women's work, and real-life nursing students must figure out how to respond to such a disparaging image of themselves in a web of gendered, professional identities. Yesterday (*Yesterday*) raises awareness of HIV in South Africa, while perpetuating cultural stereotypes. Jamie (*Won't Back Down*) advocates for her daughter in school while supporting an anti-union message. Zoey (*Nurse Jackie*) benefits from mentorship while enabling another nurse to hide her drug addiction.

The learning themes in the book, as discussed in this Introduction, centre on *Doing Research, Living in/Thinking about Contemporary Globalization, Health(y) Work(ers)*, and *Social Identity*. The first theme of *Doing Research* was intentional, as we aimed for a collection that was grounded methodologically. However, we did not set out with the remaining themes in mind; they emerged from the work of the contributors. The following eight chapters and these themes that they raise demonstrate the ways in which scholars in the field of adult education apply their work to contemporary issues as they engage in popular culture analysis and pedagogy.

NOTES

[1] For other discussions by adult educators about public pedagogy, see Clover & Bell (2013), Jarvis (2000, 2003), Jubas (2005, 2006, 2010), Mojab and Taber (2015), Sandlin (2007), Sandlin, Schultz, and Burdick (2010) or Sandlin, Milam, and Wickens (2007).

² Referencing and citing films and television shows or episodes can be challenging, given APA's direction to use a combination of producers', writers', and directors' names, which can be numerous for a given title. All authors have done their best to adhere to this protocol respectfully and responsibly. Some titles, which authors might mention in passing only, are not included in their References lists.

REFERENCES

Armstrong, P. (2008). Learning about work through popular culture: The case of office work. In V. Aarkrog & C. H. Jorgensen (Eds.), *Divergence and convergence in education and work* (pp. 379–402). Bern, Switzerland: Peter Lang.

Brown, T. (2011). Using film in teaching and learning about changing societies. *International Journal of Lifelong Education, 30*(2), 233–247.

Clover, D. E., & Bell, L. (2013). Contemporary adult education philosophies and practices in art galleries and museums in Canada and the UK. *Adult Learner (0790-8040): Irish Journal of Adult and Community Education, 1*(1), 29–43.

Currie, D. H. (1999). *Girl talk: Adolescent magazines and their readers.* Toronto, ON: University of Toronto Press.

Giroux, H. (2000). Public pedagogy as cultural politics: Stuart Hall and the "crisis" of culture. *Cultural Studies, 14*(2), 341–360. doi:10.1080/095023800334913

Giroux, H. (2004). Cultural studies, public pedagogy, and the responsibility of intellectuals. *Communication and Critical/Cultural Studies, 1*(1), 59–79. doi:10.1080/1479142042000180926

Guy, T. C. (2007). Learning who we (and they) are: Popular culture as pedagogy. *New Directions for Adult and Continuing Education, 115,* 15–23. doi:10.1002/ace.263

Jarvis, C. A. (2000). Reading and knowing: How the study of literature affects adults' beliefs about knowledge. *International Journal of Lifelong Education, 19*(6), 535–547. doi:10.1080/ 02601370050209069

Jarvis, C. A. (2003). Desirable reading: The relationship between women students' lives and their reading practices. *Adult Education Quarterly, 53*(4), 261–276. doi:10.1177/0741713603254029

Jarvis, C. A., & Burr, V. (2010). *TV teacher: How adults learn through TV viewing.* Paper presented at the 40th Annual SCUTREA Conference, 6–8 July, 2010, University of Warwick, Coventry, England. Retrieved September 1, 2013 from leeds.ac.uk/educol/documents/191647.doc

Jubas, K. (2005). A *fine balance* in truth and fiction: Exploring globalization's impacts on community and implications for adult learning in Rohinton Mistry's novel and related literature. *International Journal of Lifelong Education, 24*(1), 53–69.

Jubas, K. (2006). Theorizing gender in contemporary Canadian society. *Canadian Journal of Education, 29*(2), 563–583.

Jubas, K. (2010). *The politics of shopping: What consumers learn about identity, globalization, and social change.* Walnut Creek, CA: Left Coast Press.

Luke, C. (Ed.). (1996). *Feminisms and pedagogies of everyday life.* Albany, NY: State University of New York.

Mojab, S., & Taber, N. (2015). Memoir pedagogy: Gender narratives of violence and survival. *Canadian Journal for the Study of Adult Education, 27*(2), 31–45.

Sandlin, J. A. (2007). Popular culture, cultural resistance, and anticonsumption activism: An exploration of culture jamming as critical adult education. *New Directions for Adult and Continuing Education, 115,* 73–82.

Sandlin, J. A., Milam, J. L., & Wickens, C. M. (2007). Spend smart, live rich: Popular pedagogy and the construction of the "good consumer" in the popular lifestyle magazine *budget living. Journal of Curriculum and Pedagogy, 4*(1), 113–135. doi:10.1080/15505170.2007.10411630

Sandlin, J. A., Schultz, B. D., & Burdick, J. (Eds.). (2010). *Handbook of public pedagogy: Education and learning beyond schooling.* New York, NY: Routledge.

Sandlin, J. A., Wright, R. R., & Clark, M. C. (2013). Re-examining theories of adult learning and adult development through the lenses of public pedagogy. *Adult Education Quarterly, 63*(1), 3–23. doi:10.1177/ 0741713611415836

Taber, N. (2007). *Ruling relations, warring, and mothering: Writing the social from the everyday life of a military mother* (Unpublished PhD dissertation). Adelaide, Australia: University of South Australia.

Taber, N. (2009). Gender in children's books written for military families: The gendered portrayal of women and men, mothers and fathers in the Canadian military. *Journal of Integrated Social Sciences, 1*(1), 120–140.

Taber, N., Woloshyn, V., Munn, C., & Lane, L. (2014). Exploring representations of "super" women in popular culture: Shaping critical discussions with female college students who have learning exceptionalities. *Adult Learning, 25*(4), 142–150. doi:10.1177/1045159514546214

Tisdell, E. J. (2008). Critical media literacy and transformative learning: Drawing on pop culture and entertainment media in teaching for diversity in adult higher education. *Journal of Transformative Education, 6*(1), 48–67.

Tisdell, E. J., & Thompson, P. M. (2007). 'Seeing from a different angle': The role of pop culture in teaching for diversity and critical media literacy in adult education. *International Journal of Lifelong Education, 26*(6), 651–673.

Williams, R. (1980). *Culture and materialism*. London, England: Verso.

Kaela Jubas
Adult Learning/Werklund School of Education
University of Calgary

Nancy Taber
Faculty of Education
Brock University

Tony Brown
Faculty of Education, Science, Technology & Maths
University of Canberra

ROBIN REDMON WRIGHT AND GARY L. WRIGHT

2. *DOCTOR WHO* FANDOM, CRITICAL ENGAGEMENT, AND TRANSMEDIA STORYTELLING

The Public Pedagogy of the Doctor

> Whovians is the given name for Doctor Who fans. In order to be a true Whovian, enthusiasts must write at least one piece of Doctor Who fan fiction in which they subvert the series' form to deal with a topical issue such as drugs, unemployment, child abuse.
> ~ TVCream.co.uk (in Jarman & Davies, 2010, p. 243)

As the opening quotation indicates, many *Doctor Who* fans care about improving lives and curing social ills. Meisner (2011) asserts that the Doctor is "an activist" who is "an example to concerned citizens everywhere" (p. 7). While scholars differ in their interpretations of the show's texts, most agree that many episodes contain overt anti-totalitarian storylines, progressive social messages, and educative political parallels. The academic arguments are often over matters of the degree to which episodes critically address issues of global, social, and political importance, or the degree to which fans internalize those messages. As critical adult educators, we set a goal to find episodes that might serve as pedagogical examples around critical analyses of entrenched social injustices, institutionalized systems of oppression, and corporate and governmental power and control.

Any study of media must begin with some sort of textual analysis. For the purposes of understanding how educators might use *Doctor Who* in critical pedagogy, we chose to analyze episodes using critical content analysis, a "social-structural analysis, derived from Marxist sociology and political economy of the media" (Hartley, 2002, p. 33) and textual analysis (Larsen, 2002; Palli, Tienari, & Vaara, 2010). Specifically, we chose textual analysis involving "close critical reading ... derived from the traditions of literary critical reading" (Hartley, 2002, pp. 32–33). We chose these methods, in part, because, as Hartley points out, textual analysis is "accessible to non-specialists ... [and] a useful pedagogic and persuasive tool" (p. 31).

We began with multiple viewings of all episodes from the last four incarnations of the Doctor, looking for scenes that were typical pedagogical moments focused on a particular social issue (Berger, 2000). We then transcribed each scene for textual analysis. Because most textual analysis holds that meaning can be found in grammar and language use (Palli, Tienari, & Vaara, 2010), it is important to transcribe verbatim with an emphasis on pauses, sounds, and mood. An analysis of such factors helped us interpret attitudes and assumptions in the text. We then looked for ways the texts relate to contemporary social structures and identified metaphors critical of those structures (Miller, 2010). Berger (2000) explains that textual analysis featuring such ideological criticism "bases its evaluation of texts, or other phenomena being discussed on issues, generally of a political or socioeconomic nature that are of consuming interest to a particular group of people" (p. 71). This chapter outlines the results of our analysis.

We chose *Doctor Who* for this study because fans are devoted; they become immersed in the pleasures surrounding the series. Television research "only quite recently recognized the full extent to which questions of [TV-watching] pleasure are implicated in many arguments ... about knowledge, information, the supporting of citizenship, provision for minority groups, and the relation of national to international" (Corner, 1999, p. 107). Because these topics are crucial to critical adult education, the discipline of adult education must recognize this point as well. The purpose of this study is to offer educators a set of illustrative examples for utilizing clips from the show to introduce, or to advance, discussion around a variety of topics related to critical social analysis.

> "I AM AND ALWAYS WILL BE THE OPTIMIST. THE HOPER OF
> FAR-FLUNG HOPES AND DREAMER OF IMPROBABLE DREAMS."
> ~ THE DOCTOR, "THE ALMOST PEOPLE" (GRAHAM & SIMPSON, 2011)

Doctor Who is the world's longest running science fiction television series. Since its inception in 1963, the program has often rendered "significant representations of the postcolonial sociopathetic abscess – the diverse but specific material uncertainties and horrors of contemporary existence that are attributable in some way to colonialism and its fallout" (Orthia, 2010, p. 209). Spawned at the BBC, and recently celebrating its 50th anniversary as a pop culture phenomenon, *Doctor Who* was initially projected against the backdrop of Cold War political ideology. Based on a vague idea for a children's "sci-fi" serial from BBC executive Sydney Newman, the show's premise was created by a committee from the drama department (Robb, 2009). Newman chose a 28-year-old Verity Lambert to produce the show, making her the first female producer in BBC history. Newman later told reporters that "she had never directed, produced, acted or written drama but, by God, she was a bright, highly intelligent, outspoken production secretary who took no nonsense and never gave any" (Robb, 2009, p. 32). Newman then appointed Waris Hussein, also 28 years old, as director for the series. As the first director of color to work for the BBC, Hussein understood Lambert's struggles to be accepted and respected by her all-male colleagues. The team of Lambert and Hussein developed a children's hero willing to fight for equality and justice.

BRIEF INTERLUDE

For the uninitiated, *Doctor Who* is a science fiction tale about a Time Lord from the planet Gallifrey who calls himself "the Doctor." The Doctor can travel anywhere in space *and* time in his space/time craft called the TARDIS (Time and Relative Dimensions in Space). If he is mortally wounded, he can regenerate, taking on a new physical appearance and a new personality, while preserving his memories of previous incarnations. This brilliant plot device allows the BBC to recast the lead actor periodically. The show ran for 26 years before it was cancelled, only to be resurrected 16 years later, in 2005, and dubbed Nu *Who* by fans. Nu *Who* introduced Christopher Eccelston as the ninth Doctor, followed by David Tennant as tenth, Matt Smith as the eleventh incarnation and, most recently, Peter Capaldi became the twelfth Doctor.

Ever since its introduction, the TARDIS has always appeared as a blue 1950s-style British police telephone box. This time machine, however, exerts a Jedi mind-trick type of influence on onlookers allowing it to blend in with any local environment. Furthermore, it is enabled by such Time Lord Technology to display unlimited space on the inside, boasting uncounted rooms, a massive library, closets filled with attire for any time or place *ad infinitum*, and a swimming pool.

The Doctor always travels with a companion (or two) – usually human – because he values their perspective and their company. He is exceedingly brilliant and, in the current series, has accrued over 2,000 years of lived experience. He was forced to send his planet into a parallel universe hidden from everyone, even himself, in order to stop a war with the Time Lord's worst enemy, the Daleks. That act left him alone – the last of his species. He abhors violence and never carries a weapon. He does, however, carry a sonic screwdriver that has the remarkable ability to open anything, measure anything, and analyze anything.

> "KEEP IT CONFUSED. FEED IT WITH USELESS INFORMATION ...
> I WONDER IF I HAVE A TELEVISION SET HANDY?" ~ THE DOCTOR,
> "THE THREE DOCTORS" (BAKER & MARTIN, 1973)

McLaren and Hammer (1996) argue that television is the primary mechanism through which "capitalism is able to secure cultural and ideological totalization and homogenization" (p. 106). In *The Saturated Self*, Gergen (1991) posits television as 1) exemplary of self-reflexivity, 2) a creator of vicarious relationships, 3) a separator of families, 4) a symbolic community for like believers, 5) a producer of inchoate narrative, 6) a hyper-reality, 7) a representation of relatedness, and 8) a tool for terrorists. Mirrlees' (2013) and Ventura's (2012) research indicates corporate entertainment media, primarily through television and film, has created a neoliberal cultural empire. Television wields "incommensurable ideological power without interference" because it "tutors us in acceptance rather than resolve" (Wagner &

Maclean, 2008, pp. 18–19). Charles (2007) argues that it shapes not only current ideology, but also that of the past. Television destroys history and stunts cultural evolution:

> It is the cultural equivalent of the atom bomb: its confusion between the old and the new, between the archived and the live, has dissolved the distance between the past and the present – has killed history at the speed of light. This is more than anachrony: this is ahistoricality. This is more than nostalgia: this is denial. Its mode of preserving the past … makes television a particularly able medium in which a late imperialist nation might hearken back to its days of glory. (p. 114)

Television is a major part of a "neoliberal corporate culture" that naturalizes a growing wealth gap and "devalues gender, class-specific, and racial injustices of the existing social order," while "subordinating the needs of society to the market" (Giroux, 2010, p. 486). Contemporary examples include Buist and Sutherland's (2015) analysis of sexist stereotypes in popular TV police shows, as well as Brayton's (2014) and Wright's (in press) analyses of class in reality TV programs.

Television is also a powerful educator. According to Wagner and Maclean (2008), television's pedagogical grip on its audience is all the more powerful because it convinces us that it is unimportant. It "is so self-reflexive, such a parody of itself, so continually broadcasting its unseriousness and meaninglessness" (p. 19) that academics often dismiss it as unimportant, and most viewers never consider the cumulative effect of its pedagogy. Scholars outside cultural studies often ignore television's impact on their students and research participants or, worse, make unsubstantiated claims of its dangers. Television's curriculum, of course, supports the status quo, fosters acceptance of neoliberalism, and promotes unbridled consumerism. It is the curriculum of a medium *created* to promote consumption. But it is also a creative industry, made up of writers, artists, and visionaries who enact a pedagogy of storytelling, and who sometimes create subversive, resistant tales.

Entertaining, engaging television stories capture the imagination and remain with audiences, enduring in their hearts and minds. Such captivating stories, with their gripping emotional scenes, occupy our thoughts and become part of our daily conversations. Romances and relationships are spawned from affinity for them, social groups are formed around them, and families relate to one another through them. Indeed, many times, they become the narratives that shape rather than reflect our cultures. Popular cultural narratives are embedded in our daily lives and seamlessly interwoven into our own developing and unfolding personal stories. Over the last couple of decades, these stories have grown tentacles, expanding into video games, internet communities, mobile apps, and Facebook pages. They introduce strangers and become the cement of friendship bonds. They are shaped into meta-narratives becoming so pervasive in our lives they begin to formulate our frames of reference.

Most of these contemporary cultural narratives depend on and, indeed, are promulgated by six multi-national corporations with goals dictated by stockholder demands for profits and executives' expectations of bloated bank accounts in the Caymans (Kunz, 2007; Miller, 2007). As Kunz (2007) points out, "with five corporations holding financial interest in close to 94 percent of the [U.S. television] program hours" and 90.28 percent of U.S. films owned by six conglomerates, "the level of concentration has reached a point that an oligopolistic structure exists" (pp. 222–223). In the US, rather than curtailing monopolization, the Federal Communications Commission (FCC) acted as "head cheerleaders for this wave of conglomeration and consolidation" (p. 223). With the departure of the G. W. Bush administration, "most of the regulations that pertain to ownership of broadcast television networks or stations and cable television services or systems are gone" (p. 223). Moreover, "there is also an unprecedented interpenetration of corporate media power, via overlapping directories" with the "118 people sitting on the boards of the top media companies [also acting as] directors of 288 other national and global corporations" (Miller, 2007, p. 16). Not surprisingly, most programming reinforces a capitalist, neoliberal hegemony of systemic inequality and institutionalized oppression, along with an ethic of consumerism and competition. As consumers of these products, viewers accept and even demand such narratives which, by sheer repetition, become common-sense reality (Wagner & Maclean, 2008). Inequality is naturalized and disseminated – just as culture has always been – by storytelling. The production output of the modern television industry is saturated with stories that support and glorify the status quo. For example, women make up 51 percent of the US population, but only 39 percent of the speaking roles on US broadcast networks (Gauntlett, 2008). Most of those roles are stereotypically domestic, and those shows that do feature successful professional women "have focused on their quests for sex, pleasure and romantic love" (Gauntlett, 2008, p. 65). Reality TV shows proliferate on cable television and "depict the working-class and the poor as (1) content, even happy, to be poor; (2) proud of their ignorance and lack of social capital; and (3) undeserving of socialistic government programs that might provide opportunities for advancement, authentic education, and a robust social safety net" (Wright, in press). However, often within genres like science fiction or fantasy, there are texts that can be interpreted as resistant; there are programs with stories that explore alternative, more humane possibilities for human evolution. By such means, *Doctor Who* offers allegories to help viewers deconstruct assumptions, question established norms, imagine egalitarian possibilities, and probe our collective conscience.

"THE DOCTOR SHOWED ME A BETTER WAY TO LIVE YOUR LIFE ... YOU DON'T JUST GIVE UP. YOU DON'T JUST LET THINGS HAPPEN. YOU MAKE A STAND. YOU SAY 'NO.'" ~ ROSE, "THE PARTING OF THE WAYS" (DAVIES, 2006)

Today, there is "a growing body of literature that explores the linkages between popular culture and world politics, arguing that popular culture, whilst reflecting political worldviews and current events, also plays an important role in producing and popularizing" (Van Veeren, 2009, p. 363) those same worldviews. Television's grip on culture and learning has increased exponentially, especially in the US, with unrelenting deregulation and escalating lobbyist influence. Yet, we argue that *Doctor Who*, which airs on BBC America, is one of those spaces of resistance embedded within popular television that sometimes provides a subtext of critical analysis, questioning the naturalness of the capitalist narratives currently produced by the Western media-military-industrial complex. *Doctor Who* offers possibilities for cross-generational living-room discussions and classroom visual aids, encouraging viewers to "take a stand."

Fascination with the Doctor

Few television shows have led to the destruction of as many trees as *Doctor Who*. The Doctor himself, a friend to and respecter of trees, would be appalled by the sheer quantity of *Doctor Who*-related books, magazines, and other paper items continually being published. In addition to the novelizations of the series, there are 2000 plus other novels, inestimable short-story collections and novellas, as well as annuals, histories, anniversary specials, dictionaries, and encyclopedias. There are official BBC-sanctioned magazines, episode guides, special publications, and comic book series. There are also numerous unofficial biographies, continuity guides, anthologies, handbooks, and compendia. Equally prolific are volumes of fan analyses, fan narratives, fanzines, and fan autobiographies (Couch, Watkins, & Williams, 2005; Gulyas, 2013; Frankel, 2013; Thomas & O'Shea, 2010). Finally, *Doctor Who* and its fandom have attracted academic interest from a variety of disciplines (Booth, 2013; Butler, 2007; Chapman, 2006; Garner, Beattie, & McCormack, 2010; Hansen, 2010; Hills, 2010, 2013; Muir, 1999; O'Day, 2014; Orthia, 2013; Tulloch & Alvarado, 1983). Scholars and fans from myriad backgrounds have all found value – whether educational, motivational, pedagogical, or inspirational – in the resistant messages found both in classic and in Nu *Who*.

A Critical Sampling

It seems appropriate at this juncture to provide a few examples of critical analyses from disciplines other than adult education. As scholarly interest in the *Doctor Who* curriculum grows, so will the number of disciplines which value and investigate its effects. For this chapter, we briefly discuss a few studies that might be of interest or useful to adult educators and learners.[1]

Scholars in media and television studies look at a wide range of topics around the show and much of their work touches on issues that concern the field of adult education. DiPaolo (2010) contends that close textual reading of both Classic *Who* and Nu *Who* reveals storylines that promote "secular humanism, cultural pluralism, and globalism," while taking a "stance against imperialism, prejudice, willful ignorance, and the bureaucratic mindset" (p. 981). Charles (2008) asserts that Nu *Who* engages "contemporary political concerns" and argues "against the totalizing strategies advanced by both sides in the war on terror" (p. 461). Robb (2009) points to *Doctor Who*'s political and cultural themes, including "satirizing consumerism and the influence of big business" (p. 222) and presenting contemporary health issues caused by "big-business exploitation" (p. 223). Gupta (2013) agrees that the Doctor deals with issues related to capitalism/consumerism and the environment, but also stresses the Doctor's "assault on the class system and privilege" (p. 45). It is noteworthy that McKee's (2004) qualitative study of *Doctor Who* fans in the UK found no such political interpretations. Fans interpreted the stories in ways that fit their already-held political beliefs, from Marxist left to extreme right wing. He concludes, then, that *Doctor Who* does not support any political ideology.

Critical race scholars like Orthia (2013) point out that *Doctor Who*'s "overt ideological frame" always "*presents itself* as opposing racist oppression, with varying degrees of success" (p. 293, italics in the original). Gupta (2013) affirms that the Nu *Who* has a racially diverse cast, but advocates for more proactivity, insisting that "what it needs to do now is to have story lines that do not blindly portray a race-free utopia but, instead, use the programme to meet the transformation of racial issues in the 21st century head-on" (p. 49). Most agree that Nu *Who* has made an effort to be racially inclusive.

Dixit (2012), an international relations scholar, argues that Doctor Who "can play a role in imagining our relations with those considered different or alien, rather than seeing them as threats to be eliminated" (p. 290). *Doctor Who* offers "possibilities for interaction and the politics of encounter" that should be studied by students of international relations (p. 292). Dixit proffers that *Doctor Who* reveals that the biggest threat to citizens is often their own government and, thus, "directs attention to the process of threat construction instead of seeing threats as external to the body politic" (p. 296). In an international war on terror, the Doctor "questions who is a threat and who is dangerous" (p. 297). As a pedagogical tool, *Doctor Who* provides a resource "for (re)imagining the study of international relations differently" (p. 304).

There are volumes written in the field of cultural studies about *Doctor Who* and its fandom, and they cover a wide spectrum of interests and issues. Amy-Chinn (2008) outlines how Rose, a companion to the Ninth and Tenth Doctors, is placed in a subservient position to the Doctor because her compassion and caring disempower her. But Magnet (2010) argues that Rose's compassion, although a traditionally gendered characteristic, helps her rise above and "even exceed the Doctor's abilities" (p. 155), although she goes on to admit that the second series "declaws" Rose and undoes any feminist progress she made. Yet, Wallace (2010) reads Rose's "domesticity" as an indication that "the programme is moving away from its patriarchal nature," and argues that Nu *Who* stories actually revolve around the new companions of Rose, Martha, and Donna, making it a "female led show" (p. 114).

On a vastly different contemporary topic, Gibbs (2013) analyzes how several *Doctor Who* storylines deal with post-traumatic stress disorder (PTSD) in the wake of the recent long wars in Iraq and Afghanistan. This recurring thread reveals the show's "commitment to the depiction of more realistic responses to trauma" which "demonstrates certain ways in which complex theoretical material is refracted through popular culture and is, in turn, further propagated" (p. 268).

The general consensus of *Doctor Who* research is it has consistently displayed varying degrees of critical cultural allegory – depending on its writers. Scholars have primarily analyzed program content or audience response with a view to themes that run through seasons, decades, or Doctors. We agree with Hills (2008) that we should "consider what is at stake when we take seriously, as scholars, notable 'moments' of sf [science fiction] television" (p. 26). There are "moments" in Nu *Who* that can represent the concepts that Brookfield (2005) argues one must learn in order to develop as a critical, questioning adult. As adult educators, we have a responsibility to teach critical theory and critical reflection "with the explicit social and political critique, and activism this implies" (Brookfield, 2005, p. 373). The use of popular culture to introduce social and political critique can help lower emotional barriers that often arise when assumptions and learned beliefs are challenged. Jarvis and Burr (2011) call for adult educators to view and discuss popular television texts infused with social and political critique to help students "consider the wider social and cultural implications" (p. 178) of structural inequalities and systems of oppression.

Hartley (2002) points out that textual and content analysis of television can stimulate discussions around myriad issues – from politics and war to sexual identity (p. 31). While textual analysis has been legitimately criticized for not going far enough in understanding the cultural phenomenon of television, it can "tease out how pleasures mix with power, emotion with reason, information with ideology, in the very tissue of sense-making" (Hartley, 2002, p. 32). For the purposes of this chapter, we will provide examples of *Doctor Who* "moments" which might be meaningful for those learning to become critical citizens, recognize and challenge ideology, unmask mechanisms of power, contest hegemony, and practice democracy (Brookfield, 2005). We take these from the four most recent incarnations of the Doctor, beginning with the 2005 reboot and the ninth Doctor. Nu *Who* was brought back to the small screen by Russell T. Davies as executive producer and writer of many of the episodes. The ninth Doctor differed from his eight predecessors, discarding the trappings of the upper class – after all, he is a Time Lord – and donning the wardrobe, appearance, and accent of contemporary working-class Britain.

The Ninth Doctor – Corporate-Media-Political Complex

In a previous work, Robin (Wright, 2010a) describes her classroom use of video clips from the ninth Doctor episode, "The Long Game" (Davies & Grant, 2006), to illustrate the dangers of media monopolies and the need for adults to critically consume news and information. "The Long Game" depicts a future where the human race has been stunted; they have become xenophobic, vicious, and paranoid chiefly because all their news comes from a single source, Satellite 5, controlled by a creature, hired by the banking industry, to manipulate the human race for its own ends. It is a thinly veiled critique of consumerism and allusion to Rupert Murdoch and his right wing pseudo-news propaganda organizations.[2]

Such commentary on media's negative effects on humankind continues a few episodes later in the two-part season finale, "Bad Wolf" and "Parting of the Ways" (Davies & Ahearn, 2006a, 2006b). When the Doctor and Rose, played by Billie Piper, revisit Satellite 5, 100 years after shutting down the bogus news operation in "The Long Game," they find the satellite broadcasting reality TV (RTV) programs on all channels, and humanity is again stunted. Hundreds of *Big Brother* houses, *Weakest Link* games, *What Not to Wear* episodes, and myriad assorted *Survivor*-type contests are broadcast 24 hours a day. Laws have been enacted requiring everyone to purchase access to the programming. Anyone may be selected to be a contestant at any moment – resistance incurs the death penalty, as does losing a game or being voted off a show. Humans live to watch RTV; their lives (and deaths) are controlled by it. Satellite 5 is owned by Bad Wolf Corporation which, the Doctor discovers, is controlled by the Daleks, the Doctor's greatest enemy. Normally detached killing machines who oppose any species except "pure" Dalek-kind, these Daleks are religious zealots worshipping a Dalek-Emperor-God and killing non-believers. The Daleks, no longer the racist fascists of the Cold War *Who,* are now the embodiment of post 9/11 terrorists.[3]

Before confronting the Dalek-terrorists, the Doctor must contend with the Dalek front organization, Bad Wolf Corporation, which controls the government, summarily executes non-Satellite 5 subscribers, and directs private security forces to arrest, sentence, and imprison citizens without trial or appeal for resisting participation in the games. The parallels of corporate media's insalubrious hold over humankind to global events in 2005, including coverage of Hurricane Katrina and the U.S. government's appalling response to it, media reactions to the London bombings, and ongoing concerns about the U.S. involvement in torture of prisoners and unlawful surveillance of citizens, are evident to even the most casual viewer.

Just as "The Long Game" is not a negative message about proper journalism, but about the abuse of corporate power and lack of critical questioning by citizens, "Bad Wolf/The Parting of the Ways" is not so much a commentary on RTV as it is on humanity's passive, uncritical acceptance of corporate entertainment media's political power. Because the Doctor broke the ideological control of single-source news/propaganda 100 years earlier, humanity became susceptible to ideological indoctrination from corporate "entertainment." Earth's inhabitants ignored corporate abuses, immersing themselves in manufactured predicaments. The following moment from "Bad Wolf" emphasizes the point. The Doctor and Lynda, a fellow escapee from a *Big Brother* house, find their way to the observation deck and stand contemplating a horribly polluted earth.

> The Doctor: So the population just sits there? Half the world's too fat, half the world's too thin, and you lot just watch telly?

Lynda: [nodding and smiling] 10,000 channels all beaming down from here.

The Doctor: The human race – brainless sheep, being fed on a diet of – mind you, do they still have that program where three people have to live with a bear? [grinning broadly] – [serious again] I don't understand; last time I was here, I put it right.

Lynda: No, but that's when it first went wrong, 100 years ago, like you said. All the news channels, they just shut down overnight. There was nothing left in their place, no information. The whole planet just froze. The government, the economy – they collapsed. That was the start of it; 100 years of hell.

The Doctor: Oh, my – I made this world. (Davies & Ahearn, 2006a)

The risks inherent in uncritical consumption of corporate-generated information, education, and entertainment are clear. While corporations make unholy alliances and engage in environmental and human rights abuses for the maximization of profits, religious fanatics and intolerant extremists wield power by infiltrating corporate structures. All the while an uncritical public simply goes along, mindlessly supporting corporate monopolies.

The first season of Nu *Who* has many moments that explore the need for citizens to be critically educated and "to ignore it is to miss educational moments when we might use the undeniable pleasures of popular culture to propose disruptive alternatives [to neoliberal hegemony] and promote liberatory learning" (Wright, 2010b, p. 249). Using such moments in classrooms can provide inroads to discussions surrounding issues of power and democracy.

The Tenth Doctor – Human Resources

The second season of Nu *Who* ushered in a new Doctor played by David Tennant with Russell T. Davies still at the series' helm as executive producer. Themes and subtexts were still culturally relevant and often critical of social inequalities, prejudices, and oligarchy. Moments from the episode "Planet of the Ood," written by Keith Temple (Temple & Harper, 2008), are useful prompts for critical discussions about equality and choice in the workplace.

Set in the 42nd century, this episode, once again, explores corporate malfeasance via abusive labor practices directed at "foreign labor." The Doctor and companion Donna Noble, played by Catherine Tate, arrive on the Ood-Sphere, homeworld of the Ood, a race of peaceful beings who are born vulnerable due to their biological design. Naturally, humans have enslaved them making them a species of servants, and for 200 years the family-owned corporation, Ood Operations (OO), has been processing and selling the Ood as labor for the military, individuals, and corporations. Ood are described as "happy to serve," but after hearing the sales pitch, Donna asks "Don't the Ood get a say in this? – Are there any free Ood?" (Temple & Harper, 2008). The Doctor and Donna soon slip away from the "showroom" and discover that the Ood are whipped and abused. They investigate a warehouse where Ood are packed into cargo containers, reminiscent of illegal immigrants who are frequently discovered in ports today.

Upon opening a cargo container to reveal a shipment of Ood standing in formation like a contingent of Emperor Qin's Terra-Cotta Warriors, Donna retches from the stench while expressing horror that humans are again building wealth by enslaving "the other."

Donna: A great big empire built on slavery.

The Doctor: It's not so different from your time.

Donna: Oi! I haven't got slaves!

The Doctor: Who do you think made your clothes? (Temple & Harper, 2008)

This moment makes the allegory clear. As the episode unfolds, corporate representatives and Mr. Halpen, the current patriarch and CEO of OO, advance familiar arguments for allowing such abuses – the Ood are better off as servants and soldiers. Solana Mercurio, OO public relations spokesperson chimes in, "We make them better" (Temple & Harper, 2008).

As the allegory unfolds, the reason for Ood acquiescence becomes clear. They are a telepathic species, born with a forebrain and a small external hindbrain, which OO removes when "processing" the Ood. The Doctor explains:

The Doctor: Like the amygdala in humans, it processes memory and emotions. You get rid of that, you wouldn't be Donna anymore, you'd be like an Ood – a processed Ood.

Donna: So the company cuts off their brains –

The Doctor: [angrily] – and they stitch on the translator. (Temple & Harper, 2008)

A third factor in the Ood's make-up is the Ood Brain – a large brain that is their telepathic center. They are a collective species by design. The Halpens have kept the Ood Brain under a dampening field since they arrived on the planet two centuries before. This kept the unprocessed Ood from communicating with the processed Ood. Educators can easily draw parallels to impoverished governments, strangled by debt, subjugated by powerful entities, and compelled to be complicit in the exploitation of their people and resources. The Ood serve in order to survive.

The Doctor saves the Ood, but he could not have done it without the Friends of the Ood, an activist group who have been working to uncover and expose abuses for decades. This hopeful subplot is positioned against apathy and willful ignorance in a conversation between Donna and Solana Mercurio.

Donna: If the humans back on Earth knew what was going on here –

Solana: Don't be so stupid; of course they know.

Donna: They know how you treat the Ood?

Solana: They don't ask. Same thing. (Temple & Harper, 2008)

Such moments afford adult educators an opportunity to broach conversations around global labor practices, consumerism, capitalism, neoliberalism, and responsibility.

The Eleventh Doctor – Our Best Hope

In 2010, Russell T. Davies and David Tennant left the program, and 27-year-old Matt Smith became the Eleventh Doctor. Steven Moffat replaced Davies as executive producer and head writer. Moffat focused less on global political issues and more on the complexity of personal relationships and individual consciences as citizens with agency. His is a more Habermasian view of what the Doctor can represent, with a focus on "common interest" and "inclusivity" of classes (Habermas, 1989, pp. 36–67). Habermas, unlike many critical theorists, felt that revolutionary change might not actually be possible, so people should "work to achieve realistic and specific social changes in particular contexts" (Brookfield, 2005, p. 222). Of course, for any positive change it is necessary to be reflexive and questioning of one's own beliefs and motives, examining one's complicity in hegemony. Moffat's characters do that in spades. Self-reflexivity and challenging one's previously held assumptions are major themes in Moffat's *Who*.

The Eleventh Doctor travels briefly with a young woman, Amy Pond, played by Karen Gillan, but soon her fiancé and eventual husband Rory Williams, played by Arthur Darvill, joins them in their adventures. Rory and Amy's relationship is a key thematic element throughout the Smith/Moffat years. Many other relationships are featured, including the Doctor's marriage to River Song, played by Alex Kingston. Interracial, inter-species, and homosexual partner relationships, conspicuously visible in the Russell T. Davies years, are normalized by their plot relevance in the Moffat era, and the cultural marginalization of a variety of other pairings is also examined. The Kingston/Smith romantic pairing, for example, rejects the deeply engrained and sexist ageism so dominant in Western cultures, since Kingston is almost twice Smith's age.

Moffat's story arcs are complex and stretch over multiple seasons. Fans can and do discuss themes across media outlets like Facebook, Twitter, blogs, fan forums, and Meet-Up Groups; however, the complexity of the arcs can make it difficult to distill moments for classroom discussion unless all students are fans. Still, while critical political allegories are not as easily encapsulated as in Davies' years, there are many scenes that offer provocative content and impetus for discussions around the Habermasian concepts of the public sphere and individuals working together for the common good.

In the episode "The Power of Three" (Chibnall & Mackinnon, 2012), for example, humanity is about to be wiped out by the Shakri, who "serve the word of the Tally." The Tally is described by the Doctor as "Judgement Day or the Reckoning." Humanity is to be erased before they "colonize space." According to the Shakri, "The human contagion must be eliminated.... The human plague – raiding and fighting and, when cornered, the rage to destroy." In fear of humanity's savagery, the Shakri are killing humans using weapons designed as small boxes that appear across the globe and are capable of stopping human hearts. The Doctor responds:

> So! Here you are, depositing slug pellets all over the Earth, made attractive so humans will collect them, hoping to find something beautiful inside, because that's what *they* are. Not pests or plague – creatures of hope! Forever building and reaching. Making mistakes, of course, every life form does, but – *but* they learn and they strive for greater and they achieve it!...You want a tally? Put their achievements against their failings though the whole of time. I will back humanity against the Shakri every time. (Chibnall & Mackinnon, 2012)

The scene cuts to Kate Stewart, head of the Unified Intelligence Task Force (UNIT), a United Nations global organization created to protect the Earth from alien threats. The Doctor left her in charge of dealing with a planet in chaos. Speaking on the phone, Kate is firm: "Tell the Secretary-General, it's not just hospitals and equipment, it's people! Our best hope now is each other" (Chibnall & Mackinnon, 2012). When people are dying in equal numbers around the globe, governments are powerless. It is the earth's citizens that must come together to save humanity. Human plague or best hope? Such reflexive questioning about potential choices for human evolution is a dominant theme in Moffat's *Doctor Who* and provides imaginative fodder for discussions about the public sphere and the importance of community.

The Twelfth Doctor – "Tell me I haven't gotten old." ~ The Doctor, "Deep Breath" (Moffat & Holmes, 2014)

The most recent incarnation of the Doctor is played by Peter Capaldi, a Scottish actor in his mid-fifties. He replaced Matt Smith, who was in his twenties when he began his tenure as the Doctor. This provided Moffat with the opportunity to expand upon the subtext of anti-ageism that the Doctor's marriage to River Song brought to consciousness. When the Doctor's young companion, Clara Oswald, played by Jenna Louise Coleman, suddenly finds herself tumbling through the time vortex with a much older Doctor, she is openly disappointed.

The regeneration process is exceedingly disorienting. After regeneration, the Doctor struggles to remember who he is, who his friends are, even how to fly the TARDIS. In the premiere episode for the 2014 season, "Deep Breath," Clara manages to get the Doctor back to his good friends, Madame Vastra, a homo-reptilian from the dawn of time, and her human wife, Jenny. Vastra, played by Neve McIntosh, and Jenny, played by Catrin Stewart, are Victorian private detectives loosely modeled on Sherlock Holmes and Dr. Watson, and are recurring characters throughout the eleventh Doctor episodes. When the three women finally manage to get the Doctor to sleep, Clara asks, "What do we do; how can we fix him?...How do we change him back?" (Moffatt & Holmes, 2014). Vastra gives her a cold look and leaves the room. Alone with the sleeping Doctor, Clara and Jenny discuss his new incarnation:

Clara: Why did he get that face? Why does it have lines on it? It's brand new. How can his hair be all gray? He only just got it.

Jenny: It's still him Ma'am, you saw him change.

Clara: I know, I really do. I know that. It's just, if Vastra changed, if she was different, if she wasn't the person you liked?

Jenny: I don't like her Ma'am; I love her. And as to different, well, she's a lizard. (Moffatt & Holmes, 2014)

This sets up the next scene wherein the women convene in Vastra's chambers:

Vastra: He regenerated, renewed himself.

Clara: Renewed. Fine.

Vastra: Such a cynical smile.

Clara: I'm not smiling.

Vastra: Not outwardly. But I'm accustomed to seeing through a veil. How have I amused you?

Clara: You said *renewed* and he doesn't look renewed; he looks – old.

Vastra: You thought he was young?

Clara: He looked young!

Vastra: He looked like your dashing young gentleman friend. Your lover even.

Clara: [laughing nervously] Shut up!

Vastra: But he *is* the Doctor. He has walked this universe for centuries untold. He's seen stars fall to dust. You might as well flirt with a mountain range.

Clara: I did not flirt with him!

Vastra: He flirted with you.

Clara: How?

Vastra: He looked young! Who did you think that was for?

Clara:	Me?
Vastra:	Everyone. I wear this veil as he wore a face – for the same reason.
Clara:	What reason?
Vastra:	The oldest reason there is for anything. To be accepted….I wear a veil to keep from view what many are pleased to call my disfigurement. I do not wear it as a courtesy to such people, but as a judgment on the quality of their hearts.
Clara:	Are you judging me?
Vastra:	The Doctor regenerated in your presence. The young man disappeared; the veil lifted. He trusted you. Are you judging him? (Moffat & Holmes, 2014)

Clara angrily denies her ageist reaction, but it is clear that Vastra has touched a nerve and has done so for a reason. While not prejudiced in her reasoned beliefs, Clara's emotional reaction to an older-appearing version of the Doctor reflects the deeply engrained glorification of youth and denigration of age prevalent in Western cultures.

"NOT SURE IF IT'S MARXISM IN ACTION OR A WEST-END MUSICAL" ~ THE DOCTOR, "THE DOCTOR DANCES" (MOFFAT & HAWES, 2006)

To understand the power of the *Doctor Who* curriculum, it is important to understand the intense connections fans have to the Doctor. Fans participate in face-to-face fan groups, social media groups, *Who*-based craft circles, and *Doctor Who* conventions. They create fan fiction (fan fic), fan videos (vidders), and fandom-based blogs. They have created their own language, *Whospeak*, for discussion about the show (e.g., squee, shippers, anorak, fanwank, retcon and the Not-We). Jenkins (2006) defined this kind of media convergence as "transmedia storytelling." Transmedia storytelling offers a "richer entertainment experience" because fans act as "hunters and gatherers, chasing down bits of the story across media channels" (pp. 20–21). This includes not only the *Doctor Who* spin-offs, *Torchwood* and *The Sarah Jane Adventures*, where *Doctor Who* characters and even the Doctor himself make appearances, but also web-based free-to-play games like *Doctor Who Adventure Games* and *Doctor Who: Worlds in Time*. These games "introduce new facts to the expanding mythos of the fictional universe" (Perryman, 2014, p. 238) as well as educational nonfiction content about history and science. They even come with Teacher Resource Packs for use in schools (Evans, 2013). The BBC produced metatextual websites and blogs intended to "extend audience engagement and encourage a two-way interaction" (Perryman, 2008, p. 25). There were TARDISodes produced for download on mobile phones and computers (Perryman, 2008). Transmedia storytelling also includes experiences in the UK such as *Doctor Who Live* (a touring stage show), *Doctor Who Proms* (the music performed live), and *The Doctor Who Experience* (an exhibition of props, costumes, and other related items). Of course, there are books, comics, and magazines. Transmedia storytelling creates a world for fans that can be accessed across platforms. Such a world, replete with critical messages in "moments" like those described above, offers imaginative educational potential for those willing to ponder it. The nature of transmedia storytelling combines the joy of discovery with possibilities for awakening critical consciousness in adults through discussions.

For adult educators, guided discussions of such moments can be powerful both to fans and to non-fans and casual watchers. It may also help create new fans who will bring their critical analytical skills to the emotionally vested members of the *Who*niverse. As Orthia (2013) points out, "*Doctor Who* is not just one of the many cultural entities worthy of scholarly attention; there is something in particular about *Doctor Who* that matters to its fan commentators" (p. 295). Its fandom is an interactive, international and expanding community. Providing those fans with the tools for critical analysis, discussion, and reflection is a pedagogical imperative.

According to Adorno (1991),

> The majority of television shows today aim at producing, or at least reproducing, the very smugness, intellectual passivity and gullibility that seem to fit in with totalitarian creeds even if the explicit surface message of the shows may be anti-totalitarian. (pp. 165–166)

Combatting cultural indoctrination is difficult and requires that viewers utilize tools provided by critical theory. But critical theory can be difficult, dull, and uninspiring to students. We live in a media saturated society where students' expectations have been constructed by the immediacy of cell phones and iPads. Classrooms have become places to be endured. Adult educators need ways to adapt to the reality of those expectations and to infiltrate the evolving transmedia communities where meaning is being debated and constructed. What people learn through their involvement with televisual and transmedia texts "can bring about learning that is far more powerful, lasting and lifelong than learning in formal educational settings" (Wright & Sandlin, 2009, p. 135). Brookfield's (2005) urgent call to teach adults the precepts of critical theory and ideological detoxification can be daunting. But there are creative, critical television writers whose work can draw the necessary pictures for us.

Marcuse (1978) advocates for withdrawing from popular culture's influence in order to see the oppression it convinces us to tolerate. In today's media-saturated world, such distance is impossible. But, as Barron (2010) observes, "the Doctor acts as a force for change ... defeating political and cultural enemies, principally those of sexism, class prejudice, racism, and homophobia, which he can observe because of his alien identity" (p. 148). Through the Doctor's eyes, we see ourselves as he sees us; that may be as close to Marcuse's isolation as is possible.

We are not claiming that the Doctor can single-handedly awaken the human race to the devastating effects of unregulated free markets, social injustices, naturalized bigotry, and undemocratic principles wrought by centuries of popular culture controlled by the owners of capital and ingrained in our collective cultural consciousness. Not single-handedly. But using *Doctor Who* moments in classrooms can help adult educators approach issues of citizenship and social action with joy rather than dread. Moffat recognizes the power of an intense, meaningful scene:

> I love a good plot, a good twist, a good gimmick, but character and emotions are more important. And most important of all? Moments! Give them moments! People will forget over time – over a week – the story, the characters, and who ended up with who ... but moments cut through and live forever. *Doctor Who* specializes in moments. (Moffat as cited in Hills, 2008, p. 27)

Traditional textual analysis focuses on popular culture texts as a whole, but as McKee (2003) argues, people do not live their lives that way. They catch bits of songs, they remember snippets of dialogue; they remember particular scenes in movies. It is "moments" that people retain and reflect upon in their meaning-making processes. There are many *Doctor Who* moments worthy of analysis. Sharing those with students can be both clarifying and memorable. That is if we, *Doctor Who* fans and critical educators, call on the Doctor for help.

NOTES

[1] For a more in-depth review of some recent *Doctor Who* scholarly anthologies, see Bould, M. (2014). Bigger on the inside, or maybe on the outside. *Science Fiction Film and Television, 7*(2), 265–286.

[2] Rupert Murdoch is an Australian-American businessman worth over $13 billion who has grown, and continues to grow, an international media empire that includes News Corp, News of the World (UK), Fox News (US), and the *Wall Street Journal*. He has been a long-time supporter of conservative politics which are prominent in his media holdings.

[3] We realize that the contexts we outline to describe useful moments in the episodes are necessarily superficial. Every episode is replete with history, allusions, intertwining subplots, intertextual references, story arcs, and intricate twists. Because of space constraints, we offer only enough detail for readers unfamiliar with the show to understand the scenes discussed.

REFERENCES

Adorno, T. (1991). *The culture industry*. London, England: Routledge.
Amy-Chinn, D. (2008). Rose Tyler: The ethics of care and the limit of agency. *Science Fiction Film and Television, 1*(2), 231–247. Retrieved from Project MUSE database.
Baker, B., & Martin, D. (Writers), & Mayne, L. (Director). (1973, January 13). The three doctors [Television series episode]. In B. Letts (Producer), *Doctor Who*. London, England: BBC.
Barron, L. (2010). Intergalactic girl power: The gender politics of companionship in the 21st century *Doctor Who* (pp. 130–149). In C. Hansen (Ed.), *Ruminations, peregrinations, and regenerations: A critical approach to Doctor Who* (pp. 248–261). Newcastle upon Tyne, England: Cambridge Scholars Publishing.
Berger, A. A. (2000), *Media and communication research methods*. Thousand Oaks, CA: Sage Publications.
Booth, P. (Ed.). (2013). *Fan phenomena: Doctor Who*. Chicago, IL: University of Chicago Press.
Brayton, S. (2014). Family matters: Neoliberal narratives of welfare capitalism in *Undercover boss*. *Studies in Media and Communication, 2*(2), 71–81. doi:10.11114/smc.v2i2.501

Brookfield, S. D. (2005). *The power of critical theory: Liberating adult learning and teaching*. San Francisco, CA: Jossey-Bass.

Buist, C. L., & Sutherland, J. (2015). Warning! Social construction zone. In A. Trier-Bieniek (Ed.), *Feminist theory and popular culture* (pp. 77–88). Rotterdam, The Netherlands: Sense Publishing.

Butler, D. (Ed.). (2007). *Time and relative dissertations in space: Critical perspectives on Doctor Who*. Manchester, England: University of Manchester Press.

Chapman, J. (2006). *Inside the TARDIS: The worlds of Doctor Who*. London, England: I. B. Tauris.

Charles, A. (2007). The ideology of anachronism: Television, history and the nature of time. In D. Butler (Ed.), *Time and relative dissertations in space: Critical perspectives on Doctor Who* (pp. 108–122). Manchester, England: Manchester University Press.

Charles, A. (2008). War without end? Utopia, the family, and the post-9/11 world in Russell T. Davies's *Doctor Who*. *Science Fiction Studies, 35*(5), 450–465.

Chibnall, C. (Writer), & Mackinnon, D. (Director). (2012, September 23). The power of three [Television series episode]. In M. Wilson (Producer), *Doctor Who*. Cardiff, Wales, England: BBC Cardiff.

Corner, J. (1999). *Critical ideas in television studies*. New York, NY: Oxford University Press.

Couch, S., Wakins, T., & Williams, P. S. (2005). *Back in time: A thinking fan's guide to Doctor Who*. Waynesboro, GA: Damaris Books.

Davies, R. T. (Writer), & Ahearne, J. (Director). (2006a, June 9). Bad wolf [Television series episode]. In P. Collinson (Producer). *Doctor Who*. Cardiff, Wales, England: BBC Cardiff.

Davies, R. T. (Writer), & Ahearne, J. (Director). (2006b, June 6). The parting of the ways [Television series episode]. In P. Collinson (Producer), *Doctor Who*. Cardiff, Wales, England: BBC Cardiff.

Davies, R. T. (Writer), & Grant, B. (Director). (2006, April 21). The long game [Television series episode]. In R. Miles & G. Rowland (Producers), *Doctor Who*. Cardiff, Wales, England: BBC Cardiff.

Dipaolo, M. E. (2010). Political satire and British-American relations in five decades of *Doctor Who*. *The Journal of Popular Culture, 43*(5), 964–987. doi:10.1111/j.1540-5931.2010.00782.x

Dixit, P. (2012). Relating to difference: Aliens and alienness in Doctor Who and international relations. *International Studies Perspectives, 13*(3), 289–306. doi:10.1111/j.1528-3585.2012.00491.x

Evans, E. (2013). Learning with the doctor: Pedagogic strategies in transmedia *Doctor Who*. In M. Hills (Ed.), *New dimensions of Doctor Who: Adventures in space, time and television* (pp. 134–153). London, England: I. B. Tauris.

Frankel, V. E. (2013). *Doctor Who, the where, what, and how: A fannish guide to the TARDIS-sized pop culture jam*. Sunnyvale, CA: LitCrit Press.

Garner, R. P., Beattie, M., & McCormack, U. (Eds.). (2010). *Impossible worlds, impossible things: Cultural perspectives on Doctor Who, Torchwood, and the Sarah Jane adventures*. Newcastle upon Tyne, England: Cambridge Scholars Publishing.

Gauntlett, D. (2008). *Media, gender and identity*. London, England: Routledge.

Gergen, K. J. (1991). *The saturated self*. New York, NY: Harper Collins Basic Books.

Gibbs, A. (2013). "Maybe that's what happens if you touch the Doctor, even for a second": Trauma in *Doctor Who*. *Journal of Popular Culture, 46*(5), 950–972. doi:10.1111/jpcu.12062

Giroux, H. A. (2010). Neoliberalism as public pedagogy. In J. A. Sandlin, B. D. Schultz, & J. Burdick (Eds.), *Handbook of public pedagogy: Education and learning beyond schooling* (pp. 486–499). New York, NY: Routledge.

Graham, M. (Writer), & Simpson, J. (Director). (2011, May 28). The almost people [Television series episode]. In S. Moffat (Producer), *Doctor Who*. Cardiff, Wales, England: BBC Cardiff.

Gulyas, A. J. (2013). *In Fandom's shadow: Being a Doctor Who fan from the 1990s to today*. Grand Blanc, MI: Deserted Moon Press.

Gupta, A. (2013). Doctor Who and race: Reflections on the change of Britain's status in the international system. *The Round Table, 102*(1), 41–50. doi:10.1080/00358533.2013.764083

Habermas, J. (1989). *The structural transformation of the public sphere: An inquiry into a category of bourgeois society* (T. Burger, Trans.). Cambridge, MA: MIT Press.

Hansen, C. (Ed.). (2010). *Ruminations, peregrinations, and regenerations: A critical approach to Doctor Who*. Newcastle upon Tyne, England: Cambridge Scholars Press.

Hartley, J. (2002). Textual analysis. In T. Miller (Ed.), *Television studies* (pp. 29–34). London, England: BFI Publishing.

Hills, M. (2008). The dispersible television text: Theorising moments of the new *Doctor Who*. *Science Fiction Film and Television, 1*(1), 25–44. Retrieved from Project MUSE database.

Hills, M. (2010). *Triumph of a time lord: Regenerating Doctor Who in the twenty-first century*. London, England: I. B. Tauris.

Hills, M. (Ed.). (2013). *New dimensions of Doctor Who: Adventures in space, time and television*. London, England: I. B. Tauris.

Jarman, C. M., & Davies, C. A. (2010). *The quotable Doctor Who: 2000 quotations about the world's favourite time lord* (Vol. 1). London, England: Blue Eyed Books.

Jarvis, C., & Burr, V. (2011). The transformative potential of popular television: The case of *Buffy the Vampire Slayer. Journal of Transformative Education, 9*(3), 165–182. doi:10.1177/1541344612436814

Jenkins, H. (2006). *Convergence culture*. New York, NY: New York University Press.

Kunz, W. M. (2007). *Culture conglomerates: Consolidation in the motion picture and television industries*. Lanham, MD: Rowman & Littlefield Publishers.

Larsen, P. (2002). Mediated fiction. In K. B. Jensen (Ed.), *A handbook of media and communication research: Qualitative and quantitative methodologies* (pp. 117–137). London, England: Routledge.

Magnet, S. (2010). Two steps forward, one step back: Have we really come that far? In L. M. Thomas & T. O'Shea (Eds.), *Chicks dig time lords: A celebration of Doctor Who by the women who love it* (pp. 154–162). Des Moines, IA: Mad Norwegian Press.

Marcuse, H. (1978). *The aesthetic dimension: Toward a critique of Marxist aesthetics*. Boston, MA: Beacon Press.

McKee, A. (2003). *Textual analysis: A beginner's guide*. London, England: Sage Publications.

McKee, A. (2004). Is *Doctor Who* political? *European Journal of Cultural Studies, 7*(2), 201–217. doi:10. 1177/1367549404042494

McLaren, P., & Hammer, R. (1996). Media knowledges, warrior citizenry, and postmodern literacies. In H. A. Giroux, C. Lankshear, P. McLaren, & M. Peters (Eds.), *Counternarratives: Cultural studies and critical pedagogies in postmodern spaces* (pp. 81–116). New York, NY: Routledge.

Meisner, M. (2011). The doctor knows best. *Alternatives Journal, 37*(2), 7.

Miller, T. (2007). *Cultural citizenship: Cosmopolitanism, consumerism, and television in a neoliberal age*. Philadelphia, PA: Temple University Press.

Miller, T. (2010). *Television studies: The basics*. London, England: Routledge.

Mirrlees, T. (2013). *Global entertainment media: Between cultural imperialism and cultural globalization*. New York, NY: Routledge.

Moffat, S. (Writer), & Hawes, J. (Director). (2006, May 12). The Doctor dances [Television series episode]. In P. Collinson (Producer), *Doctor Who*. Cardiff, Wales, England: BBC Cardiff.

Moffat, S., & Holmes, R. (Writers), & Wheatley, B. (Director). (2014, August 23). Deep breath [Television series episode]. In N. Wilson (Producer), *Doctor Who*. Cardiff, Wales, England: BBC Cardiff.

Muir, J. K. (1999). *A critical history of Doctor Who on television*. London, England: McFarland & Company.

O'Day, A. (Ed.). (2014). *Doctor Who, the eleventh hour: A critical celebration of the Matt Smith and Steven Moffet Era*. London, England: I. B. Tauris.

Orthia, L. (2010). "Sociopathetic abscess" or "yawning chasm"? The absent postcolonial transition in *Doctor Who. The Journal of Commonwealth Literature, 45*(2), 207–225. doi:10.1353/chq.0.0475

Orthia, L. (Ed.). (2013). *Doctor Who & race*. Chicago, IL: University of Chicago Press.

Pälli, P., Tienari, J., & Vaara, E. (2010). Textual analysis. In A. J. Mills, G. Durepos, & E. Wiebe, (Eds.), *The encyclopedia of case study research* (pp. 923–925). Thousand Oaks, CA: Sage Publications.

Perryman, N. (2008). *Doctor Who* and the convergence of media: A case study in transmedia storytelling. *Convergence: The Journal of Research into New Media Technologies, 14*(1), 21–39. doi:10.1177/ 1354856507084417

Perryman, N. (2014). "I am the Doctor!" Transmedia adventures in time and space. In A. O'Day (Ed.), *Doctor Who, the eleventh hour: A critical celebration of the Matt Smith and Steven Moffat era* (pp. 228–245). London, England: I. B. Tauris.

Robb, B. J. (2009). *Timeless adventures: How Doctor Who conquered TV.* Harpenden, UK: Kamera Books.

Stanish, D., & Myles, L. M. (Eds.). (2012). *Chicks unravel time: Women journey through every season of Doctor Who.* Des Moines, IA: Mad Norwegian Press.

Temple, K. (Writer), & Harper, G. (Director). (2008, May 9). The planet of the Ood [Television series episode.] In S. Liggat (Producer), *Doctor Who*. Cardiff, Wales, England: BBC Cardiff.

Thomas, L. M., & O'Shea, T. (Eds.). (2010). *Chicks dig time lords: A celebration of Doctor Who by the women who love it.* Des Moines, IA: Mad Norwegian Press.

Tulloch, J., & Alvarado, M. (1983). *Doctor Who: The unfolding text.* London, England: Macmillan.

Van Veeren, E. (2009). Interrogating *24*: Making sense of US counter-terrorism in the global war on terrorism. *New Political Science, 31*(3), 361–384. doi:10.1080/07393140903105991

Ventura, P. (2012). *Neoliberal culture: Living with American neoliberalism.* Abingdon, England: Ashgate Publishing. Retrieved from http://www.ebrary.com

Wagner, J. N., & Maclean, T. B. (2008). *Television at the movies.* New York, NY: Continuum Books.

Wallace, R. (2010). "But Doctor?" A feminist perspective of *Doctor Who*. In C. Hansen (Ed.), *Ruminations, peregrinations, and regenerations: A critical approach to Doctor Who.* Newcastle upon Tyne, England: Cambridge Scholars Press.

Wright, R. R. (2010a). Narratives from popular culture: Critical implications for adult education. *New Directions for Adult and Continuing Education, 126,* 49–62. doi:10.1002/ace.371

Wright, R. R. (2010b). Unmasking hegemony with *the Avengers*: Television entertainment as public pedagogy. In J. A. Sandlin, B. D. Schultz, & J. Burdick (Eds.), *Handbook of public pedagogy: Education and learning beyond schooling* (pp. 139–150). New York, NY: Routledge.

Wright, R. R. (in press). If it quacks like a duck…: The classist curriculum of Disney's reality television shows. In J. A. Sandlin & J. M. Maudlin (Eds.), *Disney, culture, and curriculum.* New York, NY: Routledge.

Wright, R. R., & Sandlin, J. A. (2009). Cult TV, hip hop, shape-shifters, and vampire slayers: A review of the literature at the intersection of adult education and popular culture. *Adult Education Quarterly, 59*(2), 118–141. doi:10.1177/0741713608327368

Robin Redmon Wright
College of Education
Penn State University
Harrisburg

Gary L. Wright
School of Science, Engineering and Technology
Penn State University
Harrisburg

ELISSA ODGREN

3. LEARNING HOW TO BUILD COMMUNITY WITHOUT FOLLOWING THE INSTRUCTIONS

Finding Pieces of Resistance in The Lego Movie

INTRODUCTION

My sole intention in watching *The Lego Movie* (Lin, Lee, Lord, & Miller, 2014) trailer was to find out why everyone else liked it so much. When the trailer began, I immediately recognized the song "Everything is AWESOME!!!" (Patterson, Bartholomew, Harriton, & The Lonely Island, 2014) that my colleagues had been singing for months. Although the musical familiarity was unexpected, it matched my preconceived notions of the film as a marketing tool to encourage consumption and conformity. The rest of the trailer, however, was nothing like what I expected. When the film's antagonist introduced himself as President Business, I was amazed that a children's movie would be bold enough to implicate politics in big business by amalgamating them together into the name of one villain. Impressed by its counter-hegemonic undertones, I realized that the film was actually a sociopolitical satire. It could have been a generic children's movie, putting minimal effort into script-writing and maximal investment into spin-off merchandising, but instead it took a major risk in Hollywood storytelling by not following the rules. The juxtaposition of resistance and reinforcement of consumer culture intrigued me, so I decided to watch the entire film through a critical lens.

I was motivated to engage in this analysis by a Master's course that I was completing. One option for the final assignment was to conduct a textual analysis of a film or a novel. I thought about *The Lego Movie*, which I had seen recently, and how much it illustrates concepts that had been covered in the course. I used ideas about the methodological approach of textual analysis presented by McKee (2003). As he explains, "Textual analysis is about making educated guesses about how audiences interpret texts" (p. 27). As McKee and other scholars who use textual analysis clarify, there is no single way to interpret any text, and all texts are "read" (or viewed) intertextually, together with other texts. In recognizing that point, I also recognize that, in the end, *The Lego Movie*, like any text, will always be associated with a range of possible meanings. Still, as McKee (2003) explains,

> There are limits on what seems reasonable in a given culture at a given time. Ways of making sense of the world aren't completely arbitrary; they don't change from moment to moment. They're not infinite, and they're not completely individual. (p. 18)

Using a careful, analytical reading of both *The Lego Movie* and relevant scholarship, I outline one possible, and conceptually grounded, interpretation of this film.

This chapter first touches on the significance of using popular media as a tool for sociological analysis and outlines my guiding questions and perspective. I then explore three major themes related to informal adult learning: transformative learning, communities of practice, and citizenship. In my discussion, I summarize recent research on popular media in adult education, and delve into the potentially transformative nature of public pedagogy. I then discuss criticisms of the film's gender representation and product placement in order to emphasize the importance of critical media literacy.

EXAMINING POPULAR MEDIA AS PEDAGOGY

Along with television, music, and social media, movies are an extremely influential component of popular culture, shaping understandings of the world and affecting the way in which people relate to one another. Giroux (2008) cautions that by branding itself as mere entertainment "the movie industry conceals the political and ideological nature of the pedagogical work it performs" (p. 7). Although interest in popular culture is growing, it is still an underdeveloped topic within the field of adult education (Sandlin, Wright, & Clark, 2013; Wright & Sandlin, 2009). Much of the existing literature focuses on the use of popular media in the classroom, leaving the question of how popular culture operates pedagogically outside formal education (Burdick & Sandlin, 2013). Jubas (2013) calls attention to the impact that fictional television characters have on viewers' lives, identities, "and, perhaps more importantly, their aspirations" (p. 130). Cultural consumption, then, becomes a form of informal and incidental learning, which "is at the heart of adult education because of its learner-centred focus and the lessons that can be learned from life experience" (Marsick & Watkins, 2001, p. 25).

Although Brookfield (2004) highlights the potential of popular media to offer counter-hegemonic messages, others discuss popular culture as "a device of inculcation and domination" (Burdick & Sandlin, 2013, p. 146), existing only to reinforce the dominant hegemony. Fürsich (2009) takes this idea one step further, noting that it is important "to analyze which spectrum of facts is permitted by this mediated reality and what is silenced" (p. 246). Furthermore, because cultural consumption is often so emotionally, rather than intellectually, oriented, it is able to educate as well as "miseducate" consumers in important ways (Tisdell, 2007). For this reason, Tisdell concludes that there are advantages to bringing popular culture into the adult education classroom, where critical reflection and analysis can be fostered. Once viewers begin to recognize the important role that popular media plays in their lives, the ability to watch movies from a critical perspective can be developed.

Because it is impossible to keep the influence of popular culture out of the classroom, it is important that adult educators and adult learners alike acknowledge that media has the "pedagogical function of culture in constructing identities, mobilizing desires, and shaping moral values" (Giroux, 2000, p. 349), which he refers to as "public pedagogy." It is within this continual reassessment of identity and values that learning takes place (Sandlin, Wright, & Clark, 2013), including around social relations. Giroux stresses the political nature of culture and reminds his readers that public pedagogy must "begin at those intersections where people actually live their lives and where meaning is produced, assumed, and contested in the unequal relations of power that construct the mundane acts of everyday relations" (p. 355).

APPROACHING *THE LEGO MOVIE* AS TEXT: QUESTIONS AND PERSPECTIVE

I am very curious about what people are learning when they watch a popular film such as *The Lego Movie*. When adults watch *The Lego Movie*, are they identifying with the characters and learning something about themselves in the process? Does the film challenge adult viewers to think critically about our current capitalist and profit-driven consumerist society? What can the film teach about how to address difficult, complex topics such as corporatization and social change? As Giroux (2008) asks of all films, what are the "social anxieties and assumptions that prompted their production and their circulation as public texts in the first place" (p. 8)? What impact, if any, does this film have on these anxieties? Answers to these questions will vary for individual viewers, but in this analysis I begin to consult relevant scholarship in order to theorize possible interpretations of this animated film, and to answer the questions based on my own viewing of it. As Sandlin and her colleagues (2013) suggest, science fiction, video games, and animated films may have more potential as sites of cultural resistance and discourse due to their inherent nature of examining scenes beyond our current reality. Films that use computer graphics, such as *The Lego Movie*, enable audience members to move past human boundaries and examine life from a new perspective. This new perspective may help them expose previously unexamined assumptions, dualities, and biases, prompting transformational change.

In this analysis, I work from a critical pedagogical framework, which "springs from a deep conviction that society is organized unfairly and that dominant ideology provides a justification for the uncontested reproduction of a capitalistic system" (Brookfield, 2003, p. 141). The concepts of transformative learning, communities of practice, and citizenship can be seen in *The Lego Movie*, and I explore them after summarizing the main characters and storyline of the film.

THE LEGO MOVIE: SYNOPSIS

The Lego Movie follows the story of an ordinary construction worker named Emmet. He lives in the city of Bricksburg and abides by all of its rules. The city, the corporations, and the media are controlled by President Business, whose alter-ego Lord Business secretly plans to glue everyone into permanent place. Emmet is unaware of this danger until he accidentally stumbles upon the Piece of Resistance at his construction site. The prophecy states that the Piece of Resistance can stop President Business, and the person who finds it is The Special – the one who will save the world. With the Piece of Resistance stuck to his back, Emmet is captured by Bad Cop, a police officer sent by President Business to kill him. Emmet is rescued by the feisty lead female character, Wildstyle, and she introduces him to a group of people called Master Builders. Because Wildstyle and other Master Builders are able to build things from Lego blocks without following instructions, they have had to go into hiding from President Business.

The Master Builders are aware of President Business's evil plan and they believe in the prophecy of The Special. Emmet is not a Master Builder and does not think that he is The Special, but he is so smitten with Wildstyle that he refuses to admit otherwise. Emmet meets Vitruvius, the wise old wizard who first told of the prophecy, and they travel to Cloud Cuckoo Land to meet with the other Master Builders. Bad Cop tracks Emmet there and then destroys Cloud Cuckoo Land, capturing many of the Master Builders in the process. Emmet, Wildstyle, Batman, and Unikitty evade capture and devise a new plan to defeat President Business. When Emmet realizes that he is capable of original thought and can therefore also build without following the instructions, he decides to break the rules and become an instrument for positive social change. Hijacking a television studio, Wildstyle reveals that President Business plans to kill everyone and she pleads for the help of all the ordinary citizens of Bricksburg in defeating this evil tyrant. The citizens are able to free the captured Master Builders and prevent some of President Business's micromanagers from gluing everyone into place, but it is Emmet who ultimately saves the day. Just as President Business is about to kill him, Emmet explains that every person has the ability to change the world. In that moment, President Business decides to change his plan and allow growth, creativity, and inclusiveness.

The film ends by revealing that it is a story within a story. In the film's metanarrative, a son wants to play with his father's Lego, but the father has glued most of the pieces in place. Like President Business, the father realizes that he has created too many rules, so he decides to unglue his Lego and play creatively and collaboratively with his son instead.

TRANSFORMATION, COMMUNITY AND CITIZENSHIP IN *THE LEGO MOVIE*: A CRITICAL ANALYSIS

Marketed as a children's movie, this major Hollywood blockbuster reveals a subtext that reflects common anxieties and, at times, assumes a subversive appearance. Recently, there has been a smattering of Hollywood-produced apocalyptic films depicting disastrous environmental consequences of capitalism on a global scale. *The Lego Movie* looks at capitalism and corporatisation, but also portrays what can be seen as a process of transformative learning. In addition to that concept, I explore the idea of community and the process of building and maintaining communities of practice, as well as the notion of citizenship and how it changes significantly throughout the film.

Transformative Learning

As Merizow explains, transformative learning is a process of examining one's habits of mind or points of view rather than simply rejecting ideas that do not match one's preconceived notions of the world. Describing transformative learning as a social process whereby "learners use their imaginations to redefine problems from a different perspective" (Mezirow, 1997, p. 10), he emphasizes that this is the very essence of adult education. Dirkx (2001) elaborates on that notion by detailing the importance of emotion in learning, pointing to the extra-rational nature of meaning-making. Dirkx (2001) also adds that, "emotionally charged images, evoked through the contexts of adult learning, provide opportunity for a more profound access to the world by inviting a deeper understanding of ourselves in relationship with it" (p. 64). Hoggan and Cranton (2015) also identify critical reflection and the developing new perspectives as key components of transformative learning.

Several adult education researchers point to popular culture's potential for developing critical social awareness as part of transformative learning (Jarvis, 2012; Sandlin & Milam, 2008; Tisdell, 2007). Educational support can make learning from popular media more effective by presenting adult learners with questions to ponder (Jarvis, 2012; Tisdell, 2008), and Tisdell further emphasizes that it is the interaction between learners that truly facilitates transformative learning. In their discussion of reading fiction as a means of transformative learning, Hoggan and Cranton (2015) conclude that the emotional and intellectual experience of wanting to emulate certain characters (or not) can move readers to "convert the overall experience from simply a cognitive understanding to a more holistic catalyst for deep learning and change" (p. 21). Wright (2009) explains that the consumption of popular media can spur learning and have lifelong effects, as viewers personally connect to characters and consequently redefine their own identities to mirror elements of behaviour or attitudes that they find empowering. When people learn that they can reconstruct at least some of their identities, engaging in personal and even social change also becomes possible.

The development of critical social awareness is one of the major themes in *The Lego Movie*, as viewers watch "crucial pedagogical moments occur with encounters with the radical other" (Burdick & Sandlin, 2013, p. 148) when the protagonist, Emmet, meets people outside his regular community. Emmet's sense of social awareness develops through his interaction with new peers, authority figures, and other characters, depicting a constructivist and context-based approach to adult learning (Brookfield, 2009). Through interactions with the radical and diverse group of Master Builders, Emmet is introduced to the concept of resistance and he begins to recognize the struggle that they face. Jarvis (2012) states that works of fiction can indeed "promote a better understanding of marginalised others, and greater critical social awareness" (p. 743). Jarvis also believes that the feeling of empathy is a necessary catalyst leading to lasting change in the frames of reference required to share in others' experiences. Her work details the empathy that viewers develop for others as they experience the world through the lenses of popular fiction characters. She draws attention to the fact that narratives confirming common, but perhaps unspoken or unacknowledged, experiences can illicit powerful empathic responses in viewers. Viewers may empathize with Emmet, the "ordinary" construction worker, or they may resonate more with one of the myriad other characters in the film, including the feisty Wildstyle, the cyborg pirate Metalbeard, the egotistical Batman, or the hauntingly helpful ghost of Vitruvius. Although viewers initially may tend to empathize with the characters most like themselves, *The Lego Movie* uses such a diverse blend of past superheroes, futuristic hybrid animals, and popular culture icons that it becomes almost impossible not to try on each character's perspective in turn. Even if the majority of viewers resonate most strongly with Emmet, the transformative learning he experiences by considering alternative points of view acts of a model for the beginnings of social change. As Brookfield (2009) explains, transformative learning experiences require "a readiness to considering radical alternatives to one's habitual ways of thinking and acting" (p. 36), and this readiness may be primed by critically examining popular media.

It is on this edge of entertainment and learning that great growth and understanding can occur. By personally connecting to and empathising with movie characters, viewers are taken on a journey of new experiences, new possibilities, and new perspectives. Witnessing social change as a collective enterprise, and seeing such a grassroots movement succeed (albeit in computer-generated animation), gives permission for viewers to reveal their inner desire for social justice, spurring dialogue and cultivating further reflection. It is at this intersection of the known and the unknown, the sophisticated and the banal, the studio's intentions and the viewer's interpretations, that the dynamism of public pedagogy is found.

Learning in Community

Community is central to the movie's plot, and the opening scenes are devoted to grounding Emmet in the city of Bricksburg, a truly "closed community" (Anderson,

1999) walled-in from other places. Viewers are bombarded by the homogeneity of everyone in Emmet's community, as he begins his day by reading instructions such as "How to Fit In, Have Everybody Like You, and Always Be Happy!" (Lin et al., 2014). The instructions on fitting in and being happy continue: "Enjoy popular music ... Drink overpriced coffee ... Always root for the local sports team." Corporate culture dictates that the citizens of Bricksburg purchase manufactured products that conform to hegemonic norms. The Octan Corporation has a monopoly in Bricksburg, and its effects on community typify Giroux's (2011) description that "dominant media largely function as a moral anaesthesia and political firewall that legitimate a ruthless and fraudulent free-market system" (p. 12). Difference is not tolerated there, as everyone is instructed to destroy anything that looks weird, and the opening scenes show construction workers knocking down several old Victorian-style buildings with flourish.

In Bricksburg, behaviour is enforced by totalitarian rule masquerading as democracy. President Business, the owner of the Octan Corporation and the world, whispers an aside during a commercial that reminds everyone to "Follow the instructions or you'll be put to sleep" (Lin et al., 2014). This euphemism for capital punishment alerts the audience to the potential danger embodied by President Business. Mass communication is monopolized by the Octan Corporation. Reminiscent of Orwell's (1949) novel *1984,* several street signs indicate the presence of government surveillance, including, "Conform – It's the norm!", "Color inside the lines," and the blatantly obvious, "I've got my eye on you!" (Lin et al., 2014). This community is completely defined by its hypercapitalistic consumer culture. It typifies Giroux's (2011) view of today's society as increasingly market-driven and privatized, focused on consumption and conformity as indicators of belonging.

The Lego Movie soon begins to poke holes in the usual narrative promoting "commodity consumption as the preeminent measure of success and happiness" (Wright, 2010, p. 50). When Emmet sees Wildstyle for the first time, he consults his instructions and decides that he must report this event because it is weird. After stumbling and falling down a hole, Emmet sees the Piece of Resistance – the very thing that Wildstyle is there to find – but is unsure of what to do. The Piece of Resistance glows and beckons him to come closer, which Emmet does, literally stepping on an instruction that says not to touch strange pieces. When Emmet awakens in the police station, Bad Cop reveals President Business's plan. Confused by what Bad Cop is saying, Emmet responds, "President Business is going to end the world? But he's such a good guy! And Octan, they make good stuff! Music, dairy products, coffee, TV shows, surveillance systems, all history books, voting machines – wait a minute" (Lin et al., 2014).

Indeed, President Business intends to end or, at least, curtail the world, by keeping Bricksburg in permanent stasis. Mistakenly believing that Emmet is The Special, Wildstyle arrives just in time to free him. During their escape, Emmet realizes that they are about to leave the walled city of Bricksburg. He shouts, "I can't do this! That is against the instructions!" (Lin et al., 2014). Although Wildstyle now realizes that Emmet is not The Special, it is too late to stop and, together, they break through the wall to other communities.

Wildstyle takes Emmet through many diverse communities on their way to Cloud Cuckoo Land, which operates in total contrast to Emmet's closed community. He expresses his nervousness by stating, "So, there's no signs or anything. How does anyone know what not to do?" (Lin et al., 2014). Emmet is clearly struggling with what Jarvis (2006) calls "disjuncture." While watching Emmet's struggle, viewers are reminded that freeing oneself from existing paradigms is often a difficult and complex process (Jarvis, 2006; Marsick & Watkins, 2001). Although each new character Emmet meets offers different perspectives and opportunities for learning, his mind remains trapped by the totalitarianism of Bricksburg, until he reaches Cloud Cuckoo Land. In that open and seemingly anarchic world, Emmet is presented with a new concept of community, which engages him in new learning. As Unikitty explains to him, "Here in Cloud Cuckoo Land, there are no rules! There's no government, no babysitters, no bedtimes, no frownie faces, no bushy moustaches, and no negativity of any kind!" (Lin et al., 2014). Noting that every example in Unikitty's statement is hypocritically negative, Wildstyle reminds viewers to listen carefully and think critically, regardless of the enthusiasm with which promises of freedom are demanded or delivered. Perhaps a community totally lacking in rules is neither technically possible nor socially ideal. Emmet is beginning to understand that, as communities become more open and organic, personal choice becomes a powerful new imperative, at the same time as it remains limited by collective interests and forces (Anderson, 1999).

Communities of practice as a space for critical learning. Clearly, Emmet learns various lessons as he encounters and engages with different sorts of communities. In *The Lego Movie*, community is an obvious site of learning. The community of practice (Wenger, 1998) is one model of learning community that becomes evident and important in the film.

A community of practice is formed as a result of collective learning that is "created over time by the sustained pursuit of a shared enterprise" (Wenger, 1998, p. 45). Their members "decide what they need to learn, what it takes to be a full participant, and how newcomers should be introduced to the community" (Wenger, 1998, p. 234), and learn and construct a sense of identity as community members through their community-based practice. Most obviously, community of practice is exemplified by the Master Builders, who demonstrate all three elements that Wenger outlines: joint enterprise, mutual engagement, and shared repertoire. In addition to their shared construction expertise and practice, the Master Builders establish a common focus on learning how to defeat President Business. Mutual engagement is illustrated when all of them convene to discuss their past experiences with President Business in order to learn from one another.

An important concept within this model is "legitimate peripheral participation," described as "the process by which newcomers become a part of a community of practice" (Lave & Wegner, 1991, p. 29). Focusing on the situated learning made possible by an apprentice-type scenario, newcomers to a community of practice spend some time on its periphery, gradually moving toward the centre as they develop knowledge, belonging, and expertise. In *The Lego Movie*, Vitruvius attempts to train Emmet before introducing him to the community of Master Builders, but Bad Cop suddenly appears and they have to flee. The normal process of movement from periphery to centre is pre-empted for Emmet. When he arrives at the Master Builders' secret headquarters in Cloud Cuckoo Land, Vitruvius pushes him into the centre of the group. As Wenger (1998) might predict, viewers witness the intensely fearful reaction of a newcomer unprepared to join a community of practice, alongside the annoyance and apathy of the old-timers in response to the newcomer's naiveté.

Just moments after meeting this community of practice, Emmet witnesses the capture of most of the Master Builders and the total destruction of Cloud Cuckoo Land. Emmet and a few others manage to escape, but they become stranded at sea. When the chance of rescue seems hopeless, a Master Builder named Metalbeard notices something strange in the water and returns to investigate. What captures Metalbeard's attention is the fantastical made real, the product of the first original thought that Emmet ever had: a floating double-decker couch. Because it looks like nothing they would expect to see, this couch is ignored by the micromanagers sent out by President Business, enabling the surviving Master Builders to hide in it and avoid being captured. While some previously considered Emmet's original ideas "so dumb and bad that no one could ever think that they could possibly be useful" (Lin et al., 2014), his fresh perspective as a newcomer enables the old-timers in the community of practice to regroup and continue working together to save the world. This suggests one short-coming of the community of practice model that others comment on: the possibility that newcomers might have something to teach experts (Fuller, Hodkinson, Hodkinson, & Unwin, 2005).

It is at this moment that Emmet becomes a fully engaged member of the community of practice, exemplifying the element of mutuality (Wegner, 1998). The film's ending thus beautifully illustrates the importance of both expert practitioners and novice innovators to a thriving community of practice. As Wegner (1998) states, the boundaries between communities of practice and the outside world "are the likely locus of the production of radically new knowledge" (p. 254). This powerful combination of expertise and innovative thinking is apparent at the end of the film when the Master Builders are working alongside the citizens of Bricksburg, disassembling existing structures and scavenging pieces to build new ones.

Wenger (1998) states that "the formation of a community of practice is also the negotiation of identities" (p. 149), and viewers may recognize that Emmet helps the Master Builders redefine their identities as well. Emmet's suggestions augment the creative expertise of the Master Builders by demonstrating innovative ways to relate to one another and work together as a team. Because practice is always changing, Wenger (1998) emphasizes that "in a world that is not predictable, improvisation and innovation are more than desirable, they are essential" (p. 233). In the final scene, when Emmet is about to be killed, he improvises and flips the script when he says to President Business,

> You don't have to be the bad guy. You are the most talented, most interesting, and most extraordinary person in the universe. And you are capable of amazing things because you are The Special. And so am I. And so is everyone." (Lin et al., 2014)

Emmet is able to move from surface learning in a superficial community to deep learning and critical consciousness as a champion of social change. Emmet reminds viewers that, "Right now, it's about you. And you – still – can change everything" (Lin et al., 2014). With its main characters working together as social activists in the spirit of community, the film ends on a happy note with the people of Bricksburg rescued and the metanarrative dispute between father and son resolved. *The Lego Movie* is a fantastic exploration of the creation of communities of practice through Emmet's eyes. For viewers thinking about joining or creating communities of practice, the film "highlights the importance of finding the dynamic set of communities they should belong to – centrally and peripherally – and to fashion a meaningful trajectory through these communities over time" (Wenger, 2000, p. 243).

Redefining Citizenship

Central characters in *The Lego Movie* are not just members of a community of practice; they are also citizens. The film acts as a narrative telling Emmet's story of growth and his realization that citizenship involves being critical and engaged. His law-abiding nature in the beginning of the film embodies a personally responsible citizen, one who follows the rules without question. Emmet's everyday life in Bricksburg is a perfect example of passive citizenship encouraged by the capitalistic, consumer-based lifestyle currently supported by neoliberal hegemony. In Jarvis's (2008) discussion of the consumer society, he points out that corporations create advertising using psychological techniques intentionally designed to "create situations in which all people learn to desire commodities themselves, especially children" (p. 20). Furthermore, the depth of citizenship tends to decrease as consumption increases, to the point where citizenship becomes "little more than electing those who will manage that state, and receiving whatever goods and services it provides" (Jarvis, 2002, p. 8). The authoritative order enforced from above and the almost irritatingly happy consent delivered from below is emphasized repeatedly in the movie's opening scenes. Viewers may immediately recognize themselves when they see Emmett being a good consumer citizen by waiting in line to buy overpriced take-out coffee. This scene typifies the "hegemonic idea that shopping and consumption are expressions of democracy" (Jubas, 2012, p. 68), but Emmet seems ignorant of any problematic notions contained therein. Early in the film, Emmet starts to question one of the messages he hears on television, but then a "sitcom" comes on and Emmet falls off the couch laughing. He pauses momentarily to ask himself, "What was I just thinking?" then decides, "Uh, I don't care" (Lin et al., 2014).

Emmet's transformative growth as a citizen begins when Wildstyle explains to him that before President Business took control, people moved freely between the worlds and they could build anything they wanted. Obsessed with order, President Business built walls to separate the people of the universe and he hired Bad Cop to capture all of the creative Master Builders who are able to build things without instructions. Emmet must unlearn that he is "just a regular, normal, ordinary guy" (Lin et al., 2014) without any original ideas, and begin thinking of himself as The Special – the one with the creativity and ability to save the world. Although Wildstyle doubts that Emmet is The Special, she does bring him to Vitruvius, the blind wizard who told her about the prophecy. When Wildstyle gets upset and exclaims that Emmet will never be a Master Builder, Vitruvius counters, "Of course not. Not if you keep telling him he can't. He needs to see that he can" (Lin et al., 2014). The inner strength Emmet needs in order to transform into a participatory citizen is repeatedly bolstered by Vitruvius. Once he recognizes that he is actually capable of having original thoughts, Emmet begins to take on a leadership role within the larger group of Master Builders. In that regard, his process resembles Brookfield's (2010) explanation that the first step towards democracy involves "acknowledging that anyone is as likely to make a valuable contribution to the community as anyone else" (p. 9). Furthermore, Emmet's learning about active citizenship parallels Brookfield's (2009) description of adult development that "entails people resisting dominant ideology and confronting structures that systematically diminish them" (p. 31).

At this point, audience members are also challenged to examine the concept of The Special critically. After all, for people concerned about equity and freedom, the entire idea that some citizens are special is problematic. The notion of a chosen one is a theme depicted in several popular media texts, including such films as *Star Wars, The Matrix,* and *Harry Potter*, as well as televisions shows like *Buffy the Vampire Slayer*. In *The Lego Movie*, The Special is prophesied to be "the greatest, most interesting, most important person of all times" (Lin et al., 2014). It is almost as if the idea of being a chosen one confers some special citizenship status, which places one above the law or removed from regular democratic and community participation. Although Emmet does not show any immediate, drastic personality changes due to his new title and unique position, viewers may observe the long-term effects of such perceived self-importance in other characters. Batman's character is shown as shockingly narcissistic and selfish, prompting viewers to wonder if individuality is often gained by sacrificing commonality with other citizens. Obsessed with his looks, his music, and his car, Batman cannot deviate from his personal script of what it means to be a superhero with privileged citizenship status. Even when several lead characters are desperately trying to build a submarine to escape Bad Cop, Batman insists on only using black Lego pieces to build his section. In the same moment, other characters demonstrate a similar lack of commitment to the collective interest or practice. Unikitty only wants pink pieces and Wildstyle simply refuses to cooperate with Emmet's idea for a collaborative escape plan. Emmet gets so frustrated by the lack of concerted effort that he exclaims, "You're all so talented and imaginative, but you can't work together as a team" (Lin et al., 2014). Here we see how even these fictional characters are touched by neoliberalism, which rejects the idea of obligation to the collective. In these examples, traditional liberal rights claims are reduced to matters of ego and personal, often superficial, preferences, and come into tension with some core values of both communities of practice and democratic citizenship.

As it nears its end, the film deals with the question of specialness when Vitruvius, mortally wounded in the battle with Bad Cop and President Business, admits to Emmet that he made up the prophecy and there is no such thing as The Special. With his new identity stripped away, his initial sense of belonging lost, and his goal seemingly out of reach, Emmet begins to express his grief for causing the death of Vitruvius and the destruction of Cloud Cuckoo Land. Wildstyle tells Emmet that she believes in him and he can still save the universe. Bolstered by her encouragement and freed from the pressure of acting like his preconceived notion of The Special, Emmet blossoms into a creative and effective citizen. Recharged by Emmet's new enthusiasm, Wildstyle comes up with a radical plan for collective action to fight injustice and effect social change. Taking over Octan Corporation's television studio, she broadcasts a message to the citizens of Bricksburg and asks them to become groundbreakers, to build whatever pops into their minds, and to fight back against President Business. Recognizing the potential of the media to offer "the rudiments of a formative culture that fosters justice, compassion, and a concern for others" (Giroux, 2011, p. 15), Wildstyle uses television to reach out to people and encourage them to do their part in realizing a new vision of community life.

The next scene opens with a shout of, "Look! It's the citizens!" (Lin et al., 2014) and the movie reaches its climax with a powerful soundtrack encouraging a rush of emotion. Viewers can then delight in the power and creativity of ordinary citizens fighting back against corporate control in a wondrous display of Lego ingenuity, in the name of active engagement and creation of democracy. Like any site of meaningful democracy, this changed Bricksburg is a place where disagreement is possible. As Giroux (2011) states, "democracy thrives on dissent" (p. 19) an idea that seems like an obvious answer to today's trend towards a "culture of deepening collective cynicism" (p. 19). It is both within this fictional movie itself and the informal discussions amongst its viewers that the potential for "the development and mobilization of counterhegemonic learning" (Burdick & Sandlin, 2013, p. 143) occurs. As Brookfield (2009) explains, "this is a developmental project, inevitably bound up with helping people realize common interests, reject the privatized, competitive ethic of capitalism, and prevent the emergence of inherited privilege" (p. 38).

LEARNING HOW TO BUILD COMMUNITY WITHOUT FOLLOWING THE INSTRUCTIONS

BEYOND AWESOMENESS

For Emmet, everything really is awesome. For those able to think critically even while watching amazing computer-generated imagery that mimics stop motion animation, a few things might stand out as being not so awesome after all. Here I would like to trouble the gender inequalities and rampant commercialism that are reinforced subtly but consistently throughout *The Lego Movie*.

Audience members may wonder why the story is told through Emmet's eyes, given that he finds the Piece of Resistance by accident and, in doing so, basically prevents Wildstyle from becoming The Special herself. This point leads me to question the film's overall lack of female characters, and Hollywood's chronic inability to portray gender ratios accurately. Although women are not a minority in terms of population, they are often treated as such in film, especially when it comes to representing heroes or other strong characters. In what appears to be a misguided effort to counter the more sexist and stereotypically demure feminine roles of the past (Jarvis, 2012), the token female role in children's movies today is often depicted as lively, feisty, and somewhat aggressive. Magowan (2013) suggests that what is known as the "Smurfette Principle," whereby children's films only script one or two female characters amongst a multitude of males, has now evolved into what she calls the "Minority Feisty." The Minority Feisty character is embodied by Wildstyle, an aggressive and talented female who seems like somebody who could have the starring role in the film, but does not. Wildstyle's primary role in the movie is to help the lead male role, Emmet, become The Special. Her secondary role is to serve as girlfriend to Batman, who misunderstands and ignores her.

Aside from Wildstyle, there are only two other female characters with speaking lines in *The Lego Movie*. Wonder Woman has two lines and, although Unikitty has several, she is a non-human hybrid animal. When some of the Master Builders reassemble after the destruction of Cloud Cuckoo Land, Vitruvius greets them all by name, but says to the lone female Master Builder, "Wonder Woman, I had no idea you'd be here" (Lin et al., 2014). The tendency to downplay the female characters' centrality or value is juxtaposed with their occasional importance. For example, during one of the final battle scenes, when Emmet is trapped and facing death once more, it is yet again a female character who rescues him.

The reinforcement of traditional gender relations and the overall lack of female characters in the film suggest residual effects of Lego's masculinised marketing strategies from the 1980s (Braizaz, 2013), which seem to be exacerbated by its two young male writer-directors. The directors may have acknowledged their implicit gender bias at the end of the film when all is good in Emmet's world and the boy in the metanarrative has reconciled with his father. After a nice hug and a particularly touching moment, the father says to his son, "Now that I'm letting you come down here and play, guess who else gets to come down here and play?...Your sister" (Lin et al., 2014). I would be surprised if gender bias is not something that they try to remedy in the sequel. This is Hollywood after all; there is always a sequel.

Even with tales of radical societal change, including the defeat of a capitalist tyrant, *The Lego Movie* is still Hollywood's version of a 101-minute toy commercial. Continuous product placement in a film that criticizes consumerism is so overtly hypocritical that it almost becomes distracting for the viewer. Even within the film when Batman suggests building a bat submarine, he quickly adds the words "patent pending" to protect his property rights. Aside from the obvious use of Lego toys with the accompanying movie and television tie-ins, the film also uses a seemingly random assortment of products including Krazy Glue®, Band-Aid®, Q-Tips®, Titleist®, iPod Shuffle®, and X-ACTO® utility knives. These products are used humourously since they are all considered relics from the human world and President Business consistently mispronounces their brand names without realizing it. This running joke may be tacitly informing the audience that anyone who does not recognize these products is an ignorant fool. The added fact that all of these items are considered relics, even though they are mostly random, disposable objects from our hyper-commodified culture, points to the extreme importance of product recognition for marketing and reception of cultural texts. In this way, the film illustrates how a text that is critical and subversive can also echo and bolster a hegemonic order, and suggests how popular culture can function in complicated ways that are never entirely controllable or predictable.

CONCLUSION

The influence of popular media is potent and pervasive; however, because it may both resist and reinforce the dominant culture, the onus is on viewers to think critically as they use it in their construction of knowledge. If audience members are to engage in that sort of critical thinking, then the onus is also on adult educators to take popular culture and critical media seriously in their work (Tisdell, 2008). Deepening the study of adult learning and popular media, this textual analysis of *The Lego Movie* used selected elements of this popular mainstream film to frame a discussion of communities of practice, citizenship, and adult learning. Working from a critical pedagogy perspective, I incorporated ideas from social justice, critical media literacy, and feminist theory in my textual analysis.

Somehow, Lin, Lee, Lord, and Miller were able to produce a mass-marketed children's movie that explores such complex social issues as community, citizenship, and adult learning, while simultaneously addressing our current anxieties about capitalism, consumerism, and corporatisation. Although the film may not bring about massive social transformation (given that its primary objective was simply to sell tickets and increase toy sales), it nevertheless offers a social critique in surprisingly creative and daring ways. By rejecting the idea of one special person that is chosen to save the world, Emmet's character leaves audience members with a feeling of hope and unlocked potential. The film also rejects the usual idea of winning by defeating a villain, and offers an empathetic alternative instead.

Although a detail such as product placement in a movie may seem trivial, it is important because it indicates and invites the beginning of critical questioning and consciousness. As Fürsich (2009) describes, popular media texts "present a distinctive discursive moment between encoding and decoding that justifies special scholarly engagement" (p. 238). Media literacy provides the tools for critical analysis and discourse is an essential component of this process. Cognitive and emotional development and transformative learning experiences are fostered by deconstructing messages found in films and exposing their truths. By critically examining the context and interplay of politics and power in film-making, adults can begin to question assumptions and rethink beliefs. Even in *The Lego Movie* itself, construction workers strike up conversations by asking each other if they watched the fictional sitcom *Where Are my Pants?* last night. The inclusion of a fictional television show within the film emphasizes the function of public pedagogy as a reinforcement of normative values as well as a potential platform for discussing social issues more critically. Other comments implying the need for critical media literacy within the film include Wildstyle's first words on air after breaking into the Octan Corporation studio: "I'm on TV, so you can trust me" (Lin et al., 2014). As popular media's reach has become much further and longer-lasting than ever expected, "the pedagogical discourse imparted by popular culture becomes enmeshed with meanings and desires that exist beyond these media's intentions and scope" (Burdick & Sandlin, 2013, p. 156). Critical media literacy education in the adult learning classroom can help decipher a range of possible meanings and implications; certainly, my own attachment of *The Lego Movie* to a graduate course clarified some important lessons for me. The story itself is clearly important, but educators and audience members alike must also think about who is telling the story, who is listening to it, and who is interpreting it.

As I suggested in the introductory section, the analysis presented here is influenced by more than my careful viewing of *The Lego Movie* and my reading about some central adult learning concepts. My personal interpretation of popular media is strongly rooted in various defining characteristics including my gender, race, age, and my life experience. All aspects of research, including analysis, are influenced by over-arching perspective – which I identified as critical pedagogy (Brookfield, 2003) – as well as the understandings that one has at the outset and other factors. For example, in the opening scenes of the movie, the construction workers talk about eating chicken wings and giant sausages after work. I have a visceral, negative reaction to that as a vegetarian, but for other viewers this part may have little impact or might actually contribute to the enjoyment of watching the film. This is part of the reason that scholars emphasize the need for critical media literacy (Tisdell, 2007; Wright, 2013): Without active discussion involving diverse individuals and multiple perspectives, any dominant discourse may simply be reinforced rather than challenged. Further to that point, Burdick and Sandlin (2013) note that the awareness of popular media's influence is only a partial one if the understanding of how viewers respond to it is absent. I can only speculate on how other adult viewers may interpret this film and if teachable moments are there for them too. As helpful and careful as my viewing of *The Lego Movie* and this inquiry might have been, there are other possibilities in interpretation and analysis that remain unexplored.

Like a set of Lego blocks, "learning is a process of continuous deconstruction of knowledge, of playing with contradictions, and of creatively and productively opening the discourse of a field to an eclectic mosaic of many truths" (Kilgore, 2001, p. 60). As a toy, Lego blocks are designed to inspire creativity and encourage imagination. As a film, *The Lego Movie* can be seen as encouraging its viewers to become Master Builders and produce new mosaics of community by deconstructing and reconstructing the parts available, once they are able to see the usefulness of all the pieces. The beauty of this film is that it follows the complex development of social consciousness not only in one individual, but also in an entire community of ordinary citizens. How these non-conformist and anti-capitalist messages were scripted into such a major Hollywood blockbuster, I still do not know. Perhaps the lucrative success of the writers' previous films granted them more creative freedom than usual. Perhaps the production company hedged their bets on few viewers being smart enough to think about the movie's counterhegemonic messages, while the majority of viewers would go out to buy new toys. Even if its teachings were messy at times, and some cultural norms were tacitly reinforced, the take-home message for me remains one of hope. Like many viewers, I see parts of myself in Emmet, and I was overjoyed to be reminded that sometimes life gets better when I stop following the instructions and choose to improvise instead.

ACKNOWLEDGEMENT

I would like to thank Kaela Jubas for her encouragement, feedback, and helpful comments on the initial drafts of this chapter.

REFERENCES

Anderson, W. T. (1999). Communities in a world of open systems. *Futures, 31*(5), 457–463. doi:10.1016/ S0016-3287(99)00005-1

Brookfield, S. (2003). Putting the critical back into critical pedagogy: A comment on the path of dissent. *Journal of Transformative Education, 1*(2), 141–149. doi:10.1177/1541344603254148

Brookfield, S. (2004). Racializing and concretizing Gramsci in contemporary adult education practice. *Interchange, 35*(3), 375–384. doi:10.1007/BF02698885

Brookfield, S. (2009). Understanding development. In G. Strohschen (Ed.), *Handbook of blended shore education: Adult program development and delivery* (pp. 27–43). doi:10.1007/987-0-387-09443-4_2

Brookfield, S. (2010). Leading democratically. *New Directions for Adult and Continuing Education, 128*, 5–13. doi:10.1002/ace.386

Braizaz, M. (2013, October 24). *Lego and gender marketing: A strategy under construction.* Retrieved from http://www.womenology.com/marketing-watch/lego-and-gender-marketing-a-strategy-under-construction/

Burdick, J., & Sandlin, J. A. (2013). Learning, becoming, and the unknowable: Conceptualizations, mechanisms, and process in public pedagogy literature. *Curriculum Inquiry, 43*(1), 142–177. doi:10.111/curi.12001

Dirkx, J. (2001). The power of feelings: Emotion, imagination, and the construction of meaning in adult learning. *New Directions for Adult and Continuing Education, 89*, 63–72.

Fuller, A., Hodkinson, H., Hodkinson, P., & Unwin, L. (2005). Learning as peripheral participation in communities of practice: A reassessment of key concepts in workplace learning. *British Educational Research Journal, 31*(1), 49–68. doi:10.1080/0141192052000310029

Fürsich, E. (2009). In defense of textual analysis: Restoring a challenged method for journalism and media studies. *Journalism Studies, 10*(2), 238–252. doi:10.1080/14616700802374050

Giroux, H. A. (2000). Public pedagogy as cultural politics: Stuart Hall and the crisis of culture. *Cultural Studies, 14*(2), 341–360. doi:10.1080/095023800334913

Giroux, H. A. (2008). Hollywood film as public pedagogy: Education in the crossfire. *Afterimage, 35*(5), 7–13.

Giroux, H. A. (2011). The crisis of public values in the age of the new media. *Critical Studies in Media Communication, 28*(1), 8–29. doi:10.1080/15295036.2011.544618

Hoggan, C., & Cranton, P. (2015). Promoting transformative learning through reading fiction. *Journal of Transformative Education, 13*(1), 6–25. doi:10.1177/1541344614561864

Jarvis, C. (2012). Fiction, empathy, and lifelong learning. *International Journal of Lifelong Education, 31*(6), 743–758. doi:10.1080/02601370.2012.713036

Jarvis, P. (2002). Globalisation, citizenship and the education of adults in contemporary European society. *Compare: A Journal of Comparative International Education, 32*(1), 5–19. doi:10.1080/ 03057920120116490

Jarvis, P. (2006). *Towards a comprehensive theory of human learning: Lifelong learning and the learning society* (Vol. 1). New York, NY: Routledge.

Jarvis, P. (2008). The consumer society: Is there a place for traditional adult education? *Convergence, 41*(1), 11–27.

Jubas, K. (2012). Critically minded shopping as a process of adult learning and civic engagement. *New Directions for Adult and Continuing Education, 135*, 61–69. doi:10.1002/ace.20027

Jubas, K. (2013). Grey('s) identity: Complications of learning and becoming in a popular television show. *Review of Education, Pedagogy, and Cultural Studies, 35*(2), 127–143. doi:10.1080/10714413. 2013.778653

Kilgore, D. W. (2001). Critical and postmodern perspectives on adult learning. *New Directions for Adult and Continuing Education, 89*, 53–62. doi:10.1002/ace.8

Lave, J., & Wenger, E. (1991). *Situated learning: Legitimate peripheral practice*. New York, NY: Cambridge University Press.

Lin, D., Lee R. (Producers), Lord, P., & Miller, C. (Directors). (2014). *The Lego movie* [Motion picture]. United States: Warner Bros. Pictures.

Magowan, M. (2013, January 28). *The Smurfette principle "evolves" into the minority feisty*. Retrieved from http://reelgirl.com/2013/01/the-smurfette-principle-evolves-into-the-minority-feisty/

Marsick, V. J., & Watkins, K. E. (2001). Informal and incidental learning. *New Directions for Adult and Continuing Education, 89*, 25–34.

McKee, A. (2003). *Textual analysis: A beginner's guide*. London, England: Sage Publications.

Mezirow, J. (1997). Transformative learning: Theory to practice. *New Directions for Adult and Continuing Education, 74*, 5–12.

Orwell, G. (1949). *1984*. New York, NY: Harcourt.

Patterson, S., Bartholomew, J., Harriton, L., & The Lonely Island. (2014). Everything is AWESOME!!! [Recorded by Tegan & Sara]. On *The Lego movie: Original motion picture soundtrack* [CD]. Sydney, Australia: WaterTower Music.

Sandlin, J. A., & Milam, J. L. (2008). Mixing pop (culture) and politics: Cultural resistance, culture jamming, and anti-consumption activism as critical public pedagogy. *Curriculum Inquiry, 38*(3), 323–350. doi:10.1111/j.1467-873X.2008.00411.x

Sandlin, J. A., Wright, R. R., & Clark, C. (2013). Re-examining theories of adult learning and adult development through the lenses of public pedagogy. *Adult Education Quarterly, 63*(1), 3–23. doi:10.1177/0741713611415836

Tisdell, E. J. (2007). Popular culture and critical media literacy in adult education: Theory and practice. *New Directions for Adult and Continuing Education, 115,* 5–13. doi:10.1002/ace.262

Tisdell, E. J. (2008). Critical media literacy and transformative learning: Drawing on pop culture and entertainment media in teaching for diversity in adult higher education. *Journal of Transformative Education, 6*(1), 48–67. doi:10.1177/1541344608318970

Wenger, E. (1998). *Communities of practice: Learning, meaning, and identity.* New York, NY: Cambridge University Press.

Wenger, E. (2000). Communities of practice and social learning systems. *Organization, 7*(2), 225–246.

Wright, R. R. (2010). Narratives from popular culture: Critical implications for adult education. *New Directions for Adult and Continuing Education, 126,* 49–62. doi:10.1002/ace.371

Wright, R. R. (2013). Zombies, cyborgs, and other labor organizers: An introduction to representations of adult learning theories and HRD in popular culture. *New Horizons in Adult Education & Human Resource Development, 25*(1), 5–17. doi:10.1002/nha.20003

Wright, R. R., & Sandlin, J. A. (2009). Cult TV, hop hop, shape-shifters, and vampire slayers: A review of the literature at the intersection of adult education and popular culture. *Adult Education Quarterly, 59*(2), 118–141. doi:10.1177/0741713608327368

Elissa Odgren
Werklund School of Education
University of Calgary

TONY BROWN

4. TEACHERS ON FILM

Changing Representations of Teaching in Popular Cinema from Mr. Chips to Jamie Fitzpatrick

INTRODUCTION

Films are an important means of conveying cultural and political stories of the times. In their narrative construction and storytelling they create a public pedagogy. For hooks (1996), "cinema assumes a pedagogical role in the lives of many people. It may not be the intent of a film-maker to teach audiences anything, but that does not mean that lessons are not learned" (pp. 2–3).

Movies are very different texts than books, for better and for worse. Distilling messages in a visual way that tells a compelling story often connects with wider audiences much more powerfully than rationally based arguments. Films' power comes from a connection to the ideas and spirit of the time. Strong popular narratives can shape the way viewers as individuals, and in their wider identity affiliations, understand the world around us and its possibilities or restrictions. Storytelling, especially in film, changes in response to the social, cultural and political concerns and interests of the time, as it also shapes that environment. The most powerful films reflect the world back to us; thus, they can become a battleground over interpretations of the social world.

After viewing numerous film representations of the practice of teachers, and the social roles expected of them, I identified five roles or categories, corresponding to the historical period of groups of films. For nearly a century teachers in films were generally portrayed in a positive light. In the first four categories the teacher is the pivotal character and whatever faults are depicted the viewer can see that they are doing their best to assist their young students to grow and take a place in the world beyond school. This depiction of teachers playing a positive role was disrupted in a series of American films in the 21st century, exemplified by *Won't Back Down*, (Johnson & Barnes, 2012), which changed the focus from the teacher to the parent/consumer, in this case an embattled underdog in Jamie Fitzpatrick. Contributing to a wider backlash against public education, it epitomised the shift from seeing teaching as a generally noble contribution to students' preparation to enter adult society to one where teachers and especially those in public education systems are the obstacle to young peoples' learning.

As popular culture texts, films contribute to re-shaping the public debate around education because they speak directly to a wide viewing audience. In this chapter I attempt to explain the backlash narrative's appeal by showing how it inverts and appropriates a progressive story of struggle. Right now they are helping to shape what ideologically committed business interests argue needs changing in education systems. These interests want governments to transfer public monies into private providers' hands, while also enabling market mechanisms to determine the purpose of education, the breadth and content of the curriculum, and resource allocations to schools. The main obstacle to this occurring and therefore the primary target has been teacher unions and teachers themselves. De-legitimising and weakening those who stand against this trend has become a multi-focused campaign. *Won't Back Down* (Johnson & Barnes, 2012) became the flag-bearer of the backlash films as part of the wider political targeting of public education.

METHOD AND PERSPECTIVE

In analysing teacher focused films I first applied Williams' (1953/1993) teaching method of developing "attentive seeing and listening" (pp. 189–191) to establish a foundation for understanding a story's inner-workings, of how it is constructed, its elements and the audience it intendeds to speak to. This dovetails with the "thick description" approach of Geertz's (1975) interpretive ethnography, which aims to explain cultures through specifying the many details, conceptual structures and meanings. Between the *thin* (surface) description, and the *thick* description (of underlying meaning) lies the object of ethnography: "a stratified hierarchy of meaningful structures" (Geertz, 1975, p. 9) Constructing an account is an "interpretive one in search of meaning" (p. 5). The intention of constructing such accounts is to serve a collective purpose of better understanding that history. Research has a social meaning and "a multiplicity of complex, conceptual structures" (p. 10) must first be grasped and then rendered. Developing the thick description of the selected films enabled me to develop the categories of teacher-types that I use here.

Secondly, I draw on educators who examined how narrative and storytelling develop affective understanding and motivate action. The pioneering constructivist Jerome Bruner (1986) refers to two modes of knowing, the logico-scientific (cognitive), and the narrative (affective). An underlying strength of the narrative form, and hence film, is its appeal to the affective, where gripping stories and their lifelikeness work with the viewer's imagination. Just how important this is becomes very clear in the character of Jamie Fitzpatrick (Maggie Gyllenhaal) in *Won't Back Down* (Johnson & Barnes, 2012). Finally, I examine how contemporary stories of teachers are shaped by and shape the political discourse of how education should be organised and funded, curriculum developed, students assessed, the impacts on teachers' work, autonomy and status, and the vested interests at play.

TEACHERS EVOLUTION ON SCREEN: FIVE CATEGORIES OF TEACHER FILMS

Filmmakers' fascination with teachers and schooling began slowly with a few significant films scattered through the early 20th century, then increasing in the 1950s and 1960s and accelerating from the 1980s onwards when numerous movies were made about teachers and schools. Among these are many where schools are essentially a backdrop to the filmmakers' real interest, which ranges from teen romance, bullying or coming of age (*Breakfast Club; Mean Girls; Ten Things I Hate about You; Grease*); to dangerous and unruly youth (*One Eight Seven; Higher Learning*); to against-the-odds sporting achievements or redemption (*Hoosiers; Coach Carter; Win Win; The Blind Side*); to the teacher as a figure of fun (*Carry on Teacher; St. Trinians* series; *Grease; Election; Ferris Bueller's Day Off; Bad Teacher*).

My interest here, however, is on narrative or fictional films where teachers, teaching and schooling is the central concern. The teacher as a shepherd guiding his young boarding school boys for their future male, and generally ruling class roles, as epitomised by the avuncular Mr. Chips in *Goodbye, Mr. Chips* (Saville & Woods, 1939), established a screen role model that endured for 20 years and still recurs in new guises into this century. Robert Donat's patrician Chips is a Latin teacher and slightly eccentric character with fixed ideas about teaching and discipline when we first meet him as an unmarried novice teacher. By the end of his career, and the film, he is married, wiser and much loved by generations of boys. This portrayal of the esteemed old figure endures. There continues to be updated versions of this narrative where a liberal education is still available for privileged British boys (*History Boys*, 2006) and the daughters of America's elite (*Mona Lisa Smiles*, 2003). The charismatic if somewhat flawed teacher is also reprised in *The Prime of Miss Jean Brodie* (1969), and *Dead Poets Society* (Haft, Witt, Thomas, & Weir, 1989).

By the 1950s in the aftermath of the second world war, with the threat of nuclear war and the rapid growth of industrialisation, a new world was being born in which characters like Mr. Chips were an anachronism. *The Browning Version* (Baird, St. John, & Asquith, 1951), a screen version of Terence Rattigan's play, prefigured a new type of teacher film of the 1950s and 1960s. It linked elements of the old with a more naturalistic depiction of the gritty contemporary times. Michael Redgrave's Crocker-Harris, the antithesis of Mr. Chips, is an unloved teacher of Greek stuck in his own rigidity and groping towards self-awareness as he is confronted by ill health and his forced resignation.

In the USA a tougher new teacher emerged who is called upon to deal with the unruly teenagers of the time. Set in the rock'n'roll post-war period *Blackboard Jungle* (Berman & Brooks, 1955), takes place in an inner city New York school with a soundtrack including Bill Haley's "Rock around the Clock" on the opening credits, and it became the pivotal film of the period. Glenn Ford's character Rick Dadier is a war veteran and new teacher at North Manual High where many of the pupils, led by Gregory Miller (Sidney Poitier) and Artie West (Vic Morrow), frequently engage in criminal behaviour. Its promotion described the setting as "teenage terror" and "teenage savages turning schools into a jungle," "fiction torn from big city modern savagery."[1] It reflected a generational fear of youth and an emerging rebelliousness, but also a sense that these kids had to be disciplined to enter the world of work. And, in case anyone might miss this point the school was not named after a notable figure like Washington, or Jefferson, but was North Manual High. There was an overt class antagonism in the story as the students were mostly white (though obviously not Poitier's character) urban, working class, violent, and disconnected from school. Now the teacher's role was one of civilizing uncontrollable adolescents. The situation called for a tough, no nonsense teacher and Ford's Dadier fitted the bill with his attempts to engage the students' interest in education, challenging both staff colleagues and pupils.

In Britain, *To Sir, with Love* (Clavell, 1967) followed *Blackboard Jungle*, this time with Sidney Poitier as the teacher who has to, miraculously, reform the school's hoodlums. While it stretched credibility, it did establish Poitier's character as a remarkable, almost mythical figure noble for his integrity and morality. Here was the beginning of a shift from the civilizing teacher to what would emerge in the 1980s in a series of films where we can identify the teacher as a heroic, self-sacrificing, saviour figure.

Dead Poets Society (Haft et al., 1989) provided a link between the periods with Robin Williams' romantic shepherd figure also sounding the death knell of the Pied Piper-esque teacher on film. The late 1980s introduced a third type of screen teacher with a series of American films that largely dealt with post-desegregation urban poor. In their way, they presented a celebration of teaching with the teacher portrayed as a hero/ine, and saviour of poorer, disadvantaged students, generally working class and from ethnic minorities, who were most likely destined for imprisonment, death through gangs or drugs, or early motherhood.

Based on the Jaime Escalante story, *Stand and Deliver* (Musca & Menéndez, 1988) is one of these films. Starring Edgar James Olmos[2] it is set in Hispanic East Los Angeles and follows a conventional story arc of kids who have been *written off* and who have low expectations, rising against the odds and showing what they are capable of if only someone will believe in them and give them a chance. That person is their teacher. It is notable because unlike many of the films of this period the teacher is also Hispanic, and while he fulfils the role of the *outsider* who enters the story with a wider view of the world, he is also an *insider*. *Lean on Me* (Twain & Avildsen, 1989), directed by John Avildsen who also made *Rocky*, gave a taste of the most recent American teacher and school films. Set in New Jersey's Eastside High and considered a *failing school* it is reminiscent of *Blackboard Jungle's* (Berman & Brooks, 1955) North Manual High. Eastside is a *school out of control* plagued by drugs and gang problems, a sort of prison with the inmates asserting their power while desperate teachers/warders try to regain control. Based on the story of Joe

Louis Clark (played by Morgan Freeman), the film portrays Eastside as a school at risk of being taken over by the state government unless test scores improve. Clark arrives as the new principal preaching and applying tough love to his mainly African-American students and extolling the virtues of personal responsibility.

In *Dangerous Minds* (Simpson, Bruckheimer, & Smith, 1995) East Palo Alto's Parkmont High is home to a mix of African-American and Latino students. The school grounds are set behind high fences and electrified gates. The shadowy hallways and corridors are dimly lit, and just like those of North Manual and Eastside, they appear to be more like a prison than a place of learning. Michelle Pfeiffer plays the role of LouAnne Johnson, an ex-Marine who tries everything to win over her hostile students. After a year she announces she is giving up only to be convinced to stay after receiving emotional tributes from her classmates.

The peak of this group of saviour films came with *Freedom Writers* (De Vito, Shamberg, Sher, & LaGravenese, 2007). It portrays teachers more as missionaries than professionals, giving up their lives and comfort for the benefit of others, without need of compensation. Hilary Swank's Erin Gruwell sacrifices money, time and even her marriage for her job. She appears to have no choice but to make these sacrifices in response to the wilful neglect of the school's administrators, who won't even let her take books from the storeroom. The implication is that she is more than just dedicated, for in order to be a good teacher, she has to be a hero.[3] Moore (2007) argues that these films are "presented as a celebration of teaching, but (the) message is that poor students need only love, idealism and martyrdom" (para. 14).

The saviour films represent American education's favourite past time – find inspirational teacher/principal and tell an uplifting/touching story about how kids from tough backgrounds beat the odds. When the messenger is someone like Hilary Swank, Michelle Pfeiffer or Morgan Freeman then it is even more appealing. The most problematic message that films like *Dangerous Minds* (Simpson, Bruckheimer, & Smith, 1995) and *Freedom Writers* (DeVito et al., 2010) promote is that what schools really need are individual heroes, the "Great Teacher." Giroux (1997) makes an important point about *Dangerous Minds'* "attempt to represent 'whiteness' as the archetype of rationality, authority and cultural standards" (p. 47), but he does not account for other films of this period which also aim to save their students where the teacher and/or film-maker is not white (e.g. *To Sir with Love*; *Lean on Me*; *Stand and Deliver; Walk-out*).

Every day teachers are blamed for what the system they are a part of does not provide: safe, adequately staffed schools with the highest expectations for all students. But that's not something that one maverick teacher, no matter how idealistic, perky or self-sacrificing, can accomplish. This idealized version of teaching will soon be cast aside early in the 21st century as teachers go from being depicted as martyrs to being represented as lazy, protected and unwilling to adapt to new challenges.

Outside the USA, a fourth teacher category can be seen in a set of recent French films where the teacher is an embattled mediator between the outside world and the classroom. In films such as *The Class* (Benjo, Scotta, & Cantet, 2008), *Skirt Day*

(Askenazi, Lesage, & Lilienfeld, 2008), and *Once in a Lifetime* (Kubel & Mention-Schaar, 2014), the teachers find themselves caught in the midst of local politics/politicians; demanding parents and cultural and racial divides; declining funding and resources; as they have to navigate social issues of unemployment, gender and racial conflict, while still trying to prepare their students to survive in what is depicted as a grim social and economic environment.[4] In these films we observe teachers behaving in ways that are less heroic and perhaps more how beleaguered teachers might act.

In *The Class* (Benjo, Scotta, & Cantet, 2008), the teachers are seen colluding in a misguided effort of self-preservation against the teenagers and their parents in a mixed race school in Paris. In *Skirt Day* (Askenazi, Lesage, & Lilienfeld, 2008) Isabelle Adjani's teacher loses control after confronting the daily grind of low-level violence, insolence and ethnic tensions in her classroom. She decides to wear a skirt to school over the objections of some of her Muslim students who consider it an inappropriate form of dress for a woman teacher. On that day she snaps and takes her students hostage. In *Once in a Lifetime* (Kubel & Mention-Schaar, 2014), also set in a mixed ethnic district of Paris (African, Arabic, Islamic, Jewish, white, Christian), the teachers have to enforce the secular prohibitions against religious identification including crucifixes and hijabs, as well as policing other dress codes by removing caps and headphones. Ariane Ascaride's class is a microcosm of the diversity of French schools and the challenges teachers face with classes comprising pupils from numerous ethnic and religious origins, who are often only just co-existing in the one room.

A feature of many teacher films, right from Thomas Hughes' schoolboy experiences captured in *Tom Brown's Schooldays* in 1916, is that they are often dramatized versions of biographical accounts of real teachers and their experiences. The *based on a true story* aspect of the films adds veracity to the accounts, making them appear real, which is such an important ingredient in the more highly charged political debates about schooling today.[5]

THE BACKLASH – TEACHERS AS OBSTACLE

A more recent set of American films aims to significantly shift the representation of teachers, and reflects a counter-narrative of education. In backlash films, instead of being seen as a saviour or hero/ine, the teacher, and especially the unionised public education teacher, is presented as an obstacle to learning, a representative of an over-regulated state, and protected by union conditions better than those of the parents whose children they tend. The teachers personify a wider system, funded by out-of-touch governments, administered by do-gooder/elite bureaucrats in collaboration with public sector unions. The system acts against the interests of parents excluding them from a say in decision-making over their children's education. The means for redressing this situation is presented as a combination of business-like educational leaders, privately operated schools and activist parents.

Even in current films where schools are essentially just a setting for another type of story the backdrop remains one of the failing school, harried and incompetent teachers doing their best but not keeping control of their students, where the facilities are poor, programs are being closed due to lack of funds, and principals are under pressure from heartless bureaucrats to shape up. *Here Comes the Boom* (Garner, James, & Coraci, 2012), essentially a sports comedy vehicle for its star Kevin James, is a good example. The notion of the failing school has become unremarkable, it is so common that it is like the wallpaper, always there in the background but hardly noticed, just taken for granted.[6]

The release of the documentary *Waiting for "Superman"* (Chilcott & Guggenheim, 2010) represented the turning tide against public education and paved the way for a series of backlash films against teachers and teacher unions. It follows several students' efforts to gain entry into a charter school run by the American entrepreneur Geoffrey Canada. At its conclusion we see the entry selection being made by a lottery, granting access to some and closing the door to others. An important change in emphasis in *Superman*, and in others that followed, is the move away from the focus on the teacher as hero/ine to the critical role of the Principal, or Chief Executive, as with Geoffrey Canada. Canada had previously established Harlem Children's Zone, which oversees several charter schools as well as health and social services for poor children and their families, before setting up his charter school company (Delbanco, 2013). The documentary received the financial backing of rich and powerful supporters, such as Walden Media's Philip Anschutz and Bill Gates, and prominent media proprietors (see Ravitch, 2013, pp. 19–31), and was an uncompromising attack on public education, teacher unions, and teachers' employment security, bringing to prominence anti-public education warriors such as Michelle Rhee.

Guggenheim, who had previously directed *An Inconvenient Truth*, and came with impeccable liberal credentials, was now transformed into one of conservative media-land's favourite filmmakers. America's populist in-house opinion writers saw *Superman* as both making the case that the nation's children had been betrayed by teachers' unions, and portraying charter schools in a hugely flattering light, two concepts that dovetailed with the case they had been trying to prosecute. For example, *The Wall Street Journal*, which had relentlessly criticized *An Inconvenient Truth* as part of its campaign to undermine concern about climate change, shifted to embrace his new film. In an op-ed piece, William McGurn (2010) called *Superman* a "stunning liberal expose of a system that consigns American children who most need a decent education to our most destructive public schools." In Rupert Murdoch's *New York Post*, film critic Kyle Smith (2010), who had also previously mocked *An Inconvenient Truth*, described *Superman* as "one of the best films of the year," a "heartbreaking yet thrillingly hopeful documentary [where] adults are finally starting to notice how badly kids have been betrayed by teachers unions." Joining in on pointing the finger at teachers was Oprah Winfrey, whose website promoted *Superman* by arguing that the students are "eager to get an education, but in a system riddled with ineffective teachers, staggering dropout rates and schools that are literally falling apart, the odds are more than stacked against them" (The shocking state of our schools," 2010, para. 1).

Tony Kaye's *Detachment* (Shapiro et al., 2012) is another of the indictment films of public education. Adrien Brody's Henry Barthes, a forlorn yet gifted supply teacher, is the story's focus, but it's the school he lands in that is the petri dish. The principal is about to be dismissed, the kids are disaffected and out of control, the staff burned-out, the parents antagonistic, and the authorities unknowing, insensitive, and in cahoots with property developers to raise the schools test scores in order to protect property values. The movie's opening graphics are reminiscent of *Blackboard Jungle* (Berman & Brooks, 1955), *Lean on Me* (Twain & Avildsen, 1989) and *Dangerous Minds* (Simpson, Bruckheimer, & Smith, 1995) as a set of prison bars merge into an hour glass conjuring up images of being locked up, serving a sentence, and applying to both students and teachers.

There is a link here between the saviour and backlash films as Henry Barthes shares some similarities with *Freedom Writers'* (DeVito et al., 2007) Erin Gruwell. Indeed, Barthes literally rescues a homeless school-age girl from working the streets and brings her to stay at his apartment until she can be re-settled at a youth home. Furthermore, Barthes gives voice to the despondency that is presented on screen as crippling to teachers. At one point he explains, "Most of the teachers here at one point thought they could make a difference" (DeVito et al., 2007), capturing a recurring element of the failing school genre, with the implication being that they have since given up. The film gradually builds a bleak picture, where there is little hope for the future and an enveloping sense of educational despair and decay.

The crest of the backlash wave is the release of *Won't Back Down* (Johnson & Barnz, 2012). It is a story of two mothers frustrated by the education their children are receiving at their inner-city school. Jamie Fitzpatrick is a single mother working a couple of jobs and trying to hold things together. Jamie's daughter Malia has dyslexia and needs some extra support. Nona Alberts (played by Viola Davis) is a disillusioned teacher with a son at the same school who is also struggling to make progress. The two women feel thwarted by the lack of attention they receive, and in particular by what the film shows as a system and a union that protects unmotivated teachers, and from an uninspiring principal. Soon they are forced to take on the school district administration, which in effect becomes a fight against city hall.

The viewer's attention is drawn to the problem from the very first scenes. In this set-up Jamie rushes to get Malia her eight-year old daughter ready for school and herself ready for work. It's a scene familiar to so many who have shared the same daily routine. Finally in class the viewers watch for the next eight minutes an expose of callous indifference by Deborah, the classroom teacher to the struggling Malia. Standing in the middle of the room surrounded by misbehaving classmates Malia battles to read a sentence on the blackboard. As the other students taunt her the audience observes Deborah texting on her phone and paying no attention to Malia. A full three minutes pass in the beginning of this painful scene and at no time does Deborah shift her gaze from the phone or offer any assistance.

In the next scene we see Breena, a fellow teacher in the staff room, refer to Deborah in a disparaging comment: "No ordinary deadbeat could pull off the highest salary and the lowest performance in school history seven years running" (Johnson & Barnz, 2012). We get the message that there is no secret that Deborah is playing the system, "the only thing the District does right is protect what it does wrong."

Eventually, Jamie decides to launch a campaign to get enough parent signatures to use the new Parent Trigger laws that can see the school move out of the public system and be handed over to a charter company. She first enlists Nona and together they wage a very successful community organising campaign. Jamie and Nona must try to win support from parents as well as the teachers. In a crucial scene later in the film Nona confronts her colleagues at a staff meeting and poses the question of what is holding them back from their passion for teaching that originally motivated them? The film's answer is clear; it is the outside forces, the third parties that get between a teacher and student. It is the union and the public system with their rules, regulations, contracts and clauses. If only they can be removed then the teachers will be liberated and free once again to exercise their professional discretion, give that extra bit more and satisfy their original passion. It is a reprise of Henry Barthes' conclusion in *Detachment* (Shapiro et al., 2012).

First passed in California in 2010, and since introduced by several other states, the Parent Trigger laws allow parents of children in an *underperforming* public school to take it over if 50 percent of parents support it in a petition. The school's administration and staff are then dismissed and parents choose a private operator to run the school. The charter details the education that will be offered and the standards to be met. The operator receives public funds, often with supplementary private support, to run the school, and is granted through renewable charters, greater freedom than conventional public schools to hire and fire teachers, accept or reject student applicants, and remove students who fail.

The laws came about as a result of successful organising by groups committed to undermining public education and teacher unions, and are presented as being progressive as they mobilise the disempowered against the powerful. In May 2009, Green Dot, a charter school company, formed Parent Revolution, a group specifically intended to lobby for parent trigger laws, and headed by Ben Austin a union-busting activist (see http://parentrevolution.org/who-we-are/). Parent Revolution, with a $1 million annual budget funded by the Gates Foundation, Walton Family Foundation, and other private foundations plans to activate parent trigger actions across the USA (Dreier, 2013), and held its first ParentPower Convention in 2014.

A companion piece to *Won't Back Down* is the documentary *We the Parents* (Takata & Takata, 2013). It follows the first group of parents to use the law at McKinley Elementary School in Compton, California. It also brings vividly into the open the behind-the-scenes methods of Parent Revolution, reminding us that it is not the method that is the important thing in community organising but what outcomes are being organised for and in whose interests. *We the Parents* is in effect a how-to primer for taking a school out of the public education system and handing it over to a privately owned charter company.

The underlying message of these films is that the school system, and in particular the public education system, is failing students and their parents, and by extension the wider society. Three themes emerge. Firstly, where once teachers could be expected to be the guardian, or civilizing agent, or in the most difficult circumstances a saviour figure, today they have become an obstacle. Cocooned by an overly bureaucratic and unresponsive administration and protected by their unions, teachers have become unreliable. Secondly, those teachers can be redeemed and can rediscover the passion for teaching that originally motivated them if they can be freed from the constraints and regulation of the public system and the unions. The third theme, or the call to action, is that the means of achieving this is to take schools out of the public system, make them operate as private enterprises and remove unions from the bargaining, pedagogy, and professional standards aspects of education.

CONTEXT OF THE BACKLASH: CAMPAIGNING AGAINST TEACHERS, UNIONS AND PUBLIC EDUCATION

This section focuses on the fifth category of films about the role of the teacher, the backlash category. It links an ethnographic analysis of the construction of the role of the teacher in the backlash films, to the socio-political context of the films. This context consists of the political and legislative framework that makes possible the weakening of public education by undermining teachers' working conditions and establishing new market mechanisms for schooling to benefit private profit-makers.

What is the Appeal of the Backlash Films?

In this book we have argued that popular culture, including films, are a means of conveying cultural stories of their times. How do we begin to understand how the backlash films work, and their appeal? Masterman reminds us that "the media ... are actively involved in processes of *constructing* or *representing* 'reality' rather than simply transmitting or reflecting it" (cited in Rodesiler, 2010, p. 166, emphasis in original).

Won't Back Down (Johnson & Barnz, 2012) works at the emotional level and has an authenticity because of its connection to the experience of many parents' alienation from and frustration with schools as well as the boredom and isolation reported by their children. It has elements from each of what Heath and Heath (2007) describe as the three core plots in narrative construction and inspirational stories. In the first, the challenge plot, the protagonist overcomes a formidable challenge and succeeds. It is the story of the underdog, of willpower over adversity, and from rags to riches. The classic example of this plot is David and Goliath. The second is the connection plot, which is about people who develop a relationship that bridges a gap, whether it is racial, class, ethnic, religious, demographic, or otherwise. It's about our relationships with other people, and is generally inspirational. The creativity plot is the third and it involves someone making a mental breakthrough, solving a long-standing puzzle, or tackling a problem in an innovative way. *Won't Back Down* primarily falls within the challenge plot genre with also some elements of the connection and creativity categories.

Stories are culture forging and identity forming. They link the individual with the communities they are part of and identify with, and at best create inspiration for action and change. A critical element in making the connection is the credibility and authenticity of the storyteller, or in film, the protagonist. The audience first observes Jamie in her private life. They see the challenges, the obstacles, and the crises she faces, as well as her efforts to overcome them. Her story might be different in its particulars to those of audience members but there is a level of recognition and empathy because we all face challenges and obstacles in our own lives. What elevates her story though is how she connects her individual situation to become a story beyond her. At first her only concern is to get her daughter more attention, then a different teacher, and then into a different school. The *system* blocks each attempt and so she begins working to organise other parents. What will be the means of making and building these connections? Jamie's first success is to recruit Nona the teacher, whose child is also struggling, away from her sense of impotence to believe that change can happen. And then we observe the door-to-door canvassing, the campaign begin to build in the local community.

Jamie's story is urgent. Will her aspirations for something new and better for Malia be achieved? Will the conflict with the authorities be won? This creates tension and the audience is drawn in to find out what will happen. Watching Jamie the audience is also working on the choices that have to be made, thinking about what should be done, what is the best way and the right way to act. What lessons will be learned? What conclusions drawn? The power of the story is firstly experienced through becoming involved with the drama confronting the protagonist, being interested in the story itself and the choices that the protagonist has to make. Will s/he accept the challenge or not? Finally there is the moral. If the audience has no identification with the protagonist then the story has little power, but once there is some identification the audience becomes engaged with the choices s/he has made. Viewers draw their own conclusions about whether the right or wrong choices were made, whether the actions were justified, the outcomes satisfactory, and so on. It becomes more than a rational assessment as it also engages the emotional attachment to the story (See Ganz, 2009, 2010).

Won't Back Down (Johnson & Barnz, 2012) is about re-framing the public consciousness on education and teachers. It inverts the left/liberal underdog narrative of struggle against the powerful by reframing who is powerful. To do so it has to undermine existing frames, which are organising principles that are socially shared and persistent over time. Frames work symbolically to meaningfully structure the social world and aren't simply a slogan repeated over and over. A century ago Walter Lippmann (1922/1965) described the effect as creating "the pictures in our heads."[7]

The *powerful* in this re-framing are the teacher unions and public officials, rather than private capital, the wealthy and their politicians. The marginalised and poor, single mothers and Hispanic/African-American people are lined up against the elites and privileged represented by public officials and unions of workers. Most cynically representative of this appropriation is that the Charter school Jamie Fitzpatrick wants to get her daughter into is the *Rosa Parks* school! Carol Lloyd (2012) proclaimed the movie "the *Silkwood* ... for education reformers," while Gyllenhaal compared her character to other famous women union and anti-nuclear campaigners Norma Rae and Erin Brockovich (Gensler, 2012).

The backlash films appropriate the language of modern progressive politics, occupying it, infusing it with conservative, anti-union, pro-market meaning. Radical or revolutionary once implied deep discontent with the basic structure of society, and a commitment to overturn it, beginning with the redistribution of wealth and re-ordering decision-making in the economic and political spheres. Now it is used to popularize the remaking of public institutions on the model of private corporations. It has already been introduced into postal services, telecommunications and human services such as aged and childcare and community services. The tools to remake education are financial incentives, rewards and penalties.

If the film can get the audience to identify against those depicted as their opponents, then it has been a successful in the campaign against public education.

The Legislative Route for Marketisation

Throughout the 21st century there has been a systematic legislative program pursued to narrow education, privatise it, reduce teachers' conditions and where possible remove teachers' rights to collectively organise. Beginning with George W. Bush's *No Child Left Behind* in 2001 it has continued with linking standardised testing results to funding, through to adopting the Common Core State Standards in 2010, and California's Parent Trigger laws. In 2011 Wisconsin's Governor Scott Walker forced through laws removing the right of public sector workers, including teachers and even firefighters and police, to collectively bargain (Kroll, 2011; see also Pray, Takis, & Williams, 2013). The method was to firstly tap into the resentment and frustration of people like Jamie Fitzpatrick – people with low quality service-sector jobs and few benefits, whose kids are stuck in struggling schools against the declining group of public employees who still have a decent deal. Walker then stripped away job security and collective bargaining with the support of a public attitude of *why should they have something I don't have?*

In 2012, Chicago's Mayor accelerated an existing program of closing *under-performing* schools that hit African-American communities the hardest. After 2015 there will be no public high schools on Chicago's south side serving African-American neighbourhoods. Students will be forced to either travel afar or seek entry into a local charter. Chicago's teachers responded with a nine-day strike in late 2012, the first strike for 25 years, protesting the neglect of public education, low pay and the system of teacher evaluations.

In 2013, Barack Obama proclaimed a National Charter School Week, ironically coinciding with Teacher Appreciation Week (Obama, 2013). Even more ironically, because many charter schools do not hire certified teachers, charter teachers do not have tenure and can be fired at will, and many charters are known for high teacher turnover due to the stress of longer school days.

Undermining Teachers

The assault on teachers is noted across the spectrum from conservative writers such as Dana Goldstein (2014), to policy activists (Ravitch, 2013), and critical educators such as Henry Giroux (2012) who writes of the war against teachers as public intellectuals.

Teachers have progressively had their autonomy over the curriculum and their classroom reduced in recent decades, and this applies as much to school classroom teachers as it does to vocational and technical educators and increasingly university academics. Teachers' status and experience as professionals and workers varies over time depending in large part on the fiscal position of the state and the economy more generally. In periods when governments allocate more resources to public goods, management "relies heavily on the promotion of teacher professionalism as a form of control" (Lawn & Ozga, 1988, p. x). In times of economic crisis and austerity, "the central state tends towards strong directive management, which imposes controls on teacher recruitment, training, salaries and status, and curriculum and examination content" (Lawn & Ozga, 1988, p. x). Beyond this cyclical dynamic, there is an underlying trend where the more emphasis on the role of education in creating a trained labour force the more the teaching labour process will be "analysed and restructured to increase its efficiency (i.e., productivity)" (Lawn & Ozga, 1988, pp. 87–88). "It is just such a prioritisation of what is calculable and universalisable in schooling that has precipitated a tendency to de-professionalise teachers" (Strain & Field, 1997, p. 146). This also serves to justify excluding educators from involvement in decisions about curriculum, pedagogy and assessment. A concerted effort to diminish school teachers standing and status is something that ultimately affects all educators.

In Whose Interests?

The U.S. education market is valued at $1.3 trillion (Simonton, 2013), and therefore offers extremely lucrative opportunities for investors that can access it. The right wing think tanks behind the school choice movement have a clear agenda, masked with deceptive rhetoric. They want to defund and privatise public schools through voucher programs, charter school expansion and online academies with as little oversight of their use of public monies as possible, while giving tax credits to corporations that fund private schools. Their aim is to upend what they identify as the education establishment using the code words of competition and choice as weapons.

A new market in schooling offers potential profits, so there are strong material as well as ideological reasons for the billionaires to invest in films that demonise public education, teachers and their unions.

Between 2005 and 2014 the Walton family (of the Walmart chain) donated $1 billion to organisations supporting privatisation including the Milton Friedman Foundation for Education Choice, Students First (headed by Michelle Rhee) and Alliance for School Choice. In Los Angeles alone the Walton Foundation donated $84 million to charter schools and organisations such as Green Dot Schools, and LA Parents Union (Brantley, 2013; Dreier, 2013).

Philip Anschutz, who Forbes listed as the 38th richest person in the US in 2013, owns Walden Media, which financed *Waiting for "Superman"* (Chilcott & Guggenheim, 2010) and then *Won't Back Down* (Johnson & Barnz, 2012). Anschutz, who is a major personal donor to anti-environmental, anti-gay, creationist and other right-wing causes, founded Walden in 2001. Originally it was best known for its children's, or family, films such as the *Narnia* (2005–2010) series, and co-productions with Disney, such as *Charlotte's Web* (2006), but more recently it moved into films that carried a moral message.

The opportunities created for technology and content providers by standardised curricula, standardised online testing and high quality digital production are enormous as is evident with the growing commercial intersection of media, high tech production, technology and education products.

Closer to the ground are the entrepreneurs who have seen the opportunities for personal financial benefit arising from privatisation. Juan Rangel typifies the profiteering and shady deals that are rife among the charter school companies As proprietor of Chicago's United Neighbourhood Organisation (UNO) Charter Schools, the largest charter school organization in Illinois and the largest Hispanic charter school company in the USA, he made a direct plea in a September 2012 speech for supporters to embrace the city's wealthiest people, who are the "focus force fuelling the school reform movement" (Burke, 2014) against vested groups pursuing their "adult interests" (Dumke, 2012). Over a five year period, UNO had received more than $280 million in public monies; however, insufficient public oversight saw millions disappear from the organisation and its network of 16 charter schools. Rangel had been a major force for busting the teachers' union, yet in a belated attempt to hold on to his job he agreed that UNO's teachers could join a union and negotiate a collective agreement (Burke, 2014).

Rangel's case illustrates the consequences of making market competition between schools the operational motivation. More significantly the logic is evident in examples of systematic abuse such as in Atlanta where administrators have been found guilty of manipulating SAT scores and other testing regimes in order to attract public monies or to fend off funding cuts (Rich, 2013). This phenomenon is not confined to the US. There are many examples from other countries of similar fabrication of test results, corrupt dealings between schools and developers, skimming off public monies for private use and unscrupulous marketing deals to recruit students ("Ministers 'failed to share findings on fraud,'" 2013).

CONCLUSION

Through cinema's history teachers have been generally portrayed in a positive light. They have been patricians, disciplinarians, charismatic pied-piper types, anti-heroes, saviours and social mediators. That is until recently when they have been caught up in the ideological and commercial battle against public education and have been transformed into obstacles standing in the way of children's learning and in need of "liberation" from unions.

In appropriating aspects of the progressive narrative backlash films such as *Won't Back Down* (Johnson & Barnz, 2012) recognised that developing engagement and attachment involves more than presenting a closely argued thesis. *Won't Back Down* works at the emotional level and has an authenticity because of its connection to the experience of parents. The key connection bringing Jamie and Nona together, despite all their obvious differences, is concern for how their children are being treated.

Understanding the way these films work, their appeal and their potency, is necessary for countering that narrative, but more so for being able to engage with those who are influenced by it. In the aftermath of the global financial crisis, the persistent unemployment especially for young adults, and the precarious position for workers more generally, means that education and schooling is often the focus of parents' hopes.

Representing teaching and learning on screen is difficult. Getting away from sentimental, heroic, or do-gooder portraits, is a challenge for writers and directors. However there are glimpses of good pedagogy in some films. Many teachers on screen have demonstrated learner-focused and student-centred approaches, where the teacher facilitates learning, offers support and guidance, and shows demonstrate their educational expertise. In *Freedom Writers* (DeVito et al., 2007), as well as other films such as *Walk-Out, Stand by Me*, and *The Wire*, we see teachers exercise flexibility and negotiation over texts and content using examples and exercises related to the real life situations of students. They attend to creating learning environments, make use of student journaling, discovery projects, group work and self-direction and create more interaction in class. These pedagogic practices, familiar to many adult educators, emerged after the 1970s in response to social movement critiques of traditional, didactic and instrumental learning, and the narrow curriculum that excluded the history, literature and culture of many people. They are the very practices most under threat from today's *education reformers* in schools, vocational education and increasingly in higher education.

Why is this important for critical educators? The public assault on teachers and public education goes beyond schools. Adult educators know education occurs in many other formal settings and in an even wider range of non-formal sites, however schooling is the easiest way of representing education to a general audience because it is the one site where everyone has personal experience.

If adult education is about facilitating mutual enquiry to develop the means of analysing the personal and social world around us, then understanding the struggle over the representation teachers and education on the big screen for general public consumption is an important and necessary skill to develop.

NOTES

[1] See the trailer at https://www.youtube.com/ watch?v=dKZcHwiv0E4
[2] Olmos would later direct the HBO film *Walk-Out* (2006) based on the little known Chicano student walk-out of LA schools in 1968 protesting the banning of Spanish speaking in schools. Michael Pena (who in 2014 starred in *Cesar Chavez*), plays Sal Castro, the teacher who supported the students.
[3] Saviour films also spawned some amusing spoofs such as MadTV's *Nice white lady* (see https://www.youtube.com/watch?v=ZVF-nirSq5s).
[4] While there is a suite of French films dealing with schools and teachers, they are not alone in Europe. Films about today's schools and teaching are also being made in, for example, Italy (*Il Russo et il Blu*, 2012, and Germany (*Fack ju Gothe*, 2013 and *Ms Mueller must go*, 2014).
[5] Other examples of films based on biographical accounts include *To Sir, with Love* (E. R. Braithwaite/Sydney Poitier); *Lean on Me* (Joe Clark/Morgan Freeman); *Sylvia* (Sylvia Ashton-Warner/Eleanor David); *Stand and Deliver* (Jaime Escalante/Edward James Olmos); *Dangerous Minds* (Louanne Johnson/Michelle Pfeiffer); *Freedom Writers* (Erin Gruwell/Hilary Swank); *The Class* (François Bégaudeau/François Bégaudeau), *Walk Out* (Sal Castro/Michael Pena); *The Red and the Blue* (Marco Lodoli/Riccardo Scarmarcio).
[6] Teacher films that address a range of thorny issues continue to be made. See, for example, *Il Rosso e il Blu* (Italy, 2012); *Molly Maxwell* (Canada, 2013, about a female student/male teacher sexual attraction); *A Teacher* (USA, 2013, about a female teacher/male student sexual relationship).
[7] Interestingly, Lippmann discusses the concept of "manufacturing consent" in this same book, well before Noam Chomsky made it common many decades later.

REFERENCES

Askenazi, A., & Lesage, B. (Producers), & Lilienfeld, J.-P. (Director). (2008). *La journee de la jupe/Skirt day* [Motion picture] France: Mascaret Films.
Baird, T., St. John, E. (Producers), & Asquith, A. (Director). (1951). *The Browning version* [Motion picture]. UK: General Film Distributors.
Benjo, C., Scotta, C. (Producers), & Cantet, L. (Director). (2008). *Entre les murs/The class* [Motion picture]. France: Haut et Court/France 2 Cinema/Canal+.
Berman, P. (Producer), & Brooks, R. (Director). (1955). *Blackboard jungle* [Motion picture] USA: Metro-Goldwyn-Mayer.
Brantley, M. (2013, January 7). Waltons expand political push on school measures. *Arkansas Times*. Retrieved from www.arktimes.com/ArkansasBlog/archives/2013/01/07/waltons-expand-political-push-on-school-measures
Bruner, J. (1986). *Actual minds, possible worlds*. Boston, MA: Harvard University Press.

Burke, C. W. (2014, January 8). The rise and fall of Juan Rangel the patron of Chicago's UNO charter schools. *Chicago Magazine*. Retrieved from http://www.chicagomag.com/Chicago-Magazine/February-2014/uno-juan-rangel/

Chilcott, L. (Producer), & Guggenheim, D. (Director). (2010). *Waiting for "Superman"* [Motion picture]. USA: Walden Media.

Clavell, J. (Producer & Director). (1967). *To Sir, with love* [Motion picture]. UK: Columbia British Productions.

Delbanco, A. (2013, October 10). The two faces of American education. *New York Review of Books*. Retrieved from http://www.nybooks.com/articles/archives/2013/oct/10/rhee-ravitch-two-faces-american-education/

DeVito, D., Shamberg, M., Sher, S. (Producers), & LaGravenese, R. (Director). (2007). *Freedom writers* [Motion picture]. USA: MTV Films.

Dreier, P. (2013, March 5). Why Are Walmart billionaires bankrolling phony school "reform" in LA? *Truth-Out*. Retrieved from http://truth-out.org/news/item/14930-why-are-walmart-billionaires-bankrolling-phony-school-reform-in-la

Dumke, M. (2012, August 30). UNO's Juan Rangel does a damn good Chris Christie impersonation. *Chicago reader*. Retrieved from http://www.chicagoreader.com/Bleader/archives/2012/08/30/unos-juan-rangel-does-a-damn-good-chris-christie-impression

Ganz, M. (2009). Why stories matter: The art and craft of social change. *Sojourners Magazine, 38*(3), 16–21.

Ganz, M. (2010). *Why David sometimes wins: Leadership, organization, and strategy in the California farm worker movement*. New York, NY: Oxford University Press.

Garner, T., James, K. (Producers), & Coraci, F. (Director). (2012). *Here comes the boom* [Motion picture]. USA: Happy Madison Productions.

Geertz, C. (1975). *The interpretation of cultures: Selected essays*. London, England: Hutchinson.

Gensler, H. (2012, September 28). Maggie Gyllenhaal talks unions, education and motherhood. *Philadelphia Daily News*. Retrieved from http://articles.philly.com/2012-09-28/news/34149452_1_anti-union-bias-teachers-union-top-charter-school

Giroux, H. (1997). Race, pedagogy and whiteness in *Dangerous minds*. *Cineaste, 22*(4), 46–49.

Giroux, H. (2012, December 17). The war against teachers as public intellectuals in dark times. *Truthout*. Retrieved from http://truth-out.org/opinion/item/13367-the-corporate-war-against-teachers-as-public-intellectuals-in-dark-times

Goldstein, D. (2014). *The teacher wars: A history of America's most embattled profession*. New York, NY: Doubleday.

Haft, S., Witt, P., Thomas, T. (Producers), & Weir, P. (Director). (1989). *Dead poets society* [Motion picture]. USA: Touchstone Pictures.

Heath, C., & Heath, D. (2007). *Made to stick: Why some ideas survive and others die*. New York, NY: Random House.

hooks, b. (1996). *"Making movie magic", reel to real: Race, sex and class at the movies*. New York, NY: Routledge.

Johnson, M. (Producer), & Barnz, D. (Director). (2012). *Won't back down*. [Motion picture]. USA: Walden Media/Gran Via Productions.

Kroll, A. (2011, March 17). What's happening in Wisconsin explained? *Mother Jones*. Retrieved from www.motherjones.com/mojo/2011/02/whats-happening-wisconsin-explained

Kubel, P. (Producer), & Mention-Schaar, M.-C. (Producer & Director). (2014). *Les heritiers/Once in a lifetime* [Motion picture]. France: Loma Nasha Films.

Lawn, M., & Ozga, J. (1988). The educational worker? A reassessment of teachers. In J. Ozga (Ed.), *Schoolwork: Interpreting the labour process of teaching* (pp. 81–98). Philadelphia, PA: Open University Press.

Lippmann, W. (1965). *Public opinion*. New York, NY: Free Press. (Original work published 1922)

Lloyd, C. (2012). *Won't back down: A movie review*. Retrieved from http://www.greatschools.org/improvement/parental-power/7033-wont-back-down-movie-review-parent-trigger-law.gs

Masterman, L. (1990). *Teaching the media*. London, England: Routledge.

McGurn, W. (2010, September 21). An even more *Inconvenient truth*: Al Gore's movie director takes on the public schools. *The Wall Street Journal*. Retrieved from www.wsj.com

Ministers "failed to share findings on fraud." (2013, November 13). *Yorkshire post*. Retrieved from www.yorkshirepost.co.uk/news/main-topics/education/ministers-failed-to-share-findings-on-frau

Moore, T. (2007, January 19). Classroom distinctions. *New York Times*. Retrieved from www.nytimes.com/2007/01/19/opinion/19moore.html?_r=1&pagewanted=all&oref=slogin

Musca, T. (Producer), & Menéndez, R. (Director). (1988). *Stand and deliver* [Motion picture]. USA: Warner Bros.

Obama, B. (2013). *Presidential proclamation national charter schools week*. Retrieved from http://www.whitehouse.gov/the-press-office/2013/05/03/presidential-proclamation-national-charter-schools-week-2013

Pray, D., Takis, K. (Producers), & Williams, A. (Director). (2013). *We are Wisconsin: This is what democracy looks like* [Motion picture]. USA: Bal Maiden Films in association with Public Interest Pictures & Peer Review Films.

Ravitch, D. (2013). *Reign of error: The hoax of the privatisation movement and the danger to America's public schools*. New York, NY: Alfred A. Knopf.

Rich, M. (2013, April 2). Scandal in Atlanta ignites debate over tests' role. *New York Times*. Retrieved from www.nytimes.com/2013/04/03/education/atlanta-cheating-scandal-reignites-testing-debate.html

Rodesiler, L. (2010). Empowering students through critical media literacy: This means war. *The Clearing House, 83*(5), 164–167. Retrieved from http://printandnewmedia.wikispaces.com/file/view/Rodesiler_Critical+Media+Literacy-War.pdf

Saville, V. (Producer), & Wood, S. (Director). (1939). *Goodbye, Mr. Chips* [Motion picture]. UK: MGM Denham Studios.

Shapiro, G., Lund, C., Gubelman, B., Stark, A., Kohn, B., Papavasiliou, C. (Producers), & Kaye, T. (Director). (2012). *Detachment* [Motion picture]. USA: Tribeca Film.

Simonton, A. (2013, December 11). How Wall Street power brokers are designing the future of public education as a money-making machine. *AlterNet*. Retrieved from http://www.truth-out.org/opinion/item/20567-how-wall-street-power-brokers-are-designing-the-future-of-public-education-as-a-money-making-machine

Simpson, D., Bruckheimer, J. (Producers), & Smith, J. (Director). (1995) *Dangerous minds* [Motion picture]. USA: Hollywood Pictures/Simpson Bruckheimer/Via Rosa Productions.

Smith, K. (2010, September 24). Film's anguished lesson on why schools are failing. *New York post*. Retrieved from www.nypost.com

Strain, M., & Field, J. (1997). On "the myth of the learning society." *British Journal of Educational Studies, 45*(2), 141–155.

Takata, J. W. (Producer), & Takata, J. (Producer & Director). (2013). *We the parents*. Las Vegas, NV: Go For Broke Pictures.

The Shocking State of Our Schools. (2010). Retrieved from http://www.oprah.com/oprahshow/The-Shocking-State-of-Our-Schools

Twain, N. (Producer), & Avildsen, J. (Director). (1989). *Lean on me* [Motion picture]. USA: Warner Bros.

Williams, R. (1993). Film as a tutorial subject. In J. McIlroy & S. Westwood (Eds.), *Border country: Raymond Williams in adult education* (pp. 185–192) Leicester, England: NIACE. (Original work published 1953)

Tony Brown
Faculty of Education, Science, Technology & Maths
University of Canberra

PAMELA TIMANSON AND THERESA J. SCHINDEL

5. DISCOURSE ANALYSIS OF ADULT AND WORKPLACE LEARNING IN *NURSE JACKIE*

Exploring Learning Processes within a Knowledge Culture

INTRODUCTION

Popular culture, particularly in the form of television, has a profound influence on understandings of the social world. Television is a source of information that not only shapes public perception (Cabaniss, 2011; Wright, 2010) but also creates a cultural space where adults can learn knowledge, attitudes, and behaviours through observing the relevant performances of others in various contexts (Brookfield, 1986; Jarvis & Burr, 2011; Jubas, 2013). Potter and Wetherell (1987) argued that "it is important to remember that virtually the entirety of anyone's understanding of the social world is mediated by discourse in the form of conversations, newspapers, novels, TV stories and so on" (p. 174). Professionals bring these understandings into their workplace; as a result, they become a part of workplace learning (Wright, 2013). Due to the presence of these understandings in the workplace and the impact they may have on human behaviour, television programs present opportunities to explore adult and workplace learning.

In 2009, the ShowTime network introduced the medical drama/comedy *Nurse Jackie*. The program is situated in the emergency room (ER) of a fictional New York City hospital, All Saints. The main character, Jackie Peyton, is a nurse leader in her department who struggles to balance aspects of her professional and personal life, including addiction to prescription drugs. There is a prominent theme of addiction woven throughout *Nurse Jackie*; many episodes highlight the character's efforts to elude detection. Jackie's clinical teaching role as mentor to Zoey, who appears at the beginning of the series as a first-year nursing student, is prevalent throughout the first four seasons. The cast of characters includes physicians (Cooper and O'Hara), nurses (Thor and Momo), administrators (Akalitus and Cruz), a pharmacist, an emergency medical technician (EMT), and patients.

Previous research on *Nurse Jackie* has largely focused on the portrayal of nurses in television programs. Spear (2010) evaluated the current image of nurses in the media, and Cabaniss (2011) examined the media representation of nurses on television to explore its impact on the image of nursing in the public domain. Both authors noted the importance of cooperation between the nursing profession and the media to promote more positive and realistic images of nurses. Cullen

(2012) studied student nurses' perspectives on the images of nurses and nursing in entertainment media. She concluded that students construct ideas of nursing from course work, practical experience, and personal values, and that these ideas are often in direct contrast to the inaccuracies portrayed in the media. Weaver, Salamonson, Koch, and Jackson (2013) studied nursing students' perceptions of the portrayal of their profession on television. Based on their findings, the authors encouraged students to critically engage with society's image of their profession. Weaver, Ferguson, Wilbourn, and Salamonson (2014) further explored the portrayal of men in nursing and the reinforcement of stereotypes. The ethics of the nursing profession were examined in the research of Kunyk and Austin (2012) with a focus on drug addiction. McHugh (2012) studied the success of *Nurse Jackie* in comparison to other television programs in terms of the representational challenges overcome in the program, with particular attention to the ethical representations of care.

This chapter presents our study of adult and workplace learning in the television program *Nurse Jackie*. While other research on *Nurse Jackie* has focused on ethics, professional relationships, and the portrayal of nurses, little is known about the adult and workplace learning depicted in the scenes, images, and practices enacted in this television drama. We explore how workplace learning is constructed and characterized in *Nurse Jackie*, relating our findings to adult and workplace learning literature. In the following sections of this chapter, we provide a discussion of learning and knowledge cultures, and an explanation of the discourse analysis method used in the study. Following analysis of selected scenes, we discuss the constructions and characterizations of workplace learning within a knowledge culture.

LEARNING AND KNOWLEDGE CULTURES

Workplaces are fertile social spaces that provide many opportunities for adults to learn from and with their colleagues through the completion of their daily work activities. Adults as members of a workplace community generate knowledge through their active participation in the workplace (Fenwick, 2010). The members of the community both influence and are influenced by the social and cultural elements of their workplace, and they learn through making connections between newly acquired knowledge and previous experiences (Magro, 2001; Merriam, 2008). The focus of our research is on workplace learning; therefore, we adopt the situated cognition perspective, as workers are embedded in an environment where knowing and learning have meaning and in which they may acquire the behaviours and beliefs of their work community (Magro, 2001). Employees establish meaning through the utilization of skills and concepts in particular situations, allowing them to gain a more in-depth understanding than they had previously (Magro, 2001).

Many researchers have examined workplace learning as a constituent of adult education, theorizing how adults learn within their work environments. There is an emphasis in the literature on content that adults are learning on a continual basis within their workplaces (Billett, 2001; Rothwell, 2002). The workplace context is important to consider because in many cases individuals are not able to "separate the learning process from the situation in which the learning is presented" (Merriam, Caffarella, & Baumgartner, 2007, p. 178). Employees are embedded in their work environments, in which they can co-construct knowledge with other employees, relating personal and work experiences to factual information. Through workplace learning, employees may grow as professionals, deepening their knowledge base through interactions with their colleagues.

Informal learning often occurs within the workplace. Although informal learning can be, and often is, organized and purposeful, such as the organization and management of teachers' professional learning (Colley, Hodkinson, & Malcolm, 2003), informal learning occurs as employees carry out their work and lacks the confines of boundaries that are associated with formal learning. It is a spontaneous form of learning as workers interact with each other in the workplace (Jurasaite-Harbison, 2009). Informal learning is embedded in work processes and occurs during work activities, providing great flexibility for employees. Eraut (2004) described it as "a combination of learning from other people and learning from personal experience" (p. 248). Marsick and Watkins (2001) further emphasized that informal learning is integrated in daily routines, triggered by an internal or external jolt, not highly conscious, haphazard and influenced by chance, an inductive process of reflection and action, and linked to the learning of others. Informal learning encompasses different processes such as mentoring, incidental learning, trial-and-error, problem solving, learning from experimenting, transformative learning, and socialization or tacit learning (Enos, Kehrhahn, & Bell, 2003; Eraut, 2004, 2012; Forman, 2004; Jubas & Knutson, 2013; Merriam, Caffarella, & Baumgartner, 2007).

To facilitate the characterization of adult and workplace learning for this study, we employed a conceptual framework of knowledge cultures. The concept of knowledge cultures extends from Knorr Cetina's (1999) research, where she completed a comparative study between two different epistemic cultures (scientists working in a physics laboratory and a molecular biology laboratory), and deduced that each culture had a unique way of constructing and warranting knowledge. Knorr Cetina's subsequent work (2001, 2006, 2007) and that of other researchers (Damsa, Kirschner, Andriessen, Erkens, & Sins, 2010; Guile, 2009; Jensen, 2007; Nerland, 2008) has advanced understandings of workplace learning and how professionals engage with and manage knowledge in their professional communities. The concept of knowledge cultures complements the work by Lave and Wenger (1991), and continues to develop understandings of how learning occurs through social processes and how communities of professionals produce, distribute, and access knowledge.

The value of knowledge produced and enacted within the workplace has greatly increased, as it is seen as helping organizations gain a competitive edge. This has led to workplaces having collective beliefs on how their knowledge will be produced and distributed throughout the organization. As such, the way employees within a workplace envision knowledge, in terms of its character, usefulness, and opportunities, is a part of their social life. Employees both influence the knowledge culture of their workplace and are influenced by it in terms of how they learn to see the world (Nerland, 2008). Thus, each profession has its own knowledge culture that is unique in terms of the practices or the ways that they manage and engage with knowledge and influence their work-based learning (Nerland, 2008, 2010). Knorr Cetina (2006) argued that these unique ways of professional work incorporate inquiry practices of validating, documenting, and legitimizing knowledge, which have traditionally been associated with scientific work. As such, employees within these other professions reinvent practices of their own to acquire knowledge (Knorr Cetina, 2001). They have distinct heuristic practices and knowledge relations that include such things as activities, instruments, and ways of envisioning knowledge (Nerland, Jensen, & Bekele, 2010).

The informal learning processes of professionals are embedded within the knowledge culture of their workplace. In this chapter, through an examination of a knowledge culture presented in *Nurse Jackie*, we will convey an understanding of how these learning processes of the professionals depicted in the program are constructed and characterized.

METHODOLOGY AND DATA

This study is anchored in social constructionism, which views individuals as constructors of knowledge and meaning as they engage with the world in which they live, interpreting their experiences through relationships, language, and social processes (Burr, 2003; Crotty, 1998). Language may be viewed as an important tool through which individuals create meaning, organize behaviours, and represent themselves to others in social settings such as the workplace. We used a discourse analysis approach based on Potter and Wetherell (1987) to analyse scenes in the television program *Nurse Jackie* wherein professionals learn about and from each other at work and the meanings associated with learning. A discourse is represented by

> a set of meanings, metaphors, representations, images, stories, statements and so on that in some way together produce a particular version of events. It refers to a particular picture that is painted of an event (or a person or class of persons), a particular way of representing it or them in a certain light. (Burr, 2003, p. 64)

Discourses not only describe things, they also accomplish things (Potter & Wetherell, 1987). Individuals use discourses to construct knowledge and meaning within a historical context. In turn, discourses shape actions of individuals and their interactions with others. This discourse analysis approach, therefore, is concerned with what individuals do with discourses and the practices with which they engage. The concrete representations of discourses are texts, and these may include conversations, transcripts, images, films, television programs, and objects.

A television program set within a hospital is a textual dataset rich with depictions of workplace learning. Building on the concept of knowledge cultures, workplace learning is abundant wherever professional communities such as nursing, medicine, and pharmacy engage in their practices. This chapter provides a reflexive space for exploring these depictions in comparison to theoretical understandings of workplace learning. Initially, we collected data together by viewing five episodes of the first season of *Nurse Jackie* to establish a common understanding of the method. We then independently watched all episodes in the first four seasons of *Nurse Jackie* available on DVD and documented instances of learning represented in the program. We noted details and concepts depicted in each episode, comparing interpretations of the scene, and identifying concepts related to knowledge cultures. We considered how professional learning in the workplace was constructed in the television program and how these constructions related to adult and workplace learning literature. We met after each season was viewed to share key findings, including our individual observations, interpretations, assumptions, and positions. We then co-constructed a list of scenes that we felt represented workplace learning in this drama, after which we created a transcript of the scenes using transcripts available from Internet websites as a starting point. One author verified the accuracy of the transcripts against the corresponding episodes. Throughout the data collection and analysis processes, we focused on how learning in the workplace was characterized based on adult learning literature and processes of legitimization, validation, and documentation within knowledge cultures. As we analysed the transcripts, we worked side-by-side to compare and contrast our interpretations of the program's dialogue related to learning in order to co-construct meanings and identify discourses of learning. To ensure the credibility of our results, we conducted repeated and prolonged review of the data together allowing time for our understandings to evolve over a period of 12 months.

FINDINGS AND DISCUSSION

In the four seasons of *Nurse Jackie* included in this study, processes of learning within a knowledge culture were depicted in the everyday activities of the workplace. These learning processes included legitimizing, validating, and documenting knowledge. Learning that was informal and situated, and aligned with adult and workplace learning, was depicted as learning from experience, reflection, peers, and mentors. Three representations of adult and workplace learning, or discourses, were identified: (1) mentor-protégé learning, (2) learning from mistakes, and (3) developing as a confident practitioner. Following an introduction to a scene related to each adult learning discourse, we elaborate further on the processes of producing knowledge and the heuristic practices within a knowledge culture represented at the fictional hospital in *Nurse Jackie*.

Mentor-Protégé Learning

In the first season, Jackie reluctantly agreed to mentor Zoey, the student nurse, in her first practical experience. Zoey was very excited to be a nurse and eager to learn. In one episode, the audience witnessed her learning about the effect of medications on pupil size. This story followed a previous experience in which Jackie saw a patient who complained of a broken finger, but who was actually seeking drugs. In this scene, Zoey told her mentor, Jackie, about a documentary film on the eye:

Zoey: Okay, so I watched this amazing program about miotic pupils. Well, it was about the whole eyeball, but still, did you know ...

Jackie: Okay, we're four short. I need you to stick with every patient I throw at you and follow up with them as if you are me.

Zoey: So I'm on my own?

Jackie: Stop smiling. The last time you were on your own, you gave Dave-the-addict six Percocets [narcotic pain medication tablets] for a non-existent broken finger.

Zoey: He cried every time I made him bend it.

Jackie: Zoey, drug seekers come in here all the time. You like pupils so much, make sure you're checking them.

Zoey: I will, believe me, because the pupil tells you everything you need to know.

Jackie: No, I tell you everything you need to know. We are way too busy today for you to be a pushover. (Flahive & Buscemi, 2009)

Throughout this episode, Zoey examined the pupils of several patients and co-workers. Armed with knowledge gained from the documentary film, her prior experience with "Dave-the-addict," and Jackie's challenge to check pupils, Zoey focussed on learning to examine pupils. Knowledge that pupil size changes in response to some medications such as narcotics was highlighted in this episode. As Zoey continued to examine pupils, Jackie became increasingly evasive and avoided eye contact with Zoey. By the end of the episode, Zoey's assessment skills progressed. She shared an observation with Jackie:

Zoey: So I think that temp [nurse] ... is on something, like a lot of Valium or Halcion.

Jackie: Zoey, you never narc on another nurse unless you are absolutely sure.

Zoey: His pupils are contracted, glassy and non-responsive to the light I shined directly in his eye after I rolled over his foot with a large man on a gurney. He didn't feel it.

Jackie: Okay, nice catch. (Flahive & Buscemi, 2009)

A knowledge culture is unique to each workplace and a part of daily work life for professionals. There are distinct heuristic practices and ways of envisioning knowledge within each knowledge culture (Nerland, Jensen, & Bekele, 2010). This knowledge is based on "sets of practices, arrangements and mechanisms bound together by necessity, affinity and historical coincidence which, in a given area of professional expertise, make up how we know what we know" (Knorr Cetina, 2007, p. 363). Within this episode, Jackie was mentoring Zoey and helping her learn the heuristic practices of the knowledge culture within the hospital. In response to Zoey's declaration that "the pupil tells you everything you need to know" when assessing a patient, Jackie asserted her authority as a mentor, stating: "No, I tell you everything you need to know." This exchange drew attention to two different meanings attributed to the pupil: to Zoey, the pupil meant anatomy of the eye, and to Jackie, the pupil meant Zoey as Jackie's protégé. Jackie was letting Zoey know that nursing knowledge does not emerge exclusively from clinical observations; after all, previous observations of a patient misled Zoey to release medication based on pain symptoms alone as opposed to a wider view of the patient including drug-seeking behaviour as part of the clinical picture. In this scene, Jackie offered Zoey professional expertise, sharing legitimized and validated knowledge with Zoey. Jackie guided Zoey's learning experience as she introduced knowledge that cannot be easily acquired from a documentary film (Billett, 2001).

Jackie's perspective also drew attention to the role of a mentor in monitoring student ability and sequencing student involvement to begin with simple tasks, then to engage in more complicated tasks, and eventually to "graduate" to full-time responsibility (Gowlland, 2014). In workplace learning, discourses such as the mentoring discourse signify that the mentor controls knowledge and can influence what is learned (Fenwick, 2001). Jackie's approach to mentoring involved control of what is learned; she restricted Zoey's activities to facilitate knowledge building and gaining of experience before taking on more critical tasks (Gowlland, 2014). In challenging Zoey to "check" more pupils, Jackie guided her to experiment with a task based on prior performance (Gowlland, 2014). Within the context of addiction in this scene, Jackie's role as a mentor permitted her to redirect Zoey's attention so that she evaded suspicion of narcotic use. Jackie also gave Zoey more independence when she allowed her to care for patients independently. However, Jackie instructed Zoey to "follow up with them as if you are me," indicating that she expected Zoey to mimic her practice and emanate the knowledge that Jackie validated and legitimized for her.

This scene highlighted Zoey's learning from her personal experiences with the documentary film, patients, and co-workers, and from a mentor (Eraut, 2004). Through her practical experiences and observations, especially those with the temporary nurse, Zoey reflected on her practice, through the verbalization of her observations and documentation of her understanding, and demonstrated what she learned in practice (Marsick & Watkins, 2001). Zoey documented the knowledge she gained from her co-workers and experiences in a personal notebook and a blog. This was a reflective process, as she returned to her notes when confronted with uncertainty or to determine how to care for a patient. Through this reflective consultation, her learning was shaped through the lens of the knowledge culture of her workplace (Nerland, 2008). Through a mentoring relationship, Zoey learned some of the heuristic practices of her knowledge culture and how knowledge is envisioned within her profession. In the learning process, she acquired the behaviours and beliefs of the workplace (Magro, 2001). The heuristic practices encompassed intended learning and unintended learning with respect to ethical issues in practice related to "being absolutely sure" of narcotic use by a co-worker. While not the primary aspect of the mentor-protégé relationship, the realization that new knowledge can be brought to the knowledge community by the protégé, or novice professional, challenged the authority of the mentor.

Learning from Mistakes

A patient named Neil Nutterman, a well-known film critic whose raison d'être "is to hold people to a higher standard" (Cleveland & Ellis, 2009), was introduced in an episode at the end of Season 1. In one scene, Nutterman was brought into the ER by EMTs and immediately evaluated by O'Hara and Jackie. It was apparent that Nutterman was in a great deal of pain, yet he still had the energy to spar with Jackie over his film reviews and her bedside manner. Jackie offered Zoey the opportunity for independence: "Zoey, you wanna take this one?" (Cleveland & Ellis, 2009). Zoey accepted the responsibility. Subsequent interactions between Zoey and Nutterman highlighted his continued discomfort and requests for pain medication. Zoey approached Jackie to ask if she could provide the medication. Jackie authorized Zoey to administer an intravenous narcotic medication under her supervision. Following administration of the medication, Nutterman developed slurred speech and respiratory distress, and then rapidly lost consciousness. O'Hara recognized that Zoey had administered five times the normal dose of the medication.

Jackie immediately dismissed Zoey from patient care duties, saying, "Okay, you're off the floor. No more patients. You can answer phones; that's about it. This is not good" (Cleveland & Ellis, 2009). Zoey was required to report the incident to the administrator, Akalitus, who pointed to Jackie, saying, "This is just as much your fault as it is hers" (Cleveland & Ellis, 2009). At the end of the episode, Zoey sought advice about her mistake from two veteran nurses, Thor and Momo. They recounted stories of their own mistakes and advised, "When you get to the other side of it Zoey, you'll be a better nurse" (Cleveland & Ellis, 2009).

The Nutterman story resumed in the next and final episode of Season 1 (Brixius, Wallem, & Ellis, 2009). Zoey appeared in the ER wearing a new, grey uniform. Her usual uniform of brightly coloured scrubs with animal patterns contrasted strongly with those of other nurses in the ER, who wore solid-coloured scrubs. In a fan blog entry, "Zoey" described the rationale for her choice: "Unlike some of my fellow nurses who can dress a little boringly sometimes, I try to pick clothes that let me be me. Colours, patterns and the occasional accessory allow any enthusiastic nurse to express themselves and bring a little cheer to their patients" (Barkow, 2011). Zoey's new uniform stimulated discussion in the show, much of which concerned the patient Nutterman and the medication error:

Jackie: What's up with your scrubs?

Zoey: They're grey.

Jackie: I can see that. I don't like them.

Zoey: I don't like them either. That's why I'm wearing them.

Jackie: That's not a good reason.

Zoey: I'm wearing them as a sign of remorse.

Jackie: I get it. I get it, Zoey. (Brixius, Wallem, & Ellis, 2009)

Throughout the episode, Zoey's mistake, represented by the grey scrubs, was shown to affect co-workers. As Zoey passed Jackie and O'Hara in the ER hallway, Jackie shouted, "Damn it, Zoey, change your scrubs," and O'Hara added, "They're really grim" (Brixius, Wallem, & Ellis, 2009). Later, Zoey is seated at the nursing station with Jackie:

Jackie: Zoey, just go to your locker, put on your happy-monkey scrubs. Please. Truly. Nutterman is gonna come out of this thing, I promise. So just go.

Zoey: Even if I don't get fired, I never want to administer meds again.

Jackie: You fall off that horse, you get right back on. (Brixius, Wallem, & Ellis, 2009)

The episode concluded with Nutterman's recovery and Zoey at his bedside wearing her characteristic brightly coloured "happy-monkey scrubs."

In this episode, viewers saw Jackie increase Zoey's independence and provide her with more patient-care responsibilities. As a student nurse, Zoey was excited to accept responsibility; she craved "a deepened understanding which propels [her] learning forward" (Jensen, 2007, p. 492). She wanted to learn the epistemic culture of her profession, and working/learning alongside Jackie motivated her to grow in her knowledge and role as a nurse. This growth was demonstrated in her desire to take on more responsibility and administer the pain medication to Nutterman, progressing her learning from strictly observing Jackie to including more practical experience.

Zoey experienced an external jolt in learning (Marsick & Watkins, 2001) when she observed Nutterman's adverse reaction to the medication she administered. Zoey wanted to provide care for Nutterman by relieving his pain, but instead she inflicted potentially significant harm on him. She turned to her colleagues to help her reflect on this mistake and learn from the experience. During the reflection process, she changed her uniform, thus both physically documenting her mistake and visibly demonstrating her emotional distress. Her ability to carry out her role and apply her accumulated knowledge became restricted. After conversations with co-workers Thor, Momo, and Jackie, Zoey was able to incorporate their learning experiences and advice into her own knowledge base, co-constructing knowledge on how to proceed. Her colleagues validated that mistakes are a part of the working culture in a hospital and it is important to learn and move on from the mistake by resuming duties as soon as possible; in Jackie's words, "You fall off that horse, you get right back on." They also legitimized the process of care for Zoey; when a mistake is made, you learn from it and try not to repeat it. Zoey learned to pay careful attention in the dosage she administers to a patient, what an overdose can look like, to accept the mistake she made, and to progress from it. As a result of these validation and legitimization processes, Zoey changed back into her usual scrubs, showing that she developed knowledge of how to confront mistakes and learn from them.

Within a knowledge culture, there are dynamic, embodied, and web-like relationships between objects and professionals in the workplace. Knorr Cetina (2001) argued, "epistemic environments cannot be understood without understanding expert-object relationships [because] knowledge cultures centrally turn around object worlds to which experts and scientists are orientated" (pp. 187–88). The reaction of Zoey's colleagues to her mistake and clothing change was a learning experience for Zoey. In their support of Zoey as a newcomer to the profession, her colleagues shared their experiences of making mistakes and they reflected together to help her learn through their experiences (Marsick & Watkins, 2001). Seeing Zoey in grey scrubs made her colleagues uncomfortable because they were a constant visual reminder of both her mistake and those they had made in the past. Although they validated and legitimized mistakes as part of their epistemic culture, her co-workers did not welcome the reminder, as mistakes can harm or kill patients, demoralizing hospital staff and undermining the basic premise of their professional practice. They wanted Zoey to change her scrubs because they wanted her to learn and grow from this experience, not to remain immersed in remorse. Zoey's colleagues shared in her experience, as Zoey progressed to being able to embrace and accept her mistake, and eventually move past it. The grey scrubs generated learning opportunities for Zoey because as her colleagues reacted to her scrubs, they shared their experiences, and Zoey was able to come to a new understanding of mistakes and the roles they have in their knowledge culture.

At the conclusion of the Nutterman story, Zoey appeared wearing her preferred attire. This change demonstrated a stage of Zoey's development as a professional, which accorded with the assertion that "objects contribute to creating and defining who we are as persons and the identities we form" (Jensen & Lahn, 2005, p. 308). For Zoey, this self-definition occurred during the process of reflecting and learning about mistakes, from which she was able to grow professionally and personally. Her co-workers shared the learning experience, as they co-constructed knowledge with her and helped her learn from her practical experience.

Developing as a Confident Practitioner

By the end of Season 2, Zoey had become a more confident student nurse, learning from a mentoring relationship and her mistakes. One scene began with Jackie asking Zoey to cover for her so that she may leave the shift early for a family vacation. Zoey enthusiastically accepted the opportunity to take on Jackie's role and be "in charge," stating "I've dreamt of this day" (Cleveland & Feig, 2010). Throughout the first two seasons of *Nurse Jackie*, Zoey's character keenly observed her mentor, Jackie, mimicking her language and behaviours. With the ER waiting room full of patients, Zoey assumed the role usually held by Jackie with much authority. She called for a patient, Kieran O'Garity, and spoke with him in a private treatment room. O'Garity and his wife had just arrived in New York following a long flight from Dublin. Following her initial assessment of O'Garity's condition, Cooper entered the treatment room:

Cooper:	Hi, I'm Dr. Cooper.
Zoey:	Mr. O'Garity got a rash on his way back from Dublin.
Cooper:	Yep, contact dermatitis, a.k.a. a rash. Let's get him some cortisone cream. Probably just an allergic reaction. (Cleveland & Feig, 2010)

Cooper left the room and Zoey returned to examining O'Garity's leg, asking further questions and learning more about his concerns:

Zoey:	Hmm. Hmm. That hurt?
O'Garity:	Yes, it does.
Zoey:	What about itching, does it itch?
O'Garity:	No.
Mrs. O'Garity:	What about his veins? They're worse than mine. What do you think about that?
Zoey:	Looks like a rash. It doesn't feel like a rash. Would you guys mind waiting here just a little bit? I think he [Cooper] might need another look. (Cleveland & Feig, 2010)

Zoey left the room to find Cooper and asked him to take another look at the leg. Cooper dismissed the idea stating, "Nah, he's good to go. You can discharge him." Next, we saw Zoey interrupt Dr. O'Hara while she was with another patient, to ask if she would see O'Garity:

Zoey:	She's gonna check one more thing. [Zoey attempts to leave the room.]
O'Hara:	No, Zoey, you should stay. It's your hunch we're following.
O'Hara:	Okay, see here? [pointing to a portable ultrasound machine] That's a small, barely perceptible, blood clot.
Mrs. O'Garity:	Blood clot? Oh my God.
O'Hara:	Yeah, you came very close to having a pulmonary embolism, which could've killed you. But luckily, you have this young lady to thank for catching it. I'll leave you in charge, Zoey. (Cleveland & Feig, 2010)

In this scene at the end of Season 2, Zoey checked and double-checked a patient's condition, potentially averting a serious medical incident. This was in contrast to the episode at the end of Season 1, when Zoey learned from her experience with a medication error. Within a knowledge culture, knowledge practices are "the utilization, enactment, and advancement of different expressions of profession-generated knowledge," and it is important to give "special attention to their ways of influencing work-based learning" (Nerland, 2008, p. 51). In this episode, Zoey both enacted and advanced her knowledge. She progressed in her development from a novice learner observing and gaining knowledge from her mentor, to a competent nurse applying her skills and knowledge (Billett, 2001). She transitioned to a state of internalized knowledge and an ability to function independently (Levine & Marcus, 2007). Zoey became an autonomous thinker and was able to critically reflect upon the heuristic practices of her knowledge culture, a development that some scholars might view as important for transformative learning (Mezirow, 1997, 2003). Zoey developed tacit knowledge throughout this process as she reasoned the aspects of a new experience with previously constructed knowledge, and validated and legitimized this knowledge with other members of her knowledge culture. This is consistent with the view of Aldoff, Gerund, and Kaldewey (2015), who wrote, "most dimensions of tacit knowledge are socially acquired and shared and hence are culturally specific" (p. 12). A conflict of opinion and assumptions within her knowledge culture provided Zoey with opportunities to construct and act on knowledge of clot development as a potential complication of air travel.

Reflecting upon her clinical observations, considering the patient's context (air travel), and using tacit knowledge that was based upon theoretical understandings, her previous practical experiences, and the knowledge constructed with her colleagues to this point, Zoey knew that O'Garity's rash was not just a rash; it was a sign of something more serious. In the process of development as a novice learner, she also gained the confidence to trust in her own knowledge and sought a second opinion from O'Hara. Zoey had progressed in her learning and developed confidence that allowed her to form a plan of action (Mezirow, 1997, 2003). Through a process of reflection and action (Marsick & Watkins, 2001), when she considered O'Garity's symptoms in relation to her tacit knowledge and previous experiences, she ensured that O'Garity received a second medical opinion. As a result of O'Hara's assessment of the patient, Zoey's "hunch" or tacit knowledge was validated. O'Hara thus legitimized Zoey's course of action in having confidence to use her tacit knowledge, acknowledging to the patient that it was Zoey who made the correct assessment. Zoey's independence was reinforced, she regained O'Hara's trust, and she progressed in her work-based learning and knowledge practices over the timeframe of these two experiences with patients. Zoey had developed and became a better critical thinker (Merriam, Caffarella, & Baumgartner, 2007).

As professionals seek to attain knowledge or solve problems, they enter a process of looping back and forth between the objects, themselves, and other professionals (Jensen, 2007; Knorr Cetina, 2001). This new knowledge upsets what they knew previously and allows them opportunities to reconstruct knowledge. Zoey critically reflected upon her observations of the patient in contrast to the assessment made by Cooper, and trusted her observations. She pursued a second opinion even though this action went against one of the heuristic practices of her knowledge culture. In this sense, she had confidence in the knowledge she had constructed within her knowledge culture and sought validation and legitimization from another physician. The difference of opinion on the assessment of the patient's condition created an opportunity for critical reflection and allowed Zoey to learn as a result of this experience, her reflections, and interactions with her colleagues.

CONCLUSION AND IMPLICATIONS

In this study, we examined adult and workplace learning in the television program *Nurse Jackie*, and observed and analyzed learning in the four seasons selected for this research. The learning processes and resulting knowledge were enacted through participation in everyday work activities. Characters working in the ER were shown to learn from each other and their patients through stories that spanned entire seasons of the program. The characters' learning from past experiences and their teaching of the student nurse align with discourses of learning in adult and workplace learning literature: informal learning in the workplace and factors that affect workplace learning (Eraut, 2012); the characterization of learning that occurs in workplace communities (Fenwick, 2010); the concept of a community of practice and how novice employees experience legitimate peripheral participation (Lave & Wenger, 1991); the characterization of informal and incidental learning (Marsick & Watkins, 2001); and consideration of the context in which adult learning occurs and that learning is multidimensional (Merriam, 2008). In this chapter, we explored scenes that depicted the following learning discourses: (1) mentor-protégé learning, (2) learning through mistakes, and (3) developing confidence as a practitioner.

Learning processes embedded within a knowledge culture (Nerland, 2008) were observed in *Nurse Jackie*. A distinct knowledge culture and its associated learning processes of documenting, validating, and legitimizing were portrayed. The characters acted out learning processes by documenting knowledge in notebooks, blogs, patient charts, and reports, validating their knowledge through conversation with patients and colleagues, seeking opinions and asking questions, and legitimizing knowledge through oral debate, contemplation, and reflection. Analysis of this knowledge culture aided our understandings of adult and workplace learning.

This project arose from a desire to reconceptualise our own knowledge and practices in research and teaching. In previous work, we have examined popular culture in research on education leadership (Timanson & Hicks, 2013) and employed popular culture in our teaching as professionals in the areas of teacher and pharmacist education. Our curiosity extended to the idea of popular culture as pedagogy not only for professional learning, but also as a cultural space in which adults learn (Brookfield, 1986; Hirt, Wong, Erichsen, & White, 2013; Jubas, 2013; Spear, 2010; Weaver, Salamonson, Koch, & Jackson, 2013). The growing interest evident in recent research on professional learning and knowledge cultures inspires new directions to pursue in the exploration of adult and workplace learning of professionals. We look forward to delving deeper into the concepts introduced in this chapter and deepening our understanding of adult and workplace learning.

REFERENCES

Barkow, Z. (2011, May 19). *Scrubs n' crocs*. [Web blog post]. Retrieved from http://nursinityo.tumblr.com/page/5

Billett, S. (2001). *Learning in the workplace*. Australia: Allen & Unwin.

Brixius, L., Wallem, L. (Writers), & Ellis, S. (Director). (2009). Health care and cinema [Television series episode]. In L. Brixius (Producer, Executive producer), *Nurse Jackie*. USA: Showtime.

Brookfield, S. (1986). Media power and the development of media literacy: An adult educational interpretation. *Harvard Educational Review, 56*(2), 151–171.

Burr, V. (2003). *Social constructionism* (2nd ed.). London, England: Routledge.

Cabaniss, R. (2011). Education nurses to impact change in nursing's image. *Teaching and Learning in Nursing, 6*, 112–118. doi:10.1016/j.teln.2011.01.003

Cleveland, R. (Writer), & Ellis, S. (Director). (2009). Pill-O-Matix [Television series episode]. In L. Brixius (Executive producer), *Nurse Jackie*. USA: Showtime.

Cleveland, R. (Writer), & Feig, P. (Director). (2010). What the day brings [Television series episode]. In L. Brixius (Executive producer), *Nurse Jackie*. USA: Showtime.

Crotty, M. (1998). *The foundations of social research: Meaning and perspective in the research process*. London, England: Sage Publications.

Colley, H., Hodkinson, P., & Malcolm, J. (2003). *Informality and formality in learning: A report for the learning and skills research centre*. London, England: Learning and Skills Research Centre.

Cullen, K. (2012). *Meaning perspectives and the effects of television portrayal of nurses on a sample of southern California generic baccalaureate nursing students: A phenomenological inquiry* (Unpublished doctoral dissertation). Colorado, CO: University of Northern Colorado. Retrieved from ProQuest Dissertations and Theses database (UMI No. 3541930).

Damsa, C. I., Kirschner, P. A., Andriessen, J. E. B., Erkens, G., & Sins, P. H. M. (2010). Shared epistemic agency: An empirical study of an emergent construct. *The Journal of the Learning Sciences, 19*(2), 143–186. doi:10.1080/10508401003708381

Enos, M. D., Kehrhahn, M., & Bell, A. (2003). Transfer of learning: How managers develop proficiency. *Human Resource Development Quarterly, 14*(4), 369–387.

Eraut, M. (2004). Informal learning in the workplace. *Studies in Continuing Education, 26*(2), 247–273.

Eraut, M. (2012). Developing a broader approach to professional learning. In A. McKee & M. Eraut (Eds.), *Learning trajectories, innovation and identity for professional development* (pp. 21–45). New York, NY: Springer.

Fenwick, T. (2001). Tides of change: New themes and questions in workplace learning. *New Directions for Adult and Continuing Education, 92,* 3–18. doi:10.1002/ace.36

Fenwick, T. (2010). Workplace "learning" and adult education. *European Journal for Research on the Education and Learning of Adults, 1*(1/2), 79–95.

Flahive, L. (Writer), & Buscemi, S. (Director). (2009). Pupil [Television series episode]. In L. Brixius (Executive producer), *Nurse Jackie*. USA: Showtime.

Forman, D. C. (2004). Changing perspectives from individual to organizational learning. *International Society for Performance Improvement, 43*(7), 1–7.

Gowlland, G. (2014). Apprenticeship as a model for learning in and through professional practice. In S. Billett, C. Harteis, & H. Gruber (Eds.), *International handbook of research in professional and practice-based learning* (pp. 759–779). Dordrecht, The Netherlands: Springer. doi:10.1007/978-94-017-8902-8_28

Guile, D. (2009). Conceptualizing the transition from education to work as vocational practice: Lessons from the UK's creative and cultural sector. *British Educational Research Journal, 35*(5), 761–779. doi:10.1080/01411920802688713

Hirt, C., Wong, K., Erichsen, S., & White, J. S. (2013). Medical dramas on television: A brief guide for educators. *Medical Teacher, 35*(3), 237–242. doi:10.3109/0142159X.2012.737960

Jarvis, C., & Burr, V. (2011). The transformative potential of popular television: The case of *Buffy the Vampire Slayer*. *Journal of Transformative Education, 9*(3), 165–182. doi:10.1177/1541344612436814

Jensen, K. (2007). The desire to learn: An analysis of knowledge-seeking practices among professionals. *Oxford Review of Education, 33*(4), 489–502.

Jensen, K., & Lahn, L. (2005). The binding role of knowledge: An analysis of nursing students' knowledge ties. *Journal of Education and Work, 18*(3), 305–320.

Jurasaite-Harbison, E. (2009). Teachers' workplace learning within informal contexts of school cultures in the United States and Lithuania. *Journal of Workplace Learning, 21*(4), 299–321. doi:10.1108/13665620910954201

Jubas, K. (2013). Grey('s) identity: Complications of learning and becoming in a popular television show. *Review of Education, Pedagogy, and Cultural Studies, 35*(2), 127–143. doi:10.1080/10714413.2013.778653

Jubas, K., & Knutson, P. (2013). Fictions of work-related learning: How a hit television show portrays internship, and how medical students relate to those portrayals. *Studies in Continuing Education, 35*(2), 224–240. doi:10.1080/0158037X.2012.738659

Knorr Cetina, K. (1999). *Epistemic cultures: How the sciences make knowledge*. Cambridge, MA: Harvard University Press.

Knorr Cetina, K. (2001). Objectual practice. In T. Schatzki, K. Knorr Cetina, & E. von Savigny (Eds.), *The practice turn in contemporary theory* (pp. 175–188). London, England: Routledge.

Knorr Cetina, K. (2006). Knowledge in a knowledge society: Five transitions. *Knowledge, Work and Society, 4*(3), 23–41.

Knorr Cetina, K. (2007). Culture in global knowledge societies: Knowledge cultures and epistemic cultures. *Interdisciplinary Science Reviews, 32*(4), 361–375. doi:10.1179/030801807X163571

Kunyk, D., & Austin, W. (2012). Nursing under the influence: A relational ethics perspective. *Nursing Ethics, 19*(3), 380–389. doi:10.1177/0969733011406767

Lave, J., & Wenger, E. (1991). *Situated learning: Legitimate peripheral participation*. Cambridge, England: Cambridge University Press.

Levine, T., & Marcus, A. (2007). Closing the achievement gap through teacher collaboration: Facilitating multiple trajectories of teacher learning. *Journal of Advanced Academics, 19*(1), 116–138.

Magro, K. M. (2001). Perspectives and theories of adult learning. In D. Poonwassie & A. Poonwassie (Eds.), *Fundamentals of adult education: Issues and practices for lifelong learning* (pp. 76–97). Toronto, ON: Thompson Educational Publishing.

Marsick, V. J., & Watkins, K. E. (2001). Informal and incidental learning. *New Directions for Adult and Continuing Education, 89,* 25–34.

McHugh, K. (2012). Nurse Jackie and the politics of care. *Nursing Outlook, 60*(5S), S12–S18. doi:10.1016/j.outlook.2012.06.003

Merriam, S. B. (2008). Adult learning theory for the twenty-first century. *New Directions for Adult and Continuing Education, 119,* 93–98. doi:10.1002/ace.309

Merriam, S. B., Caffarella, R. S., & Baumgartner, L. (2007). *Learning in adulthood: A comprehensive guide* (3rd ed.). San Francisco, CA: Jossey-Bass.

Mezirow, J. (1997). Transformative learning: Theory to practice. *New Directions for Adult and Continuing Education, 74,* 5–12.

Mezirow, J. (2003). Transformative learning as discourse. *Journal of Transformative Education, 1*(1), 58–63. doi:10.1177/1541344603252172

Nerland, M. (2008). Knowledge cultures and the shaping of work-based learning: The case of computer engineering. *Vocations and Learning, 1,* 49–69. doi:10.1007/s12186-007-9002-x

Nerland, M. (2010). Transnational discourses of knowledge and learning in professional work: Examples from computer engineering. *Studies of Philosophy in Education, 29,* 183–195. doi:10.1007/s11217-009-9170-2

Nerland, M., Jensen, K., & Bekele, T. A. (2010). *Changing cultures of knowledge and learning in higher education: A literature review.* Oslo, Norway: University of Oslo, Department of Educational Research. Retrieved from http://HEIK-Utd2020-Part2-Changing_cultures-3.pdf

Potter, J., & Wetherell, M. (1987). *Discourse and social psychology: Beyond attitudes and behaviour.* London, England: Sage Publications.

Rothwell, W. J. (2002). *The workplace learner.* New York, NY: American Management Association.

Spear, H. J. (2010). TV nurses: Promoting a positive image of nursing? *Journal of Christian Nursing, 27*(4), 318–321. doi:10.1097/CNJ.0b013e3181ed9f1a

Timanson, P., & Hicks, D. (2013, June). *Leading roles: A discourse analysis of the school principal as leader in television and in principalship standards.* Paper presented at the Annual Conference of the Canadian Association for the Study of Educational Administration, Victoria, BC.

Weaver, R., Salamonson, Y., Koch, J., & Jackson, D. (2013). Nursing on television: Student perceptions of television's role in public image, recruitment and education. *Journal of Advanced Nursing, 69*(12), 2635–2643. doi:10.1111/jan.12148

Weaver, R., Ferguson, C., Wilbourn, M., & Salamonson, Y. (2014). Men in nursing on television: Exposing and reinforcing stereotypes. *Journal of Advanced Nursing, 70*(4), 833–842. doi:10.1111/jan.12244

Wright, R. R. (2010). Narratives from popular culture: Critical implications for adult education. *New Directions for Adult and Continuing Education, 126,* 49–62. doi:10.1002/ace

Wright, R. R. (2013). Zombies, cyborgs, and other labor organizers: An introduction to representations of adult learning theories and HRD in popular culture. *New Horizons in Adult Education & Human Resource Development, 25*(1), 5–17.

Pamela Timanson
Faculty of Education
University of Alberta

Theresa J. Schindel
Faculty of Pharmacy and Pharmaceutical Sciences
University of Alberta

KAELA JUBAS

6. GIVING SUBSTANCE TO GHOSTLY FIGURES

How Female Nursing Students Respond to a Cultural Portrayal of "Women's Work" in Health Care

INTRODUCTION

This chapter discusses a Canadian qualitative case study of the pedagogical function of popular or "pop" culture. The study focused on "incidental" adult learning (Malcolm, Hodkinson, & Colley, 2003; Marsick & Watkins, 2001) – the unanticipated and often unrecognized learning which occurs as part of daily life. In this study, undergraduate nursing and medical students in Canada considered how they integrated cultural messages about their field of study and future work into what was being taught in their professional education programs. I used the American-produced television shows *Grey's Anatomy* and *Scrubs*, both of which are set in a hospital and feature interns (or residents) and doctors, to frame discussions with participants.

In this chapter, I concentrate on the 20 nursing student participants, all of whom were female. I also limit my discussion to *Grey's Anatomy*, which has enjoyed relatively high ratings, especially among female viewers; for some seasons, the show has been even more highly rated in Canada than in the US ("Separated at Birth," 2010). Overall, it was watched by more participants than *Scrubs*, a fact amplified among the nursing students. As a scholar located in the field of adult education and learning, I was fascinated by the portrayals of work-related learning and teaching that are not just featured, but highlighted, in both of these shows. That emphasis, it seemed to me, was rather unique in televisual texts.

My aim here is to connect a burgeoning professional identity with broader social identities which begin to develop early in life. To that end, I explore portrayals of gender relations in *Grey's Anatomy*, and how nursing student participants related those portrayals to their experiences and the ongoing stereotype of nursing as a feminine profession. Extending a discussion published elsewhere (Jubas & Knutson, 2012), I assert that audience members learn something about nursing and nurses as they watch the show, and nursing students – whose learning encompasses understanding themselves as gendered professionals-in-the-making – incorporate the show's representations into understandings of their selves and their experiences. The persistent emphasis on differences between formal and informal learning turns attention away from the reality that students bring knowledge developed through experience outside the classroom into the classroom, and vice versa.

There are three central points in my analysis. First, professional learning involves purposeful, monitored learning and incidental learning about everything from technical knowledge and skills, to social relations and identities, and both sorts of learning occur within and beyond educational programs. Moreover, learning is holistic or multi-dimensional; what is learned is both intellectually and emotionally oriented (Dirkx, 2008; Ellsworth, 2005). Contrary to the inclination to separate formal from informal learning, I concur with Malcolm, Hodkinson, and Colley (2003) that "attributes of formality/informality are present in all learning situations, but … the inter-relationships between such formal and informal attributes vary from situation to situation" (p. 315). A similar point is made by Billett (2006), who notes that "learning experiences are shaped by structural factors associated with work practices. These regulate and are reproduced by the division of labour and by the distribution of opportunities for participation in work, and learning about it" (p. 32). When I use "informal learning," I refer to activities and processes outside the classroom. At the same time, I recognize that there is a back-and-forth relationship between what people see, do, and learn outside the classroom and what they see, do, and learn inside the classroom, and that classroom walls are more porous than they might seem.

Another way of thinking about the limited distinction between formal and informal learning comes from cultural studies' notion of intertextuality (Allen, 2011). That term captures the reality that texts and information are never received singularly and in isolation. Rather, any given text is received in juxtaposition to other texts.

The connection between pop culture and adult learning about the social and professional self is worthy of examination. Herein lies the third point: Despite a discourse of meritocracy, in which social relations and identities become irrelevant, gender, race, and class remain evident and potent. Contrary to the claim that gender has been neutralized, then, cultural texts such as *Grey's Anatomy* and lived experiences such as those of the participants in my study expose the duplicity of meritocracy and its contemporary neoliberal discursive sibling, "post-feminism" (McRobbie, 2004). After conceptualizing identity, particularly gender, more explicitly, I review some of the relevant literature to help ground and contextualize my inquiry, before moving into a discussion of my study and findings. I close the chapter by reiterating key points from my analysis, and considering implications of my inquiry for the broad (and broadening) field of adult education and learning.

THINKING ABOUT GENDER

The construction, expression, assignment, and interpretation of identity, including gender identity, is one process of adult learning that plays out in both formal and informal learning settings. Individuals develop understanding of themselves and others through encounters in and with real-life and cultural texts. Identity, then, is relational in nature (Knowles, 2003), in two senses. As I note elsewhere, identity "is produced continually as individuals relate to one another in varied social contexts, and any dimension of identity exists in relation to other dimensions" (Jubas, 2013, p. 131). Here, I focus on gender, but gender identity and relations are always also connected to race or class or other facets of identity. In that earlier article, I outline the idea of a translucent crystal as a metaphor for thinking about identity: Although I might peer through one facet of the crystal, that facet is inseparable from other facets. Facets of identity, such as gender, can be discussed discretely in an examination of social life; however, peering through any facet always yields an incomplete, distorted view. This is consistent with McCall's (2009) proposition of "intercategorical complexity," which "provisionally [adopts categories] to document relationships of inequality among social groups and changing configurations of inequality along multiple and conflicting dimensions" (p. 50).

Of course, like any metaphor, this one has limitations (Jubas, 2013). Although a crystal can develop and change over time, it is not alive and social in the way that human beings are. People's identity involves degrees of both constraint and agency, is dynamic, and is never entirely predictable. What appeals to me about the metaphor of the crystal is that it reminds me that there are always multiple identities, which are always joined but never combinable.

Thinking further about the facet of gender, I find the writing of McRobbie (2004) on contemporary times helpful. She writes about today's post-feminism as "an array of machinations, [through which] elements of contemporary popular culture are perniciously effective in regard to ... [the] undoing of feminism, while simultaneously appearing to be engaging in a well-informed and even well-intended response to feminism" (McRobbie, 2004, p. 255). Similarly, Douglas' (2010) phrase "enlightened sexism" refers to the

> response, deliberate or not, to the perceived threat of a new gender regime. It insists that women have made plenty of progress because of feminism – indeed, full equality has allegedly been achieved – so now it's okay, even amusing, to resurrect sexist stereotypes of girls and women. (p. 9)

In applying the concepts of post-feminism and enlightened sexism to *Grey's Anatomy* and participants' responses to the show, I highlight how pop culture uses women's inroads into previously masculinized fields to assert that feminism's aims have been met. In so doing, it encourages audience members both to support women's continued advancement *and* to comply with well-entrenched stereotypes and attitudes that favour men and high-status masculinized professional fields. Through its representations of gender relations, pop culture delivers lessons to fans about social life and functions as one of many sources of information that fans can use – sometimes in unanticipated ways – to construct their understandings of themselves as gendered, learning, professional adults.

LEARNING CULTURE

Contemporary (Western) times and places are characterized by rhetoric of a "learning culture," which directs people to engage in continual learning, within and beyond the classroom. Cultural consumption itself is a learning process, as audience members form emotional connections to the fictional characters whose trials and successes they witness. In other words, adults live in a learning culture, and learn about and through cultural texts and practices. Often, the learning associated with cultural consumption is about social relations. This argument has been made for decades, and is associated both with the writing of Antonio Gramsci (1971) and feminist scholarship. As Luke (1996) explains,

> Gender identity and relations cannot be apprehended or theorized on their own abstracted terms….Similarly, "pedagogy" cannot be conceived of as an isolated intersubjective event since it too is fundamentally defined by and a product of historical, political, sociocultural, and knowledge relations. (p. 1)

Sometimes, cultural texts illustrate the conceptual point made by Billett (2008) and Malcolm, Hodkinson, and Colley (2003), by disrupting the boundary between formal and informal learning. For example, in their discussion of the television show *Buffy the Vampire Slayer*, Fisher, Harris, and Jarvis (2008) outline experiences of learning outside the classroom which, for the main character, affords lessons about how gender and class structure everyday life, and how she understands herself and her place in the world. As she embarks on her unique vocation, Buffy challenges stereotypes about women, even as she encounters tensions between her commitment to rejecting and maintaining feminine norms.

Other examinations of cultural texts that upset gender norms include Wright's (2010) analysis of a season of the British espionage series *The Avengers*, produced in the early 1960s. Wright centres on the impact of the physically and mentally agile lead character Cathy Gale on fans' understanding of second-wave feminism and challenges to restrictive ideas about women's capabilities. Kruse and Prettyman (2008) use the musical *Wicked* (based on Gregory Maguire's novel), an alternative telling of the story of *The Wizard of Oz* that recasts the relationship between the good witch Glinda and the Wicked Witch of the West as a friendship. For Kruse and Prettyman, one lesson is that women who aspire to be leaders must weigh the need to adopt masculine habits against pressures to enact a stereotypically feminine demeanour. Female characters (and, presumably, viewers) are reminded that women who go too far in defying hegemonic gender norms – such as the Wicked Witch – stand a poor chance of success.

In addition to their messages about and representations of gender relations, these cultural texts also relate to work-related identity and learning. That is Armstrong's (2008) emphasis in his analysis of varied versions of the television show *The Office*. Armstrong argues that the different versions of this show reflect national and cultural variations in discourses of office work. He concludes that, when people begin their careers, they already have ideas of what lies ahead for them. These ideas come from numerous sources, including cultural texts, and both converge with and diverge from lived experience. In order to become popular, pop culture does not need to provide a fully accurate representation of work and the workplace; rather, it must resonate with audiences in sufficient and meaningful ways. This point is reiterated by other scholars, and summed up in the following statement:

> Even the smartest and most aware television consumers can experience television in two seemingly contradictory ways. On the one hand, most of us know and can articulate the fact that programs we are watching are fictional. Yet simultaneously and often less than consciously, we believe and internalize the subtle and often subliminal message we are receiving. (Holtzman & Sharpe, 2014, p. xvi)

In large part, these analyses suggest that pop culture's pedagogical function is to reflect and reiterate hegemonic ideologically-based "common sense" (Gramsci, 1971) ideas about work and social relations, including gender. From a Gramscian perspective, this educational process exemplifies how everyday culture operates ideologically in the service of the social status quo, and illustrates the blurriness of the line between "formal" and "informal" adult learning. In the case of gender relations, patriarchal structure does not determine cultural representations or interpretations of them entirely; however, it does inform representations and interpretations to some degree.

Although much pop culture tries to enlist consumers in accepting a world view, not all cultural producers align with hegemonic ideology and the associated common sense about social life. Pop culture and cultural consumption function dialectically (Gramsci, 1971), as they echo hegemonic ideas and interests *and* open up potential for challenge among audiences. Moreover, some producers attempt to convey different stances, turning them into deliberate critical pedagogues for audience members, whether in the theatre, the living room or the classroom. Regardless of the convictions of a producer or author, though, any given cultural text can both reiterate and challenge hegemonic discourse by presenting characters who represent varied perspectives. Moreover, as reception theory argues, even if producers intend to sway their audiences, audience members might not receive messages according to producers' intentions (Jarvis, 2012; Trend, 2008). Still, as Trend (2008) reminds his readers, constructing meaning is not a limitless process; rather, there is a "mediated character of all representation and consequent ability of people to invent new or consequent readings" (p. 146). Adults are neither "fully autonomous, agentic beings" nor "the wholly passive creations of the culture industries" (Sandlin, Wright, & Clark, 2013, p. 3), and their learning through cultural consumption is tied to other learning sources and contexts.

Some scholars promote incorporation of critical pop culture into the classroom. Brown (2011) recounts how provocative films have facilitated discussion in his classes. Fiction, he argues, has pedagogical potency because it appeals to audience members on a distinctly emotional level. In his words, "stories do not persuade us, they either 'move' us, or they don't. When they do, it is through an empathetic identification with the characters in the story" (p. 236). Discussing her study about using the film *Crash* to spur critical reflection on diversity and oppression, Tisdell (2008) echoes Brown's point. In their conversations with fans of *Buffy the Vampire Slayer*, Jarvis and Burr (2010) found that diverse characters helped audience members deepen their sense of empathy. Jarvis (2012) suggests that promotion and expression of empathy is important to adult educators guided by the humanistic purpose of personal development, the progressivist purpose of creating ties among citizens, and more radical purposes related to social transformation.

Even pop culture that seems to hold no critical aim can be brought into the critical classroom. Tisdell (2008) argues that critical media literacy teaching can use pop culture to help students get past their initial sense of pleasure in exploring the problematic aspects of cultural texts. Likewise, Jarvis (2012) notes that, although pop culture can facilitate the deepening of empathy in any setting, the evocation of empathy can become tricky. Viewers might empathize with characters whom they like and enjoy, but who behave in troubling ways.[2] She concurs with Tisdell's conclusion that purposeful discussion in the adult education classroom offers something important to both the critical pedagogue and the adult learner. As I go on to explore, participants in my study shared points of critically-oriented learning that occurred as they watched *Grey's Anatomy*, moving in and out of their classroom and clinical placement settings.

METHODOLOGY AND PARTICIPANTS

My interdisciplinary inquiry exemplifies instrumental qualitative case study (Stake, 1995), undertaken to build knowledge about issues apparent within a case rather than about the case itself. It incorporated a range of methods, illustrating the flexibility of qualitative approaches for research conducted from the interpretive/critical theory paradigm (Guba & Lincoln, 2008). In the study's first phase, I conducted a textual analysis of the first six seasons of *Grey's Anatomy*. I viewed the episodes on DVD, and partially transcribed them. Transcribed segments relate to three themes, identified at the outset as areas of interest and important in professional education: identity, ethics, and pedagogy/learning. The resulting data helped me develop focus group guidelines as well as the code book being used to analyse participant based data. Viewing the show was, then, a data gathering and an analytical process, as well as a process that helped me prepare to gather data in the second phase of the study.

In treating *Grey's Anatomy* as a text to be analyzed, I took up core ideas of the critical/feminist discourse analysis approaches of Gee (2011) and Naples (2003). I agree with Naples that, rather than sharply dividing modernism and postmodernism or poststructuralism, working with insights from both perspectives can yield a deeper understanding of a complex phenomenon. Following Gee (2011), I looked to *Grey's Anatomy* for examples of discourse as

> socially accepted associations among ways of using language, of thinking, valuing, acting, and interacting, in the "right" places and at the "right" times with the "right" objects (associations that can be used to identify oneself as a member of a socially meaningful group or "social network"). (p. 34)

Next, I held focus groups or interviews with 41 participants during 2011 and 2012, in a small number of locations that moved me across much of Canada's vast territory: Victoria/Vancouver, British Columbia; Calgary, Alberta; and Toronto, Ontario. The inclusion of participants in this study helped me consider how a show produced in the US and featuring representations of health care workers and settings in that country is received by audiences in another country – albeit one that is connected by a long border, a common language (at least outside Quebec), and many cultural texts. In considering real-life participants important in deepening an understanding of what texts *mean* and how they *function*, I echo Burdick and Sandlin (2013), who write that

> the flows of popular culture cannot be understood from their local contexts alone....[W]hereas a more direct heuristic might be applied in cases of films, music, and television created for and viewed by a particular nation's audience, a far more nuanced understanding of pedagogical transfer must be taken up as audiences outside of this nation take up these media." (p. 156)

The participants in my research were studying in an undergraduate nursing or medical program in one of those areas, and were recruited through flyers posted and distributed through student association Facebook pages or online contact lists. The participants discussed in this chapter are the 20 nursing students, all of whom were female.

Sessions were guided by the same series of questions, which were introduced by segments from episodes that I had highlighted during the first phase. Participants could discuss other episodes or segments that they remembered and that seemed relevant to our discussion. Participants were asked to consider representations that they saw in clips shared during their focus group or other memorable parts of the show, and how those representations related to what they were learning and experiencing through their educational programs. In discussing the show's portrayals and messages, in-class lessons, and experiential learning during clinical placement, participants were encouraged to think about issues ranging from self-image and the image of members of both the medical and nursing professions, to the meaning and importance of ethics in practice, to how doctors and nurses enact "good" teaching practice, to how they as students engaged in learning. Sessions were audio and video taped for transcription, and I took notes. Whenever possible, a research assistant co-facilitated sessions. All participants were offered the option of choosing a pseudonym for themselves and those who declined to choose a name had one assigned. Data analysis was aided by NVivo software, and employed a combination of codes generated during the earlier textual analysis of *Grey's Anatomy* and emerging (sub-)codes which seemed noteworthy as I worked with participants' comments.

GREY'S ANATOMY: THE CULTURAL TEXT

Grey's Anatomy is set at the fictionalized Seattle Grace Hospital (renamed Seattle Grace Mercy West and, more recently, Grey-Sloan Memorial) and focuses on people preparing to become or practising as surgeons. The show is an example of the prime-time drama genre, which uses an episodic structure, focuses on intimate relationships, and relies on audience loyalty (Geraghty, 1991). It has enjoyed consistently high ratings among the general public as well as nursing and medical students (Czarny, Faden, Nolan, Bodensiek, & Sugarman, 2008) who are encountering or contemplating scenarios presented in the show.

This summary is restricted to Seasons 1 through 6, the span used in the study. The show's main character and namesake is Meredith Grey, a complicated, attractive, insecure woman living in the shadow of her mother who had been a surgeon at Seattle Grace. Her best friend, the brilliant, driven, unsentimental Cristina Yang, plans to become a cardiothoracic surgeon. A Korean-American woman, Cristina is distinct among the others on her team as a member of a minority racial group. Raised in a warm, working class family, George O'Malley is a decent, kind man who meets a sad but noble demise at the end of Season 5, moments after enlisting to serve in Iraq. Also at the end of that season, Izzie Stevens, a romantic blonde beauty who worked her way out of poverty by modelling, marries Alex Karev, a "man's man" who was raised in an emotionally and physically abusive family.

Miranda Bailey begins the show as the competent supervisor of these interns. She is unique as a black woman in a still largely white, masculine domain, and, for several seasons, as a parent raising a young child. Derek Shepherd, the handsome, white, popular, and respected neurosurgeon, is Meredith's on-again/off-again partner until they marry. Richard Webber, the Chief of Surgery, is notable as a black man in a senior position and the long-ago lover of Meredith's mother. Callie Torres is an orthopaedic resident from a wealthy Latino family, who comes out as bisexual. Over time, as some of these characters leave the show for various reasons, and new residents and attending surgeons come to Seattle Grace, building a large complement of characters who are introduced over the show's lengthy history, and the ones featured in segments shared during sessions.

GENDERED TEXTS, LEARNING, AND WORK

According to the model that I laid out above, gender is one facet of identity which can be seen as separate from and joined to other facets, including professional affiliation. Central to this discussion is what participants had to say about portrayals of gender relations in health care work, and how those portrayals meshed with what they were discussing in their classes and learning through clinical placements. I highlight two images that emerged in conversations with some participants: the nurse as a second-rate professional and what I refer to as a "phantom figure."

The Feminized Profession as Second-Rate

Grey's Anatomy focuses on surgical residency, one of the most masculinized specialities in the historically masculine medical profession. Although (Canadian) medical school students are now fairly evenly divided along male/female gender lines, a greater gender imbalance remains in place for surgical specialities (Burton & Wong, 2004). The continuing gendered make-up of surgery is reflected from the very beginning of the show, as Meredith comments to Cristina about the few women entering the surgical residency program with them: "Only six women out of 20" (Rhimes & Horton, 2005a). Later in the same episode, Cristina uses stereotypes of masculinity to convey the view of surgery as inherently and positively gendered: "Surgery's hot. It's the marines. It's macho, it's hostile, it's hard work" (Rhimes & Horton, 2005a).

In contrast, the nursing profession has long been feminized and, while the gender imbalance in that profession is narrowing, it persists (Sedgwick & Kellett, 2015). Despite its focus on surgical residents and attending surgeons, *Grey's Anatomy* offers images of nurses and references to nursing; they are, however, often obscured and disrespectful, and always problematic. In keeping with real-life statistics, for the most part, nurses in the show are female. Indeed, in my repeated viewings of the show and participants' recollections, only one male nurse was memorable to all of us. The real problem with *Grey's Anatomy*'s representation of nurses, especially in relation to doctors, lies in the implication that the medical profession is more intellectually demanding and superior, and that the superiority of medicine is determined by gender.

Dismissive, gender-based attitudes toward nurses are evident among at least some residents in the show from the series' very beginning, a fact that reflects Armstrong's (2008) assertion that people enter the workplace with ideas about it already formed. In the very first episode, Alex encounters an experienced nurse who is concerned that he might be misreading a patient's symptoms. Turning to Meredith for a sympathetic ear, he is surprised when she wonders if the nurse is correct:

Alex: 4B's got post-op pneumonia. Start antibiotics.

Nurse: Are you sure that's the right diagnosis?

Alex: Well, I don't know, I'm only an intern. Here's an idea – Why don't you go spend four years in med school and then let me know if this is the right diagnosis? She's short of breath, she's got fever, she's post-op – start the antibiotics. [walks toward Meredith] God, I hate nurses.

Meredith:	... She may not have pneumonia, you know. She may be splinting or have a PE [pulmonary embolism].
Alex:	Like I said, I hate nurses.
Meredith:	What did you just say? Did you just call me a nurse?
Alex:	Well, if the white cap fits. (Rhimes & Horton, 2005a)

In that instant, Alex's disdain is directed at both nurses and women, and he handily conflates professional and gender identity. Even Meredith, who initially does not seem to share Alex's attitude toward nurses, is offended at his final jibe. In her mind, she is no "nurse," and she resents the insinuation that her femaleness limits her medical expertise and authority, both of which are – in Alex's mind – amply demonstrated by him.

Alex is not the only resident who speaks about nurses and nursing in this way, nor is the disrespect shown to nurses restricted to the male residents and surgeons. Cristina, who quickly is established as the character most likely to speak her mind bluntly and acerbically, also makes disparaging comments. In an episode in the second season, when Alex is embarrassed about having to retake a test that he has failed, Cristina tells him, "You can nurse your pride, key word being 'nurse,' or you can pass your test and be a doctor" (Vernoff & Horton, 2005). The implication here is that Alex needs to "man up," study hard, and accept help from others who have passed the test, without letting feminine feelings of anxiety or self-doubt stand in his way. Even Meredith, a gentler, more sensitive character than Cristina, has moments when she resorts to stereotypical views about gender. When George takes her to the maternity ward after a long shift so that they can watch the sleeping newborns for few peaceful moments, she looks at him and says, "You're such a woman" (Rhimes & Horton, 2005b). The most overtly caring and sympathetic man on the surgical team, George is subject to routine, albeit often cryptic, jabs at his masculinity and, by extension, his sexual orientation. In the second season, when the nurses go on strike, the surgical residents must decide whether or not they will cross the picket line. First across the line is Cristina, and most of the other residents soon follow. When George, the son of a teacher and a truck driver, from a solid working class family, hesitates and chooses to stand in solidarity with the nurses, instead of being described as loyal or noble, he is insulted by Cristina who tells another resident that George is "hiding behind the picket line like a girl" (Clack & Paymer, 2006).

Through such statements and scenarios, major characters convey beliefs that the historically masculinized field of medicine is superior to the historically feminized field of nursing and that, if not maleness, then a stereotypically masculine approach to work and problems is the key to success in the sought-after "man's world." Interestingly, even female characters participate in the diminishment of traditionally feminine work; like their male colleagues, they hear and use the term "nurse" as an insult. This corresponds to the conundrum faced by female characters in other cultural texts for whom alignment with femininity and masculinity involves delicate, continual negotiation (see Fisher, Harris, & Jarvis, 2008; Kruse & Prettyman, 2008; Wright, 2010).

More often, though, nurses seem to be taken for granted in the show. This is consistent with the steady supply of television shows which centre on physicians, and the reality that few shows focus on nurses. The few shows that do centre squarely on nurses tend to be relatively short-lived ("10 Great TV Series," 2011). What tends to be left open for nurses in medical dramas, then, is their incorporation as minor characters who serve physicians. Such portrayals reflect and help maintain traditional gender-based hierarchical relations between doctors and nurses. Except for an episode in which Liz, a favourite nurse who worked with Seattle Grace, is admitted as a patient, participants and I could remember only two nurses who are taken seriously enough by the writers to be named: Olivia and Rose. It did not seem coincidental to participants that both of these nurses have affairs with major characters in the show. In other words, nurses' stature is raised a notch when they become sexual partners to the residents or doctors. Even so, that extra bit of importance is not sustained; neither Olivia nor Rose becomes a long-term partner and, when they outlive their usefulness to the show's residents or surgeons, they exit the show.

Other than serving as sexual partners or, on very rare occasion, offering a clinical opinion, what do nurses *do* in *Grey's Anatomy*, given that most of the bedside care is undertaken by the residents or surgeons? Overall, nurses are more likely to act as surgeons' handmaidens than as vital members of the health care team. That image is highlighted in the following scene, as Derek Shepherd prepares to go into surgery:

Nurse: [hands a small cup to Derek] Here you go, triple espresso, not too hot.

Derek: [takes a sip] Oh, I love you, seriously. (Koenig & Martin, 2005)

The image of the nurse as little more than an on-site barista available to fetch coffee for doctors is not one which is presented repeatedly in the show. More commonly, when nurses do appear in the operating room (OR) or in a patient's room, they have a quiet, fleeting presence and unclear purpose. Often silent and filmed with their faces away from rather than toward the camera (when working bedside) or behind masks (when in the OR), nurses are easy to ignore and forget. In the following section, I turn my attention to what participants made of such portrayals.

From Ghostliness to Corporeality, and Second-Rate to Top-Notch: Participants' Responses and/as Learning

For participants, the scenes noted above seemed exaggerated and out-of-date, given what they were learning about in their programs of study and, to some extent, experiencing in their hospital placements. Paradoxically, such scenes also seemed to reflect ideas common among members of the non-nursing general public and even some of the participants' experiences during placements. Participants recognized that, perhaps largely because of how medicine and nursing are represented in pop culture texts such as *Grey's Anatomy*, the general public knows little about nurses' scope of practice.

Even so, for most of these participants, the troubling representation of nurses and nursing in *Grey's Anatomy* was not enough to dissuade them from watching the show. In this regard, Claire was in the minority. As she progressed through her nursing studies, she increasingly found that the show's artificiality with regard to nursing made it difficult for her to relate to it and its characters. Although other participants agreed that the show treats nurses inaccurately, many actually found that (mis)representation of health care work helpful because, although tasks are falsely assigned to doctors in the show, nursing students understood that what they were watching was really *their* work.

In my conversations with the nursing student participants, a distinct impression began to emerge of the nurse as a "phantom figure" in both pop culture and the public imagination. That image captures the concurrent presence and invisibility of nurses in *Grey's Anatomy*. As Lisa explained, "I see myself as part of the show because I'm in health care, but I'm not represented." In another session, Claire used similar language to describe the feeling that she got when she watched the show, describing nurses in the show as "a ghost in the background." Echoing Lisa and Claire, Cassie made these comments:

> Yeah the nurses are pretty uninvolved, they don't interact with patients very often on the show and when they do interact with the doctors it's brief and short and they kind of are portrayed almost as a shell of a person, not as important.... I guess you can call them a flat character. So they are not a predominant, they are not a developed character in the show.... There is one nurse that I can recall ... that was more of a character and she ended up dating one of the guys. So ... they don't really usually play a huge role in the patients' care and they don't seem to show much of a huge role with the doctors as well. Yeah, they are barely even there, you can go through an entire show and they are there kind of as background but they are not really shown as playing an important role.

Participants connected the show's tendency to overlook nurses as vital and skilled health care professionals with the historical feminization of their profession. During one session, Jane noted her initial discomfort with the idea of entering a field that was so highly feminized:

> I think I probably struggled with that too when I went into nursing. I was saying to someone, like, "The only thing that bothers me is that it's traditionally regarded as women's work."... And I think whoever I was talking to was like, "Oh please, that's so ridiculous!" But I think that's one of the reasons why I was sort of conflicted too. I mean it wasn't a huge problem, but I think that was one of the little things.

Others echoed Jane's message that the regular portrayal of nurses on the sidelines of health care reflects a pervasive ignorance among the general public about the "scope of practice of a nurse." Clara recounted conversations in which her family members and friends would ask her, "'So, are you ... thinking about med school?' ... Yeah I still get it all the time, and it's almost as if, like, but you're so smart it's such a waste." Ironically, participants agreed that much of what audience members see surgical residents or surgeons do on the show and what might seem interesting to viewers is actually nurses' work. As Claire noted, surgical residents in the show "spend so much time with the patients, like taking blood pressure and giving needles, but doctors never do that in the hospital."

In discussing overtly disrespectful behaviour of residents or surgeons toward nurses, one participant, Rosalita, agreed that such behaviours and attitudes were not inaccurate, but "it's usually not that blatant." The suggestion here is that the diminishment of nursing might have become more polite and subtle, without having been eliminated altogether. Some participants thought that the recent encouragement of inter-professional learning enhanced communication and respect between physicians and nurses, and broke down extreme attitudes. Nursing student participants also acknowledged that the gendered make-up and relations in both medicine and nursing were changing, as more women entered the former and more men entered the latter field; however, these changes did not mean that historical norms of masculinity and femininity were disappearing.

As the dialogue between the characters of Cristina and Alex discussed above suggests, both men and women are brought into patriarchal relations as they embody and enact gender stereotypes and relations. Some participants saw stereotypes related to both gender and profession, and the interplay between the two facets of identity, pop up in their classes and placements. Clara described this phenomenon in her remarks about how one male nurse behaved more assertively with female residents than their male colleagues:

> I just think [that] ... because medicine and nursing historically have been so gender-specific, absolutely there is still hangover from that. And I think now ... we are getting [to] a point where there is so much more mixing in both professions, it's interesting. I see the male nurses on my unit push the female resident harder than they would the males. ... Like ... a patient who they would have stood up for and said something [about] to a male resident, they will be screaming at a female resident.

Clara was describing how these male nurses call on patriarchy's allowance of men's assertiveness and, sometimes, aggression in encounters with women. These sorts of gendered power plays can be made even if class-oriented hierarchies assign a lesser status of men to women in certain circumstances, and make it easy to predict a more deferential response. In other words, this comment suggests that, within both nursing and medicine, individuals position themselves in relation to professional *and* gender identities, in ways that can simultaneously challenge and confirm historical norms and stereotypes. Taken together, these participants' comments suggest how the nursing students could recognize elements of *Grey's Anatomy* from their real-life classes, placements, and conversations with acquaintances, even as they realized that other elements of the show did not represent nurses and nursing properly.

In portraying opportunity and meritocracy for women who work hard and choose wisely, notably the female residents and surgeons, *Grey's Anatomy* illustrates how contemporary mainstream (North American) culture adopts a neoliberal perspective which emphasizes personal responsibility and autonomy. Jennifer, who had just completed her nursing program by the time her session was held, explained, "I'm really ambitious, and there were a lot of female characters on the show....And they're all very smart and very competent and competitive. And I definitely identify with that too." The show's tendency to turn (female) nurses into phantoms who maintain a vague, mysterious presence in health care settings illustrates the extent to which gender continues to shape learning and work, even as that shape is masked by rhetoric of equal opportunity and gender-neutrality. Not only do stereotypes of femininity and masculinity remain active, but historically feminine contributions to health care work and work-related learning are diminished.

Even when they recognized its representation of nurses as highly problematic, sexist and unrealistic, most of the nursing student participants enjoyed *Grey's Anatomy*, and found various realistic, positive points in the show. Participants spoke of looking past the main characters' professional identities as residents and surgeons, and relating to characters' personalities. For many of the participants, characters such as Meredith and Izzie, who brought caring and compassion to their work, resonated with them as nursing students and women, because those qualities are viewed as stereotypically feminine attributes valued in to their feminized profession. Most of these participants welcomed the opportunity to work in a profession which emphasized being "personable" and "getting to know people and getting to know their stories." Michelle, a first-year nursing student, was an exception in this regard. She noted that she found too great an emphasis on interpersonal, relational matters in nursing classes, and identified with the no-nonsense Cristina character. As she explained during her session,

> I ... got really frustrated almost to the point of leaving nursing in my first semester because ... I found all our lectures were really like focusing super-heavily on caring.... So I got pretty frustrated thinking, I didn't come here to, like, hone my maternal instincts ... so it was kinda nice that ... Cristina Yang is ... extremely competent in what she does but she's not sentimental.

Although *Grey's Anatomy* concentrates on surgeons, it portrays numerous surgical sub-specialities, another point that the nursing student participants appreciated. The participants themselves expressed interest in various specialties, and agreed that, although nursing continues to draw predominantly women, certain specialties are perceived as masculine. More masculinised specialties include surgical, trauma and emergency nursing, and participants accepted *Grey's Anatomy*'s portrayal of surgery as "sexy" and "macho" (Rhimes & Horton, 2005a). Claire added that doctor-nurse relations have nuances related to specialty, hospital, and ward, so that sexist attitudes toward nurses are not equally pervasive or consistently manifested across the entire health care sector in any locale. Although attitudes and practices might discourage some female residents from choosing certain medical specialties, an issue that I do not discuss here, the situation in nursing seems different. There are so many women in nursing that the masculinization of some specialties is relative, and did not seem to deter participants from considering specialties that interested them, regardless of how they are gendered.

Nursing student participants who were interested in masculinized specialties enjoyed learning about and performing clinical procedures, and appreciated the extent to which *Grey's Anatomy* focuses on procedures. On the one hand, they recognized the show's inaccuracies and points of offence; on the other hand, they found scenes in the operating room exciting. Makaela, a second-year student interested in surgical nursing, chuckled as she commented, "it makes me jealous when I watch it – I want to be in those surgeries." Jillian, a classmate considering trauma or emergency nursing, mentioned, "I really like the idea of ... not really knowing what to do and having to ... problem-solve. I really like seeing those situations when someone comes in and you have to ... come up with, on the spot, what you need to do."

Regardless of their anticipated career paths and personal dispositions, nursing student participants found that *Grey's Anatomy* illuminates how gender relations surface in health care. The show offered a glimpse into their future professional lives and selves. Diverse characters helped them understand themselves in the context of gender relations, and their chosen profession as gendered terrain. At times seen as objectionable and inauthentic, at other times portrayals of and implications about gender relations in the health care field were seen as helpful and reflective of the remnants of nursing's (and medicine's) gendered history.

CONCLUDING THOUGHTS

This inquiry contributes to the adult education scholarship being undertaken in the area of culture as pedagogy. It bolsters the claim that pop culture is an important source of adult learning about identity and work, as well as social life in general. Responses of nursing student participants illustrate that, regardless of any messages that cultural producers might intend to convey, audience members also respond to cultural texts in ways that are broadly shared and particular to their sociocultural contexts.

In the case of *Grey's Anatomy*, portrayals of the advancement of professional opportunities for women and the benefits of a meritocracy are weighed against nursing students' and nurses' experiences in school, at work, and at home, and suggest how cultural texts are infused with post-feminism (McRobbie, 2004) and enlightened sexism (Douglas, 2010). Whether they are female or male, nursing students are entering a feminized occupation, and must find ways to combine a new professional identity with long-standing gender identities in ways that promote and protect their own interests. That is, as I suggest throughout my discussion, a challenge complicated by intellectual awareness and emotional pleasure. Clearly, participants' ability to relate to, empathize with, and enjoy *Grey's Anatomy*'s characters and storylines is crucial in determining their interest in, loyalty to, and learning from the show. Because of these factors, learning, especially about who one is or should be, can produce confusion and inconsistency just as easily as it can produce certainty and coherence. This point runs counter to conventional discourse of learning, especially the humanist version of transformative learning (Mezirow, 1997, 2003), although it is consistent with the poststructural insight that knowledge, like identity, is always partial and tentative. From this perspective, the generation of new questions can be just as important as the development of answers. Related to this idea, Ellsworth's (2005) notion of "the learning self" contributes to an understanding of how *Grey's Anatomy* portrays adult learners not just as "pre-formed individuals who construct knowledge as they go" (Jubas, 2013, p. 130), but as learners, workers, gendered beings whose previous and emerging knowledge combine in the ongoing construction of their selves, and how participants in the study echoed that conceptualization.

Another point emerging from this inquiry is that, rather than looking for sharp distinctions between formal and informal learning, it is possible to find "attributes" (Malcolm, Hodkinson, & Colley, 2003) of formality and informality in all learning. As I have established, regardless of whether it enters the classroom or remains something consumed in leisure settings, pop culture can become integrated into lessons learned during professional education, and professional education can become connected to cultural consumption. Ultimately, it can be very difficult to pinpoint where and when learning has occurred, and to separate learning spaces which, on the surface, seem quite distinct. I agree with Tisdell (2008) and Jarvis (2012) that facilitated discussion about pop culture in the adult education classroom is important in deepening learners'/consumers' critical media literacy and critical responses to cultural texts; indeed, I have begun to see my sessions with participants as somewhat pedagogical for both participants and me.

There are two limitations to this inquiry that I will note. First, I reiterate my caution that, although it is useful to view social life through one facet of identity, facets do not exist singly. Any exploration of a facet of identity, such as gender, yields an incomplete and distorted view of social life. Second, this study explored responses among Canadian audience members to an American cultural text; as Armstrong (2008) concludes, pop culture is both produced and consumed in specific cultural contexts, including the context of the nation-state. Although it remains an American production, *Grey's Anatomy* might elicit rather different responses among nursing students and other fans beyond Canada and North America.

Clearly, the preceding discussion establishes that pop culture's pedagogical sway does not rely entirely on its ability to replicate real-life. Audience members' awareness that characters and storylines are fictions does not necessarily diminish their pedagogical power. Ultimately, it is pop culture's resonance with consumers, its ability to create lasting connections, largely emotional in nature, which creates opportunities for learning. Through those connections, cultural texts help consumers imagine themselves in varied relationships and situations, and reconsider aspects of their own lives. Of course, cultural texts do offer up messages and do reflect something of social life, even as they might help consumers analyze, reimagine, and (re)create it. In Gramscian terms, pop culture and cultural consumption exemplify the dialectical nature of social life – the dynamic tension between culture or ideology and material relations or socioeconomic structures, between agency and constraint, between change and status quo.

Methodologically, this inquiry illustrates how approaches can be mixed to explore how popular culture helps audiences learn about themselves and their world. It contributes to the re-bridging of the now-distinct (albeit historically connected) fields of adult education and cultural studies. Ultimately, I hope that it contributes to qualitative research as a rigorous, creative undertaking among scholars in and across a range of academic fields concerned with culture, education, and gender.

NOTES

[1] This study received funding from the Social Sciences and Humanities Research Council of Canada (File #410-2010-1370) and a University of Calgary Starter Grant (File #1014097). I thank Patricia Knutson, whose work as Graduate Research Assistant was instrumental during data collection and analysis.
[2] Jarvis (2012) goes on to disrupt the romanticization of empathy and its promotion among adult educators, an important point but one which is beyond the scope of this chapter.
[3] One of these exceptions is Nurse Jackie, discussed elsewhere in this anthology.
[4] Inter-professionalism is a growing trend in health care, and there is a coinciding body of literature emerging on this topic. It is, however, beyond the scope of this chapter for me to explore this topic.

REFERENCES

10 Great TV Series about Nursing. (2011). Retrieved October 3, 2011, from http://lpntornbridge.org/2011/10-great-tv-series-about-nursing/
Allen, G. (2011). *Intertextuality: The new critical idiom* (2nd ed.). Abingdon, England: Routledge.
Armstrong, P. (2008). Learning about work through popular culture: The case of office work. In V. Aarkrog & C. H. Jorgensen (Eds.), *Divergence and convergence in education and work* (pp. 379–402). Bern, Switzerland: Peter Lang.
Billett, S. (2006). Constituting the workplace curriculum. *Journal of Curriculum Studies, 38*(1), 31–48. doi:10.1080/00220270500153781
Brown, T. (2011). Using film in teaching and learning about changing societies. *International Journal of Lifelong Education, 30*(2), 233–247. doi:10.1080/02601370.2010.547615
Burdick, J., & Sandlin, J. A. (2013). Learning, becoming, and the unknowable: Conceptualizations, mechanisms, and process in public pedagogy literature. *Curriculum Inquiry, 43*(1), 142–177. doi:10.1111/curi.12001

Burton, K. R., & Wong, I. K. (2004). A force to contend with: The gender gap closes at in Canadian medical schools. *Canadian Medical Association Journal, 170*(9), 1385–1386. doi:10.1503/cmaj.1040354

Clack, Z. (Writer), & Paymer, D. (Director). (2006, January 29). Break on through [Television series episode]. In S. Rhimes (Executive producer & Creator), *Grey's anatomy*. Los Angeles, CA: ABC Studios.

Czarny, M. J., Faden, R. R., Nolan, M. T., Bodensiek, E., & Sugarman, J. (2008). Medical and nursing students' television viewing habits: Potential implications for bioethics. *The American Journal of Bioethics, 8*(12), 1–8. doi:10.1080/15265160802559153

Dirkx, J. (2008). The meaning and role of emotions in adult learning. *New Directions in Adult and Continuing Education, 120*, 7–18.

Douglas, S. J. (2010). *The rise of enlightened sexism: How pop culture took us from girl power to girls gone wild*. New York, NY: St. Martin's Press.

Ellsworth, E. A. (2005). *Places of learning: Media, architecture, pedagogy*. New York, NY: Routledge.

Fisher, R., Harris, A., & Jarvis, C. (2008). *Education in popular culture: Telling tales on teachers and learners*. London, England: Routledge.

Gee, J. P. (2011). *An introduction to discourse analysis: Theory and method* (3rd ed.). New York, NY: Routledge.

Geraghty, C. (1991). *Women and soap opera: A study of prime time soaps*. Cambridge, MA: Polity Press.

Gramsci, A. (1971). *Selections from the prison notebooks* (Q. Hoare & G. Nowell Smith, Ed. & Trans.). New York, NY: International Publishers.

Guba, E. G., & Lincoln, Y. S. (2008). Paradigmatic controversies, contradictions, and emerging confluences. In N. K. Denzin & Y. S. Lincoln (Eds.), *The landscape of qualitative research* (3rd ed., pp. 255–286). Thousand Oaks, CA: Sage Publications.

Holtzman, L., & Sharpe, L. (2014). *Media messages: What film, television, and popular music teach us about race, class, gender, and sexual orientation*. New York, NY: M. E. Sharpe.

Jarvis, C. (2012). Fiction, empathy and lifelong learning. *International Journal of Lifelong Education, 31*(6), 743–758. doi:10.1080/02601370.2012.713036

Jarvis, C., & Burr, V. (2010). *TV teacher: How adults learn through TV viewing*. Paper presented at the 40th Annual SCUTREA Conference, 6–8 July 2010, University of Warwick, Coventry, England. Retrieved September 1, 2013, from leeds.ac.uk/educol/documents/191647.doc

Jubas, K. (2013). Grey('s) identity: Complications of learning and identity in a popular television show. *Review of Education, Pedagogy and Cultural Studies, 35*(2), 127–143. doi:10.1080/10714413.2013.778653

Jubas, K., & Knutson, P. (2012). Seeing and be(liev)ing: How nursing and medical students understand representations of their professions. *Studies in the Education of Adults, 44*(1), 85–100.

Knowles, C. (2003). *Race and social analysis*. London, England: Sage Publications.

Koenig, K. (Writer), & Martin, D. (Director). (2005, May 8). The self-destruct button [Television series episode]. In S. Rhimes (Executive Producer & Creator), *Grey's anatomy*. Los Angeles, CA: ABC Studios.

Kruse, S. D., & Prettyman, S. S. (2008). Women, leadership, and power revisiting the wicked witch of the West. *Gender and Education, 20*(5), 451–464. doi:10.1080/09540250701805797

Luke, C. (1996). Introduction. In C. Luke (Ed.), *Feminisms and pedagogies of everyday life* (pp. 1–27). Albany, NY: State University of New York Press.

Malcolm, J., Hodkinson, P., & Colley, H. (2003). The inter-relationship between informal and formal learning. *Journal of Workplace Learning, 15*(7/8), 313–318. doi:10.1108/13665620310504783

Marsick, V. J., & Watkins, K. E. (2001). Informal and incidental learning. *New Directions for Adult and Continuing Education, 89*, 25–34.

McCall, L. (2009). The complexity of intersectionality. In E. Grabham, D. Cooper, & D. Herman (Eds.), *Intersectionality and beyond: Law, power and the politics of location* (pp. 49–76). Abingdon, England: Routledge-Cavendish.

McRobbie, A. (2004). Post-feminism and popular culture. *Feminist Media Studies, 4*(3), 255–264. doi:10.1080/1468077042000309937

Mezirow, J. (1997). Transformative learning: Theory to practice. *New Directions for Adult and Continuing Education, 74*, 5–12.
Mezirow, J. (2003). Transformative learning as discourse. *Journal of Transformative Education, 1*(1), 58–63. doi:10.1177/1541344603252172
Naples, N. (2003). *Feminism and method: Ethnography, discourse analysis, and activist research*. New York, NY: Routledge.
Rhimes, S. (Writer), & Horton, P. (Director). (2005a, March 27). A hard day's night [Television series episode]. In S. Rhimes (Executive Producer & Creator), *Grey's Anatomy*. Los Angeles, CA: ABC Studios.
Rhimes, S. (Writer), & Horton, P. (Director). (2005b, April 3). The first cut is the deepest [Television series episode]. In S. Rhimes (Executive Producer & Creator), *Grey's Anatomy*. Los Angeles, CA: ABC Studios.
Sandlin, J. A., Wright, R. R., & Clark, C. (2013). Re-examining theories of adult learning and adult development through the lenses of public pedagogy. *Adult Education Quarterly, 63*(1), 3–23. doi:10.1177/0741713611415836
Sedgwick, M., & Kellett, P. (2015). Exploring masculinity and marginalization of male undergraduate nursing students' experience of belonging during clinical experiences. *Journal of Nursing Education, 54*(3), 121–129. doi:10.3928/01484834-20150218-15
Separated at birth: American and Canadian TV audiences. (2010, November 19). Retrieved from http://thetvaddict.com/2010/11/19/separated-at-birth-american-and-canadian-tv-audiences/
Stake, R. E. (1995). *The art of case study research*. Los Angeles, CA: Sage Publications.
Tisdell, E. J. (2008). Critical media literacy and transformative learning: Drawing on pop culture and entertainment media in teaching for diversity in adult higher education. *Journal of Transformative Education, 6*(1), 48–67.
Trend, D. (2008). *Everyday culture: Finding and making meaning in a changing world*. Boulder, CO: Paradigm Publishers.
Vernoff, K. (Writer), & Horton, P. (Director). (2005, December 11). Grandma got run over by a reindeer [Television series episode]. In S. Rhimes (Executive Producer & Creator), *Grey's Anatomy*. Los Angeles, CA: ABC Studios.
Wright, R. R. (2010). Unmasking hegemony with *The Avengers*: Television entertainment as public pedagogy. In J. A. Sandlin, B. D. Schultz, & J. Burdick (Eds.), *Handbook of public pedagogy: Education and learning beyond schooling* (pp. 139–150). New York, NY: Routledge.

Kaela Jubas
Adult Learning/Werklund School of Education
University of Calgary

ASTRID TREFFRY-GOATLEY

7. NARRATIVES OF ILLNESS IN SOUTH AFRICAN CINEMA

What Can Popular Culture Teach Us about HIV?

INTRODUCTION

In 1994, South Africa made international history when the backward, racially segregated apartheid state was overthrown and, for the first time in history, the country became a democracy. Under the leadership of former-activist Nelson Mandela, the African National Congress (ANC) stepped into this celebratory atmosphere and took on the task of making the South African "miracle" of peaceful transformation a continuous reality. The progressive Constitution of 1996 envisioned a society of equality, multiculturalism, reconciliation and freedom. However, more than 400 years of colonial rule and 46 years of apartheid had resulted in a severely divided society and the radical transformation envisaged could not be possible without the application of the nation's imagination (Saks, 2003). Expressive forms have been shown to assist in the "refashioning of personal and collective identities and in the rediscovery of a common humanity" (Barber, 2001, p. 177). Accordingly, the state targeted the industries of popular culture, as a key mechanism to facilitate public learning about and identification with this society in transition.

A key challenge faced by the new government was the rapidly growing HIV epidemic. Yet, although this virus posed a grave threat to the nation, officials were preoccupied with planning for the new state and failed to prioritise the control of HIV (Nattrass, 2007, pp. 38–39). Indeed, rather than adopting an appropriate public health strategy, the state responded with denialism and confusion. For instance, the ANC's seminal document, *Ready to Govern* (ANC, 1992), only devoted four lines to AIDS (Sparks, 2003, p. 284). After many years of denialism and confusion, the state eventually came to the table and, in April 2004, the public rollout of antiretroviral treatment (ART) commenced. Initially, this was a painfully slow process and the drugs reached only a small percentage of those in need (Horne, 2005); however, South Africa currently has the largest ART programme in the world with approximately 2,002,000 (31.2%) individuals having been exposed to ART by mid-2012 (Shisana et al., 2014, p. xxviii).

Over the years, the state, national bodies, and filmmakers have harnessed popular culture, in particular the mass media, to raise awareness of HIV. Indeed, popular culture has become an important, recognized site of public pedagogy internationally with contemporary sites of education shifting from formal schools to public spaces such as the wider screen culture of electronically driven audiovisual media (Giroux, 2008; Sandlin, Schultz, & Burdock, 2010). Another term for this phenomenon, "entertainment-education" is the "intentional placement of educational content in entertainment messages" (Singhal & Rogers, 2002, p. 117). The key assumption behind these interventions is that cultural texts can spark debate amongst audiences about relevant issues, which can lead to collective social change (Papa & Singhal, 2009). Entertainment-education has been a popular vehicle for raising awareness about HIV amongst the general South African population and international audiences. For instance, the television, print and radio programmes produced by the non-profit entity The Soul City Institute are prime examples of HIV entertainment-education media (Fourie, 2011).

In addition to targeted entertainment-education programmes, there have also been a number of feature films about HIV that have facilitated public engagement with this epidemic in different ways. Brown (2011) has argued that by exposing viewers to detailed accounts of everyday life, films, in particular dramas, have the potential to connect audiences "with the lives and stories of everyday people," create "bridges of understanding and solidarity," and challenge "viewers to think in new ways" (p. 245). This chapter examines the concept of adult learning about HIV through popular culture and cultural consumption. The chief premise is that post-apartheid cinema is a site of public pedagogy and that it has the potential to play a key role in shaping public understandings of HIV and sparking critical thinking and debate about this complex social phenomenon. Drawing on research conducted for my PhD (2007–2010) on the political economic conditions of post-apartheid cinema (Treffry-Goatley, 2009), and current research on HIV entertainment-education media at Africa Centre for Health and Population Studies, I explore post-apartheid cinema as a site public pedagogy and, posing the following questions: (1) What can post-apartheid feature films teach the public about HIV? (2) How might historical and contemporary political economic conditions, such as neoliberalism, influence this pedagogical process?

METHODS

Case study methodology is the principle research strategy adopted in this study, with films comprising the cases. Case studies are best suited to answering descriptive (what has happened) and explanatory (how/why did it happen) questions, and can provide rich descriptions or insightful explanations of phenomena (Yin, 2013, p. 4). I explore *what* post-apartheid feature films can teach the public about HIV and *how* neoliberalism might influence this pedagogical process. This methodology involves an empirical investigation of a contemporary phenomenon within its real-life context (Mills, Durepos, & Wiebe, 2010; Yin, 2013). Case study research can include single and multiple case studies and tends to rely on multiple sources of evidence (Thomas,

2011). This study has a multiple case study design since it refers to analyses of six post-apartheid feature films about HIV including *Yesterday* (Singh & Roodt, 2004), *Beat the Drum* (McBrayer, Shapiro, Shaw, & Hickson, 2006), *Izulu Yami* (Frederikse & Ncayiyana, 2008), *Life, Above All* (Schmitz, 2008), *Themba* (Souvignier et al., 2010), and *Tsotsi* (Fudakowski & Hood, 2006). However, the main focus here is on the analysis of *Yesterday*, which was selected as the key case due to my inherent interest in this text as one of the first commercial South African features to directly acknowledge HIV. Reference to the five other films adds a greater diversity of themes and perspectives to this in-depth analysis. Further evidence was also drawn from additional sources including, a review of relevant academic and commercial media and numerous qualitative interviews with film industry professionals including the writer and director of *Yesterday*, Darrel James Roodt, and co-producer Helena Spring.

In terms of case selection, the first criterion for inclusion was films have wide distribution to the national public through mainstream distribution channels, since the study is concerned with the mediation of or teaching about HIV to the general public through film. Secondly, as this study concerns post-apartheid cinema, I selected films that were released locally post-1994.[1] The third aspect that informed the selection was my choice to use feature films rather than documentary or short films. This decision is indicative of my concern with "popular" or "mainstream" commercial production, distribution and exhibition practices rather than alternative or subversive cinema. The last criterion relates to subject matter. Given my preoccupation with explorations of HIV in cinema, I decided to focus on works that highlight HIV in South Africa. However, although I attempted to make a representative selection of relevant texts, it is important to note that the six films included in this study are by no means an exhaustive list of all post-apartheid features that mention HIV and there may indeed be other relevant, pedagogically interesting films that have been overlooked.

Analytic Framework

In case study methodology, the case (film) is approached as "the *subject* of the inquiry" and the "analytical frame an *object* within which the study is conducted and which the case illuminates and explicates" (Thomas, 2011, p. 511, italics added). The analysis presented here is framed within the discipline of adult education, where film has been approached as a form of public pedagogy and our interaction with this media has been understood to influence "who we are and how we think both about ourselves and about other people" (Tisdell & Thompson, 2007, p. 1). In this regard, cinema as a cultural tool might be viewed as both a space for reflecting society and also creating it (Giroux, 2011, p. 60).

In my detailed analysis of the cinematic texts, in particular the detailed analysis of *Yesterday*, I work on two different levels: (1) a contextual level where I consider the wider "national" forces and the production context of the film, and (2) a textual level, where I analyse the text itself in detail. Context is important for case study research, which "assumes that examining the context and other complex conditions related to the case(s) being studied are integral to understanding the case(s)" (Yin, 2013, p. 4). However, it should be noted that, although I believe that this contextual information can provide significant insight into the films under analysis, I view such understandings as subjective, "inherently *partial* – committed and incomplete" (Clifford, 1986, p. 7, italics added).

Nevertheless, production contexts *are* important to cinematic analysis since, "as forms of public pedagogy, films must be understood in terms of their political and educational character and how they align with broader social, racial, economic, class, and institutional configurations" (Giroux, 2008, p. 7). Economic factors are particularly significant to consider in the analysis of feature film production since this is such a capital-dependent art form. Moreover, it is important to understand the hierarchies of power in cinematic production, since "we live at a time in which the educational force of the larger culture [neoliberalism]" is dominant and has become a "major force in producing subjectivities, desires and modes of identification necessary for the legitimation and functioning of a neoliberal society" (Giroux, 2011, p. 686). Therefore, political-economics are important in the analytical framework adopted and are highlighted in the brief introduction to the post-apartheid film industry below and in the analysis of *Yesterday*.

SOUTH AFRICAN FILM INDUSTRY

South Africa has a well-established industry of over 100 years in age (Botha, 2006). However, since the beginning, national exhibition and distribution structures have been monopolised by international forces and the success of the industry has been challenged by a small, racially skewed audience, a lack of infrastructure in traditionally black residential areas and a shortage of black and female filmmakers. The state has introduced various strategies to grow and improve this industry (Treffry-Goatley, 2009). Nevertheless, these have largely been framed within the prevailing political ideology of neoliberalism, a formula that has been adopted by the main international agencies, including the World Bank and the International Monetary Fund (IMF), to help "developing countries get on the high road to greater prosperity" (Sparks, 2003, p. 208). Giroux (2004) describes the pervasive influence of neoliberalism in the twenty-first century, and argues that it has not only had an "unparalleled influence on the global economy, but has also "redefined the very nature of politics and sociality" (p. 495). Neoliberalism is not known to encourage state intervention or permit variations or to make concessions to accommodate local circumstances and, therefore, the adoption of this framework might be seen as a challenge to the realisation of the post-apartheid vision of a democracy and multiculturalism and influence the ways in which HIV has been shared with and understood by audiences (Sparks, 2003).

CASE STUDY: *YESTERDAY* (SINGH & ROODT, 2004)

Released in 2004, *Yesterday* (Singh & Roodt, 2004) was written and directed by one of South Africa's most prolific filmmakers, Darrell James Roodt, and was produced by the local filmmaker Anant Singh. Singh has been an important partner for Roodt over the years. They met as anti-apartheid filmmakers, felt a connection, and have been making films together ever since. Singh has worked as a producer on many of these films, and the distribution arm of his company, Videovision, has also been responsible for certain international and local sales. Videovision, as the production company for many of these films, has also been an important source of finance for Roodt, who noted on the director's commentary for *Yesterday* that he is very lucky to have Singh's support because he has sometimes financed entire productions such as *Faith's Corner* (Singh & Roodt, 2005). "What director gets to make a silent film in this day and age?" he questioned in his DVD commentary for *Yesterday*.

The support provided to Roodt by Videovision over the years has allowed him a certain freedom to push cinematic and social boundaries and to explore politically charged and sometimes controversial themes. For example, Luc Renders (2007) has described Darrell Roodt as an accomplished director and screenwriter who has courageously brought taboo subjects into the public forum. *Place of Weeping* (Singh & Roodt, 1986), which is recognised to be one of the first anti-apartheid films to be made in South Africa is a good example of this work. And, as one of the first commercial feature films to be released in Zulu and to directly confront the human impact of the HIV national epidemic at the height of HIV denialism, *Yesterday* is no exception to this tradition.

Yesterday was shot on location in the Drakensberg region of KwaZulu-Natal in 2003. Roodt and Singh were initially planning to make two versions of the film, one in English and the other in Zulu. However, according to the film's DVD commentary, "it became clear to Roodt once filming began, that the Zulu version was far more powerful and authentic." As the commentary further notes, from a commercial point of view, he wanted to make a "subtitled art film the world could see like *City of God*."

Yesterday is part of a new wave of low budget films in South African cinema made possible by advances in digital technology. The film had a relatively low budget of R5 million (approximately $625,000 USD). Singh (cited in Larkin, 2006) explains that they had to "'pretty much'" finance it on their own, because people were rather adverse to the idea of a Zulu film about HIV. Nevertheless, they persevered and, in the end, the production also received the support of M-Net, the National Film and Video Foundation of South Africa (NFVF) and the Nelson Mandela Foundation. Yet, despite industry scepticism of the film's subject matter, *Yesterday* was relatively well received by the public and received numerous awards including the Human Rights Film Award at the 61st Venice International Film Festival, nominations for Best Foreign Language Film at the 2005 Academy Awards, an Emmy Award (the first South African film to do so), and a 2005 Peabody Award in New York. It was also the second highest grossing South African film of 2004 (Tomaselli, 2006, p. 51).

In comparison to many South African films, *Yesterday* had a very wide local and international reach. It was shown numerous times on national television (SABC and M-Net), at national and international festivals, in local and international cinemas, at AIDS Awareness events and on the entertainment screens of the national air carrier, South African Airways. It was also released on 3 September 2004 on local cinema circuits by Ster Kinekor, on 1 December 2005 (World AIDS Day) international circuits by HBO and was also screened at numerous HIV events by the Nelson Mandela Foundation and at a number of HIV awareness events by the South African government. Indeed, *Yesterday* has frequently been employed by national and international agencies to raise awareness of HIV in South Africa, and, therefore, it is significant to investigate what this popular cultural product might teach the public about HIV.

It is important to note that although *Yesterday* is explicitly linked to HIV in South Africa, Roodt is careful to point out in his DVD commentary remarks that it was not his intention to make a documentary or a docu-drama. On the contrary, he wanted to make a piece that was illuminating and poetic. He wanted to make s simple story about a complex issue. In the same interview Roodt relates *Yesterday* to Neorealist filmmaking, such *The Bicycle Thieves* (aka *Ladri di Biciclette*). A circle of film critics in Italy developed Neorealism after the Second World War. These included Antonioni, Visconti, Pasolini and Zavattini. Neorealist films tend to have a sociological or ideological purpose and focus on the lives of the poor, are shot on location, use local dialects, employ non-professional actors and favour socially orientated narratives.

Yesterday opens with a black screen and a legend that reads, "*Ehlobo*" (Summer). This screen fades into a picturesque, rural scene of a mountain range filmed at ground level. As the camera slowly tracks from left to right, it reveals a barren, rural landscape of dust, stony ground, dry, windswept grass, a broken barbed wire fence and hazy mountains. This desolate, somewhat hostile environment combines with sound effects – the sound of the wind, the repetitive plucking of a jaws harp and breathy, guttural vocals – creating a feeling of tense anticipation and unease.[2] As the camera pans to the right, a dirt road is revealed, and two distant figures become apparent. The camera remains still as they approach. "The length of time this takes indicates the length of their journey and the unhurried pace of life" (Horne, 2005, p. 173). As they come nearer, a conversation between the two figures – a woman dressed in a brightly patterned pinafore and her young child – becomes audible. The little girl, Beauty, asks her mother in their native tongue, Zulu, why she is not a bird, explaining that if she were, then she would be able to fly places and it would not be necessary to walk so far.

Set in contemporary South Africa, 10 years after the arrival of democracy, *Yesterday* follows the life of an illiterate woman called Yesterday (Leleti Khumalo), who lives in a rural village in the KwaZulu-Natal province of South Africa. The narrative details the impact of poverty, disease, inadequate medical care, physical abuse and societal discrimination on her life. The opening sequence of this film introduces us to some key elements of the narrative. For example, the legend *Ehlobo* (Summer) is indicative of the temporal frame in which the action is set and the structure of the narrative, which, like the lives of these rural people, is connected to the passing seasons. Horne (2005) argues that the sequencing device – the chronological, seasonal structure of the narrative – "creates a sense of the relentlessness of the passage of time and the inexorability of death" (p. 172). The severity of the landscape serves to create a sense of unease – a warning of the tragedy about to unfold and also teaches the audience about the social hardship and poverty of the people. This theme of poverty is further emphasised in the dialogue, which "calls attention to how poor they are: travelling by motorized transport seems as much of a possibility as flying" (Horne, 2005, p. 173).

On the road, Yesterday and her daughter come across two women who are also travelling by foot. Through a brief conversation, Yesterday learns that they are teachers and that they have been on the road, searching for work for almost two years. When they ask where the closest village is, Yesterday replies that it is her village, Rooihoek, and that it is "not too close, but not too far" (Singh & Roodt, 2004). They have been walking for about two hours, she explains. This scene serves to reiterate the theme of poverty and hardship and also introduces the theme of education, which becomes a central motif as the narrative develops. For example, one of these two women finds work as a teacher in Rooihoek and becomes a close friend of Yesterday's. Although the character of the teacher remains unnamed (acted by Harriet Lenabe), she becomes a pivotal character in the story. As an educated and employed outsider, she has the agency to actively assist Yesterday and her family in the face of poverty and HIV discrimination at the hands of their community.

After a long, dusty walk, Beauty and Yesterday arrive at a churchyard to find a queue of people waiting in the sun. From a conversation that she has with the lady in front of her, Yesterday learns that this is the line to see the doctor, and that if she wanted to be seen today, she should have arrived much earlier. And indeed, after hours of waiting, Yesterday and many others are sent home. In the director's commentary, Roodt notes that this scene makes the audience aware of the harsh reality of life for the poor in South Africa, where access to medical care is a continual struggle. Although Yesterday's face shows her disappointment, like the other unlucky patients, she accepts her fate with graciousness and starts the long walk home. This stoic attitude echoes the hopefulness of the two teachers discussed above and is indicative of Roodt's intention to make viewers aware that poor people like Yesterday are accustomed to these inadequate medical services and that they seldom complain about their dire situations.

It is clear, however, from Yesterday's persistent nightly cough that she is in serious need of medical attention. Her weak physical state is evident when she collapses the following day when hoeing the field in preparation for planting. Nevertheless, although she attempts to see the doctor again the following week, when she and

Beauty arrive at the clinic they encounter the same long queue and are once again turned away. The device of repetition, where the director shows her going through the same futile process week after week, builds concern for Yesterday and serves to make viewers explicitly aware of the inadequacy of the health services available to many of the poor in South Africa (Horne, 2005).

After the second failed attempt to see the doctor, Yesterday decides to consult the local *sangoma* (traditional healer). Threatening rain clouds precede a scene inside a dark hut where the *sangoma* throws a bag of divination bones onto the floor. Here, Yesterday learns her illness is caused by repressed anger. When the *sangoma* asks Yesterday what she is angry about, she replies that she is not angry. Unsatisfied with the answer, the *sangoma* repeats her question. Once again Yesterday affirms that she is not angry. This repetitive exchange continues until the *sangoma* gives up, warning her that if she does not let go of this anger, she will never recover.

Yesterday's new friend, the teacher, arranges a taxi to collect Yesterday and take her to the clinic and, eventually, Yesterday is early enough to see the doctor. Here one can see how the teacher, as an outsider, is able to step into this situation and make important changes to ordinary life (see Brown, 2011). When the doctor examines her chest, she looks concerned and asks if she can do a blood test. Yesterday is alarmed. Perhaps to her, a blood test suggests that her illness is serious. It also appears that she finds the concept of "taking blood" itself to be very strange and frightening. Her anxiety increases when she is given a consent form to read and sign. Her lack of education and naivety are emphasised when viewers realise that she is illiterate. Horne notes that the print on the form is "deliberately out of focus so we also see it as illegible and share her experience of illiteracy" (Horne, 2005, p. 174). When the doctor realises Yesterday's dilemma, she accepts her verbal agreement instead and proceeds to take a blood sample. The emphasis on illiteracy in this scene points again to the theme of education mentioned previously.

One week later, we find Yesterday back in the doctor's room. The scene opens with an extreme close-up of her face. This blurred, distorted image and ominous, ambient sounds combine to reflect her state of being as she sits in a swirling cloud of horror and disbelief. The doctor asks Yesterday a number of questions about her sexual habits. It is clear from Yesterday's answers, that she has "no awareness of her possible cause of infection, and that she finds it difficult and uncomfortable to answer the doctor's questions" (Horne, 2005, p. 174). For example, when the doctor inquires whether she uses a condom, her "bewildered expression and naive question 'but why? I am a married woman'" indicate that she thinks of condoms "only for the purposes of contraception, has never doubted her husband's fidelity and has been completely faithful herself" (p. 175). In response to the doctor's question, Yesterday explains that her husband works in a mine in Johannesburg and affirms that, when he is home, they enjoy a healthy sex life.

These two scenes are quite significant from a pedagogical perspective since, in a dramatized form, they raise a number of important topics relevant to HIV in South Africa. These topics include the scarcity of health services in poor rural areas, the role of male promiscuity in HIV transmission, the vulnerability and disempowerment of uneducated rural women in the context of the migrant labour system and the importance of safe sex in this context.

Following the doctor's question about her husband's whereabouts, the conversation comes to a halt and ominous music builds as Yesterday contemplates her situation. She asks fearfully whether this means that she will "stop living" (Singh & Roodt, 2004). The doctor looks down and presses her lips together tightly. Her silence is confirmation that this is indeed true. This silence can be seen as an aural signifier of the "treatment vacuum that exists for people like Yesterday [leaving] the audience to wonder why no treatment or information is offered at this critical moment, since without treatment, Yesterday's premature death is inevitable" (Horne, 2005, p. 175). It is important to note that a similar theme can be found in four of the five other case studies where HIV infection is the end of life and no treatment options are even mentioned. Among the 6 other films considered in my analysis, only *Themba* (Souvignier et al., 2010) mentions ART when a young HIV-positive boy called Themba helps his mother to access ART when he learns that she is also positive. The absence of ART in post-apartheid cinema is a direct reflection of the many years of state denial and lack of treatment access in South Africa.

The music in *Yesterday* swells as the camera rises to produce a series of cut and paste, awkward shots. The two figures below become smaller, and the viewer looks further and further downwards at Yesterday and the doctor in the small consulting room. The final high camera angle makes them seem trapped at the bottom of what resembles a pit. This technique creates dramatic awareness of the helplessness of professional and patient in this situation. The lighting in this sequence is also significant. A side window allows light to fall dramatically onto the doctor, while Yesterday sitting opposite her, remains in darkness as if death has already enveloped her.

Upon Yesterday's arrival in Johannesburg, a series of shots follow her as she moves through the city walking through crowds, sitting wide-eyed on the bus clutching her suitcase and standing at the foot of monstrous skyscrapers. At the mine, images of "whirring machines towering above her further emphasise Yesterday's alienation and anxiety, as well as the dehumanizing nature of the mine's mechanics" (Hodes, 2008, p. 12). When Yesterday confronts John with the news of her status, he reacts violently and beats her severely. The violence and alienation that Yesterday is subjected to in Johannesburg affirms the dystopic nature of the city. This country bumpkin theme is in keeping with the South African cinematic tradition of the rural protagonist's "epic voyage" to the dangerous city and is explored in four of the five other case studies considered in this chapter. For example, in *Beat the Drum* (McBrayer, Shapiro, Shaw, & Hickson, 2003), the orphan, Musa, travels by foot to the city to search for his uncle and the truth about HIV. Like the AIDS orphans of *Izulu Lami* (Frederikse & Ncayiyana, 2009), Musa is confronted by a perilous and immoral life on the streets surrounded by gangs of other orphaned child. The films *Themba* (Souvignier et al., 2010) also trace a journey of children protagonists in search of their diseased mothers who have escaped to the anonymous city to mask their HIV status from their rural communities. The spatial dichotomy that is developed in the films between the city as a place of violence and disease and the village as a place of calm and peace might be seen to feed into a preconception that black people should maintain a traditional way of life in the rural areas. This discourse is most problematic since it is directly linked to the separatist, oppressive system of apartheid. Nevertheless, if one considers that Yesterday's rural home later becomes a site of a sinister, silent violence at the hands of her community, it is also arguable that Roodt actually challenges this dichotomy in the film.

Upon Yesterday's return to the village, the time-marker *Ubusika* (winter) appears, functioning "semiotically as an omen of a harsher world and approaching death. The environment is now even more arid, windswept and bleak" (Horne, 2005, p. 177). In the opening scenes of this section, we watch Yesterday in her struggle to keep up with her everyday chores. After returning home one day from chopping firewood, she finds her husband sitting outside her hut. "His skeletal frame and blemished skin serve as fatal signs of full-blown" (Horne, 2005, p. 177). That night, in a close-up interior scene, we witness a tender encounter between husband and wife as he recounts his experience of degradation and humiliation at the mine. As John explains how the foreman eventually sent him to the doctor who did tests and confirmed what she had told him, he breaks down completely and cries like a child. At this point, Yesterday rises quickly and embraces him. Yesterday's display of compassion at this point serves to develop a greater sense of audience identification with her character. Firstly, because she has displayed the likeable qualities of kindness of forgiveness and secondly, because the power relations have been shifted. She has become the stronger character in the film: our heroine.

The focus on a single protagonist in the narrative of *Yesterday* links this work to the restorative structure of classical filmmaking and shows that this film to be blend of mainstream and neorealist filmmaking (Dancyger & Rush, 2002). This cinematic choice has attracted certain criticism since it fails to acknowledge the key role of family support and it gives the impression that Yesterday's and her husband's illnesses are unusual within their respective rural and urban communities. This, however, does not accord with the national statistics of HIV/AIDS (Horne, 2005). Nevertheless, Roodt's choice to make a rural woman the protagonist of a heroic story is in keeping with neorealist trends and is indicative of the desire to challenge established racial hierarchies in the media (Horne, 2005). A second example of a female protagonist is the resilient character of Chanda in Schmitz's (2010) *Life, Above All*. Silent and tough in the face of death, HIV and community gossip, this young woman stands for what is right and stays true to her mother and ostracised best friend. If one considers the other five case studies under discussion, one finds that, with the exception of *Beat the Drum* (McBrayer, Shapiro, Shaw, & Hickson, 2003), where a young white lawyer becomes infected with HIV, all of these films highlight HIV infection amongst the black, South African community. While one might argue that these films feed into the typecast of HIV as a "black person's" disease, these depictions are also reflective of the reality of the uneven demographic distribution of HIV in South Africa (Shisana et al., 2014).

Subsequently, we find Yesterday inside her humble home cooking supper. The teacher friend comes to visit and requests to speak urgently. She informs Yesterday that everyone in the village is talking about her husband. They do not want him to stay in the village because they say that he has HIV. "Is it true?" she asks (Singh & Roodt, 2004). Yesterday confirms that indeed it is so and confides that she too is infected. When the teacher asks why she has never told her, Yesterday shares a story about a young university student from the nearby town of Bergville who was stoned to death "when it became known that she was HIV positive" (Horne, 2005, p. 177).[3] This story is indicative of the fear that Yesterday feels about disclosing her status to the community due to the widespread denial and stigma associated with HIV in South Africa (Horne, 2005). When she learns that her friend is HIV positive, rather than shunning her, she attempts to teach the villagers about the transmission routes of HIV and to remind them that they cannot become infected by living near HIV positive residents like Yesterday and her husband. Therefore, the teacher gathers the villagers together and attempts to educate them about HIV and assures them that it can only be transmitted through surgical needles or sex. However, the women do not listen and insist that Yesterday's husband must leave the village. This is a scene when adult education and learning are portrayed for the characters and, presumably, the audience, and the theme of education is emphasised.

The communal water pump serves as a space of informal learning where the women discuss the problem of HIV. "Your husbands are bringing it to you," one says. "Yes, we get it from them" replies the other. Another bickers, "you must see how she coughs!" (Singh & Roodt, 2004). The message in this exchange is clear. Once again the city is shown to be "the source of the disease, and that migrating husbands are the vectors" (Hodes, 2008, p. 14). As Yesterday approaches the pump, the women scramble away. She is an outcast. The representation of the villagers in such scenes has attracted certain criticism. It has been argued that these individuals have been stereotyped as small-minded, mean characters with no knowledge of HIV (Wozniak, 2007). Similar representations of rural personas can be found in *Beat the Drum* (McBrayer, Shapiro, Shaw, & Hickson, 2003) where the villagers are shown to know nothing about HIV and in *Life, Above all* (Schmitz, 2010), where the inhabitants of a small town called Elandsdoorn, soon become mean and even violent when they suspect that 12-year-old Chandra's mother is HIV positive.

The reaction of the villagers drives Yesterday to approach a local hospital to enquire whether her husband might be admitted. However, she learns that they are full to capacity – another reminder of the inadequate medical services available to the poor in South Africa – and Yesterday decides to take the situation into her own hands. She starts to build a "hospital" for her husband. She and Beauty go around the village collecting material: bits of wood, corrugated iron and scraps of metal. They hammer these items together to create a rudimentary hut. In the director's commentary, Roodt notes that this is a very important, symbolic sequence in the film.

Through the accomplishment of this seemingly impossible task, Yesterday displays "independence, resourcefulness and courage" and this serves as evidence that she has taken control over her situation and shows that she refuses to "live fearfully and be at the mercy of the villagers' intolerance" (Horne, 2005, p. 179). Inside this lonely, humble abode, John spends his final days as Yesterday waits patiently at his side, nursing him as his life force slowly fades.

The legend *Ehlobo Futhi* (Summer again) serves as a somewhat paradoxical announcement at this tragic point in the narrative that summer has returned. In the opening sequence, we see Yesterday, dressed in black, standing at her husband's grave. The teacher approaches her and they discuss the opening of school the following week. Yesterday explains that she is very excited because she was never able to attend school herself. Here education surfaces as symbol of hope for the future reiterating the importance of this theme in the narrative. In this intimate moment, her friend assures her that when the end comes; she will love Beauty as her own daughter.

The teacher's adoption of Beauty serves to give this film a somewhat more uplifting ending. However, it masks the fate of the millions of orphaned and abandoned children who end up in ill-equipped, over-populated hospitals and homes throughout sub-Saharan Africa.[4] This "false" resolution to the film is also evident in the film *Tsotsi* (Fudakowski & Hood, 2006) where the lead character, a young vagabond called Tsotsi, returns the child that he mistakenly stole in a car hijacking to its parents and willingly hands himself over to the police. It is important to mention that, while *Yesterday* fails to detail the plight of AIDS orphans in South Africa, other post-apartheid features, including *Tsotsi*, *Beat the Drum* (McBrayer, Shapiro, Shaw, & Hickson, 2006), *Izulu Lami* (Frederikse & Ncayiyana, 2009), *Themba* (Souvignier et al., 2010) and *Life, Above All* (Schmitz, 2010), all deal directly with the human consequences of the loss of a parent or both parents due to HIV. Moreover, Yesterday provides a very moving account of a mother's pain of losing a full life with her daughter.

In the penultimate scene of the film, we find Yesterday sitting on Beauty's bed in a state of deep sadness as she watches her brushing her teeth over an enamel basin. She calls Beauty over to her and offers her a gift. It is a school suitcase with a uniform inside it. Beauty is delighted with the present. In the final scene, we find her at school wearing her new attire. She stands in a long line with other children as they wait to enter the building. She waves at her mother and smiles. "A close up view of her [Yesterday's] face behind the padlocked gate, which functions as a symbol of the barrier that will soon part them for ever, shows her smile of greeting slowly dissolve into an expression of profound sadness" (Horne, 2005, p. 181). Yesterday has effectively reached her reason for being. Beauty's triumph also symbolises her demise. She stays there, watching her daughter for some time, before retreating slowly. As she walks away, the camera rises up and within a few seconds, she has become a tiny, indistinct figure in the vast rural landscape. The volume of the music reduces to a whisper as she disappears, and the screen fades to black for the credits.

CONCLUSION

In this chapter, I have examined the concept of adult learning about HIV through popular culture and cultural consumption. The key premise is that post-apartheid cinema is a site of public pedagogy and that it can potentially play a key role in shaping public understandings of HIV and sparking critical thinking and debate about this complex social phenomenon (Sandlin, Schultz, & Burdock, 2010). In this analysis, I have used case study methodology to explore what post-apartheid feature films can teach the public about HIV, and how historical and contemporary political economic conditions, such as neoliberalism, might influence this pedagogical process. Overall, post-apartheid feature films such as *Yesterday* appear to have the potential to play an important pedagogical role in the context of HIV. By exposing viewers to detailed accounts of everyday life, these dramas can certainly connect audiences "with the lives and stories of everyday people," create "bridges of understanding and solidarity," and challenge "viewers to think in new ways" (Brown, 2011, p. 245).[5] Horne (2005) argues that Roodt "succeeds in using Yesterday's story to show – in an understated way – how intimately AIDS is tied to socio-economic and cultural dynamics such as stigma, poverty, migrant labour, income inequalities and gender relations" (p. 193).

Yesterday (Singh & Roodt, 2004) can indeed be viewed as a deliberate, epidemiologically informed response to HIV in South Africa. The film is set in Kwazulu-Natal, the province with highest HIV infection rate in the country. It focuses on the plight of rural black women, the population group most affected by the disease. These features highlight the inaccessibility of medical services at the time. The other five films add to the picture painted by Roodt by emphasising the economic and social impact of the epidemic on South African families, by highlighting the link between domestic violence and HIV, by drawing attention to the adverse role of stigma on people infected and affected by HIV and by drawing attention to the lack of ART for many individuals in need. Therefore, from a content point of view, these productions can be seen to have the ability to raise public awareness of the human impact of HIV in South Africa.

When one considers the wider context of the post-apartheid film industry, however, certain challenges emerge. As noted above, filmmaking and film viewing in South Africa have long been subject to racial stratification and there are very few black filmmakers or cinema houses in "black areas" (Botha, 2006). Although the state has introduced a number of strategies to "grow" the local industry, these have all been framed within the discourse of neoliberalism, which does not favour direct state interventions, or protection of local markets (Treffry-Goatley, 2010). Consequently, black people in South Africa, the population group most affected by HIV, have little access to filmmaking or film consumption (Shisana et al., 2014). Perhaps some of the cultural stereotypes evident in some of the aforementioned films, including the relatively negative depiction of rural Zulus, the simplistic portrayal of traditional healers and the dystopic vision of the cities, might have been shown differently if black filmmakers were more involved in creating these representations or if the films were more targeted at local, black audiences.

The market-orientation typical of neoliberalism has resulted in a proliferation of light-hearted, slap stick comedies on the local scene that have proven success with audiences and few filmmakers have had the courage or financial freedom to broach subjects that are difficult to talk about such as HIV. Those who have accepted this challenge have tended to frame their work within conventional formats and have tailored their products to meet the cultural expectations of local white or international audiences. Roodt's relative artistic freedom to experiment in this context – his application of neorealist narrative elements, the avoidance of didacticism and his use of an indigenous language – might be linked to *Yesterday's* small, locally funded budget and the long-term support of his filmmaking partner, Singh.

Nevertheless, this is not to say that *Yesterday* is a "perfect" or "pure" film which tells the "truth" and is free from any outside influences, commercial objectives or export orientations. Typical features of mainstream filmmaking in *Yesterday* and the other five feature films discussed here include a focus on single protagonists and a trend of restorative endings. These features are quite problematic in the context of HIV education since they do not give due recognition to the role of the extended family and community in supporting those affected/infected by HIV and can mask widespread reality of suffering in favour of "feel good" conclusion.

In conclusion, post-apartheid cinema is indeed a site of public pedagogy and does have the potential to play a key role in shaping public understandings of HIV and sparking critical thinking and debate about this complex social phenomenon. Nevertheless, although cinema, as a form of popular culture can be a valuable tool for raising public awareness and sparking critique, the commercial nature of this industry and the particular socio-economic and historic circumstances of South Africa might limit what post-apartheid feature films can teach us about HIV and which audiences these films can reach. Ultimately, *Yesterday* is best viewed as a hybrid product and as an epidemiologically informed, yet personal interpretation of the human impact of HIV in a rural community of South Africa, and a cultural text that functions in pedagogically and artistically complex ways.

NOTES

[1] I attempted to work according to the date of local release. However, it has not always been possible to determine which date is being referred to in the relevant documentation and thus there may be some contradictions in this regard.

[2] The jaws harp is also known as mouth harp, Ozark harp, trump and juice harp. It is a plucked idiophone that consists of a flexible tongue or reed that is attached to a frame. It is made of metal or bamboo and is played by plucking the reed while holding the frame against the performer's mouth for resonance. The change in shape of the mouth cavity changes to the tone of the note and produces harmonics.

[3] This scene makes reference to a real incident that took place in 1998, in which a university student Gugu Dlamini was stoned to death by her community in her hometown of KwaMacinza (Horne, 2005).

4   In 2012, the number of orphans in South Africa among those 0-18 years of age and younger was estimated to be 16.9% (3,132,041). This level has largely remained the same since the survey of 2008 (Shisana et al., 2014).
5   For example, Julie Frederikse the co-writer and producer of Izulu lami, has stated that although influence of HIV is evident in the story, they did not "want to make this a key theme of the film," but rather a subtext that is evident in the death of the mother, the symbolic of use of red in the main character's dress and the number of children living without parental care (Dercksen & Frederikse, 2009).

REFERENCES

African National Congress. (1992). *Ready to govern: ANC policy guidelines for a democratic South Africa*. Retrieved from http://www.anc.org.za/show.php?id=227

Barber, K. (2001). Cultural reconstruction in the new South Africa [Review of the book *Senses of culture: South African cultural studies*, Edited by S. Nuttall & C. A. Michael]. *African Studies Review*, *44*(2), 177–185. doi:10.2307/525581

Botha, M. P. (2006). 110 years of South African cinema (part 1). *Kinema: A Journal for Film and Audiovisual Media*, Fall. Retrieved from http://www.kinema.uwaterloo.ca/article.php?id=46&feature

Brown, T. (2011). Using film in teaching and learning about changing societies. *International Journal of Lifelong Education*, *30*(2), 233–247. doi:10.1080/02601370.2010.547615

Clifford, J. (1986). Introduction: Partial truths. In J. Clifford & G. E. Marcus (Eds.), *Writing culture: The poetics and politics of ethnography* (pp. 1–26). Berkley: University of California Press.

Dancyger, K., & Rush, J. (2002). *Alternative scriptwriting: Successfully breaking the rules*. Boston, MA: Focal Press.

Dercksen, D., & Frederikse, J. (2009). *Proudly South African filmmaking: Izulu lami/My secret sky* [Interview]. Retrieved from http://www.writingstudio.co.za/page2696.html

Fourie, L. (2011). The value of entertainment-education: The case of Soul City. In K. Tomaselli & C. Chasi (Eds.), *Development and public health communication* (pp. 316–342). Cape Town, South Africa: Pearson Education.

Frederikse, J. (Producer), & Ncayiyana, M. (Director). (2009). *Izulu lami* [Motion picture]. South Africa: DV8 & Vuleka Productions.

Fudakowski, P. (Producer), & Hood, G. (Director). (2006). *Tsotsi*. South Africa & Germany: Industrial Development Corporation of South Africa/Moviworld.

Giroux, H. A. (2004). Public pedagogy and the politics of neo-liberalism: Making the political more pedagogical. *Policy Futures in Education*, *2*(3/4), 494–503.

Giroux, H. A. (2008). Hollywood film as public pedagogy: Education in the crossfire. *Afterimage: The Journal of Media Arts and Cultural Criticism*, *35*(5), 7–13.

Giroux, H. A. (2011). Breaking into the movies: Public pedagogy and the politics of film. *Policy Futures in Education*, *6*(4), 686–695. doi:10.2304/pfie.2011.9.6.686

Hodes, R. (2008). Diseased dystopias? HIV/AIDS and the South African city in *Yesterday* and *Tsotsi*. *Postamble*, *4*(2), 1–16.

Horne, F. (2005). *Yesterday*: AIDS, and structural violence in South Africa. *Communicatio: Southern African Journal for Theory and Research*, *31*(2), 172–198. doi:10.1080/02500160508583001

Larkin, M. (2006). *Yesterday*. *The Lancet Infectious Diseases*, *6*(3), 136–137.

Macarow, K. (2008). Transmission routes: The global AIDS epidemic in South Africa and France. *The Global South*, *2*(2), 92–111.

McBrayer, W. D., Shapiro, K. S., & Shaw, R. (Producers), & Hickson, D. (Director). (2003). *Beat the drum* [Motion picture]. South Africa & United States: Z Productions.

Mills, A. J., Durepos, G., & Wiebe, E. (Eds.). (2010). *Encyclopedia of case study research*. Thousand Oaks, CA: Sage Publications.

Nattrass, N. (2007). *Mortal combat: AIDS denialism and the struggle for antiretrovirals in South Africa*. Scottsville, NY: University of KwaZulu Natal Press.

Papa, M., & Singhal, A. (2009). How entertainment-education programmes promote dialogue in support of social change. *Journal of Creative Communications, 4*(3), 185–208. doi:10.1177/ 097325861000400304

Renders, L. (2007). Redemption movies. In M. Botha (Ed.), *Marginal lives and painful pasts: South African cinema after apartheid* (pp. 221–254). Parklands, South Africa: Genugtig! Press.

Saks, L. (2003). The race for representation. In I. Balseiro & N. Masilela (Eds.), *To change reels: Films and film culture in South Africa* (pp. 132–159). Detroit, MI: Wayne State University Press.

Sandlin, J. A., Schultz, B., & Burdock, J. (Eds.). (2010). Understanding, mapping, and exploring the terrain of public pedagogy. *Handbook of public pedagogy: Education and learning beyond schooling*. New York, NY & London, England: Routledge.

Schmitz, O. (Producer & Director). (2010). *Life, above all* [Motion picture]. Germany & South Africa: Dreamer Joint Venture Film Production.

Shisana, O., Rehle, T., Simbayi, L. C., Zuma, K., Jooste, S., Zungu, N., Labadarios, D., & Onoya, D. (2014). *South African national HIV prevalence, incidence and behaviour survey, 2012*. Cape Town, South Africa: Human Sciences Research Council Press.

Singhal, A., & Rogers, E. M. (2002). A theoretical agenda for entertainment-education. *Communication Theory, 12*(2), 117–135. doi:10.1111/j.1468-2885.2002.tb00262.x

Singh, D. (Producer), & Roodt, D. (Director). (1986). *Place of weeping* [Motion picture]. South Africa: Videovision.

Singh, D. (Producer), & Roodt, D. (Director). (2004). *Yesterday* [Motion picture]. South Africa: Videovision.

Singh, D. (Producer), & Roodt, D. (Director). (2005). *Faith's corner* [Motion picture]. South Africa: Videovision.

Sparks, A. (2003). *Beyond the miracle: Inside the new South Africa*. Johannesburg & Cape Town, South Africa: Jonathan Ball Publishers.

Souvignier, M., Souvignier, I., Steinberger, J., Olën, B., de Mardt, M., (Producers), & Sycholt, S. (Director). (2010). *Themba* [Motion picture]. South Africa & Germany: Zeitsprung Entertainment, Rheingold Films & DO Productions.

Thomas, G. (2011). A typology for the case study in social science following a review of definition, discourse and structure. *Qualitative Inquiry, 17*(6), 511–521. doi:10.1177/1077800411409884

Tisdell, E. J., & Thompson, P. (2007). Editors' notes: Popular culture, entertainment media, and adult education. *New Directions in Adult and Continuing Education, 115*, 1–4. doi:10.1002/ace.261

Tomaselli, K. (2006). *Encountering modernity: Twentieth century South Africa cinemas*. Pretoria, South Africa: UNISA Press.

Treffry-Goatley, A. (2009). South African cinema after apartheid: A political-economic exploration. *Communicatio, 36*(1), 37–57. doi:10.1080/02500160903525023

Treffry-Goatley, A. (2010). *The representation of national identity in the production of post-apartheid, South African cinema* (Unpublished doctoral dissertation). Cape Town, South Africa: University of Cape Town, South Africa.

Wozniak, J. (2007). Interpretations of old beliefs and modern lifestyles in a selection of recent South African films. In M. Botha (Ed.), *Marginal lives and painful pasts: South African cinema after apartheid* (pp. 317–342). Parklands, South Africa: Genugtig! Press.

Yin, R. K. (2013). *Case study research: Design and methods* (5th ed.). Thousand Oaks, CA: Sage Publications.

Astrid Treffry-Goatley
Africa Centre for Health and Population Studies
University of KwaZulu-Natal

NANCY TABER

8. PEDAGOGIES OF GENDER IN A DISNEY MASH-UP

Princesses, Queens, Beasts, Pirates, Lost Boys, and Witches

INTRODUCTION

I have always loved fairy tales due to their magical plots and fantastical settings. I grew up watching these tales, as adapted into Disney movies and television programs, continuing to enjoy them into adulthood. Over the years, I have come to prefer fairy tale reimaginings, such as those that turn the antagonist into the protagonist (i.e., Gregory Maguire's *Wicked* novel, 2007) and those told from a feminist pespective (i.e., anthologies compiled by Zipes, 1989, and Walker, 1996). As an academic, my work has gradually come to explore the ways in which fairy tales are implicated in adult learning. Adults interact with fairy tales in relation to their own childhood memories, with the children in their lives, and for their own enjoyment. Certain fairy tales are iconic in western society; one would be hard pressed to find someone unfamiliar with the prince's kiss that wakes Sleeping Beauty, Rumplestitlskin's ire when his name is discovered, or the glass slipper Cinderella leaves behind.

Several prime time television programs and movies based on fairy tales and created for young adult or adult audiences have been released recently to the North American market. They include television series such as *Beauty and the Beast*, *Grimm*, *Sleepy Hollow*, *Once Upon a Time*, and *Once Upon a Time in Wonderland* and films such as *Hansel and Gretel: Witch Hunters*, *Snow White and the Huntsman*, and *Red Riding Hood*. The success of these popular culture artefacts based on fairy tales points to the ways in which adults continue to embrace the fairy tale genre, demonstrating Zipes' (1979/2002a) argument that fairy tales are not solely created for children. Adults are not passive consumers of these tales, but actively participate in meaning-making as they engage with them. Adult educators are increasingly exploring how learning and popular culture intersect (Jarvis & Burr, 2011; Tisdell, 2008; Wright & Sandlin, 2009a, 2009b).

In this chapter, I explore how meaning-making is entwined with pedagogies of gender in *Once Upon a Time* (produced by ABC Studios, a division of Disney-ABC Television Group). I have chosen this program because of the ways in which it is a "mash-up" of Disney characters in a variety of fairy tales. I have enjoyed watching this program, often with my teenage son, due to its strong central female characters and twists on traditional tellings. At the same time, a critical analysis is required to problematize gender representations. In my argument, I first explore literature addressing the fairy tale genre and Disney adaptations. Second, I explain my methodological approach of feminist discourse analysis. Third, I briefly describe *Once Upon a Time* (*OUAT*). Fourth, I discuss pedagogies of gender as relates to romantic love, representations of family, and intersections between childhood, adulthood, fantasy, and reality. I conclude with a discussion of the ways in which fairy tales can be educationally used for social critique.

FAIRY TALES AND DISNEY ADAPTATIONS

The field of adult education is often assumed to be based on the fact that children and adults learn differently. For me, it is not so much about age, but about context, with a focus on the ways in which learning occurs in everyday life. With respect to the everydayness of popular culture, Tisdell (2007) states, "for good or for ill, we are constantly being bombarded by messages that affect who are and how we think, whether we are conscious of those messages or not" (p. 8). It is therefore crucial for adult educators to critique these messages, raising awareness of the ways in which learning occurs in interaction with popular culture. In so doing, educators can "help people think about issues and assumptions [in popular culture and society] in new and creative ways" (Tisdell, 2008, p. 52). Fairy tales are not often taken up by adult educators, but their ubiquitousness in western society makes this genre an important site of adult learning.

Fairy tales have a long history which has evolved over time (Zipes, 1979/2002a); the stories that are now told are "versions of versions, narratives spun and respun for hundreds of years" (Harries, 2001, p. 4). Fairy tales began orally, with various writers eventually putting pen to paper. Gradually, the diversity of fairy tale writers and content narrowed, with the work of women writers (which was often quite complex with respect to form and gender), all but vanishing (Harries, 2001). The most well-known fairy tale writers are arguably the Grimm Brothers, who (re)wrote over 210 stories (Zipes, 2003). Out of these stories, Baker-Sperry and Grauerholz (2003) found that the highest reproduced tales were ones that emphasized a feminine beauty ideal that was linked to passiveness. As such, the rich history, forms, plots, and characters that once populated fairy tales have been eclipsed by a constricting focus on a very specific pattern that includes a dangerous threat and rescue from a (masculine) protector (Harries, 2001).

As Zipes (1979/2002a) argues, "large media conglomerates" such as Disney have become "a determining factor in the transmission of folk and fairy tales, ... [with] power in shaping art forms and their transmission" (p. ix). Indeed fairy tales and Disney have become almost synonymous in western society, with "Disneyfied" (Dong, 2006, p. 227) stories as prominent tellings. Disney is a "megacorporation" that "focuses on popular culture and continually expands its products and services to reach every available media platform" (Giroux & Pollock, 2010, p. xiii). For instance, *Once Upon a Time* is a television program with an accompanying website and DVD sets, as well as the companion guide *Once Upon a Time: Behind the Magic* (Titan Books, 2013), the novel *Reawakened: A Once Upon a Time Tale* (Beane, 2013), and a graphic novel *Once Upon a Time: Shadow of the Queen* (Thomsen & Bechko, 2013). One can also buy *Once Upon a Time* T-shirts, mugs, gym bags, and other associated paraphernalia.

In addition to a commodification of culture, Disney's "manufacture of fantasy" (Wasko, 2001, p. 219) supports "conservatism, homophobia, Manifest Destiny, ethnocentricity, cultural insensitivity, superficiality, lack of culture" (Wasko, p. 224). I would also add traditional gender roles and glorification of violence to Wasko's list. Despite some exceptions, characters are typically either beautiful, white, young, and good or ugly, old, and evil (Baker-Sperry & Grauerholz, 2003). Marriage between a prince and a princess is a celebration of true love and happy endings (Baker-Sperry, 2007) while alternative family forms are denigrated with evil stepmothers and mean step-sisters. There is an overall tendency in Disney animated films to demonize others, categorizing them as good or evil (Fouts, Callan, Piasentin, & Lawson, 2006), where the death of evil characters at the hands of good ones is often the goal. Although, over the years, Disney princess heroines have "expanded to incorporate some traditionally masculine characteristics" (England, Descartes, & Collier-Meek, 2011, p. 566), they have nonetheless "retained ... femininity" (p. 566) while male characters have changed little. *Once Upon a Time* complicates and replicates these gendered discourses, as I argue through my use of feminist discourse analysis.

FEMINIST DISCOURSE ANALYSIS

My research is framed by the methodology of feminist discourse analysis, which explores "how gender ideology and gendered representations of power are (re)produced, negotiated and contested in representations of social practices, in social relationships between people, and in people's social and personal identities in text and talk" (Lazar, 2005, p. 11). It explores how societal relations of gender are "taken-for-granted" in a way that "mystifies or obscures the power differential and inequality at work" (p. 7). As popular culture fairy tale artefacts are often assumed to be *just entertainment*, feminist discourse analysis (FDA) is particularly helpful in problematizing not only their content, but how certain stories are told over others. Furthermore, as *OUAT* does not follow a straight-forward stereotypical script, FDA assisted my exploration of the "subtle and complex renderings of ideological assumptions and power relations" (p. 13) within the program.

The dataset for my analysis includes the *OUAT* television series (Seasons 1–3) and *Once Upon a Time: Behind the Magic*, companion guide for Seasons 1 and 2 (Titan Books, 2013). In my analysis, I focused on plotlines and character development, asking questions such as: Who are the main characters? How are women represented? Who is evil and who is good? How does *OUAT* connect to fairy tales and Disney stories? I identified main themes that arose in addressing these questions and then classified them into the gendered discourses of true love and familial love. I discuss how these discourses function in relation to romance, representations of family, and intersections between fantasy, reality, childhood, and adulthood.

PLOT SUMMARY

Disney characters are central to the plot of *Once Upon a Time*. Although the program began with a focus on Snow White and appeared to be largely relying on tales first popularized by the Grimm Brothers (such as *Rumplestiltskin*), it began to incorporate stories from other sources which have become Disney movies (such as *Alice in Wonderland, Mulan, Peter Pan, Pinocchio* and, most recently, *Frozen*). In the latter half of its third season, it also drew in characters from the *Wizard of Oz*. The program not only mashes-up characters and plots from different sources, but revises the tellings and provides back-stories to many characters, which changes the ways in which they are viewed by the audience.

In *OUAT*, Snow White and Prince Charming must send their newborn daughter, Emma, away from Fairy Tale Land so that she can escape a curse unleashed by the Evil Queen. The amnesiac curse sends most everyone to magic-free Storybrooke, Maine. Twenty-eight years later, Emma is found by her 10-year-old son, Henry, whom she gave up for adoption. Henry has been adopted by Regina (the Evil Queen) and is convinced Emma is the saviour who can break the curse, bring magic back, and restore everyone's memories. As they encounter various threats, the story shifts from present-day Storybrooke to past- and present-day Fairy Tale Land, as well as to Neverland and Oz. Table 1 (see below) provides a list of central characters and related stories.

FINDINGS: COMPLICATING AND REPLICATING GENDER

OUAT features complex female protagonists and antagonists with detailed backstories that further develop their characters. The plot revolves around discourses of true love, a battle between good and evil, and familial connections. Discourses of love are represented not only as romantic love (as exemplified in the relationship between Snow White and Prince Charming), but as love between mothers and children (as exemplified by Emma's and the Evil Queen's love for Henry). In other research, I have specifically explored the performance of gender in Season 1 of *OUAT* (in connection with Season 1 of another series, *Grimm*)[2] as relates to "characterizations of heroic hunters and saviors, who are also estranged mothers and sons" (Taber, 2013, para. 2). In my conclusion, I stated,

> *Grimm* and *Once* engage in similar ways with militaristic societal ideals. Fights, violence, and battles are viewed as accepted and required, save for the occasional voice of conscience through Jiminy Cricket. Men and women perform a certain balance of hegemonically masculine traits, working to ensure the protection of innocents. Evil continues to lurk nearby, with good always ready to respond. And yet both programs also provide space for critiques of

Table 1. Characters and plots incorporated in OUAT[1]

Tale	Characters
Snow White and the Seven Dwarfs	Snow White/Mary-Margaret, Prince Charming/Davis, the Evil Queen/Regina, Seven Dwarfs, Magic Mirror (Sidney Glass), the Huntsman/Sheriff Graham
Beauty and the Beast	Beauty/Belle and the Beast (Rumplestilskin/Mr. Gold, also known as The Dark One), Lumiere, Gaston
Peter Pan	Peter Pan (who is also the Pied Piper), the Lost Boys, Captain Hook/Killian, Smee, The Crocodile (Rumplestitlskin), Tinker Bell, Wendy, John, Michael
The Wizard of Oz	Wicked Witch of the West/Zelena, Glinda the Good Witch of the South, Witch of the North, Witch of the East, Dorothy, the Wizard, Flying Monkeys
Robin Hood	Robin Hood, Merry Men, Marian, Sheriff of Nottingham, Little John, Friar Tuck
Mulan	Mulan
Alice in Wonderland	Mad Hatter, Queen of Hearts (The Evil Queen's mother, Cora), Knave of Hearts, Caterpillar
Little Red Riding Hood	Little Red Riding Hood/Red (who is also The Wolf), Granny, Woodsman
Pinocchio	Pinocchio/August, Geppetto/Marco, Jiminy Cricket/Archie
The Little Mermaid	The Little Mermaid (Ariel), Prince Eric, Ursula
Sleeping Beauty	Sleeping Beauty (Aurora), Prince Philip, Maleficent
Frankenstein	Dr. Frankenstein/Dr. Whale, Igor
King Midas	King Midas
Jack and the Beanstalk	Giant, Jack the Giant Killer
Rumplestiltskin	Rumplestiltskin, The Miller's Daughter (who is also Cora)
Cinderella	Cinderella, Fairy Godmother, Prince Thomas
Knights of the Round Table	Lancelot
Hansel and Gretel	Hansel and Gretel, the Woodcutter
Rapunzel	Rapunzel
Aladdin	Genie of Agrabah (becomes trapped as Magic Mirror)
Fountain of Youth	Dead Man's Peak
Sirens	Siren
Blackbeard	Blackbeard
Frozen	Elsa, the Snow Queen – Season 4

the ways in which western society views men and women, good and bad. It is this space that will hopefully develop as the programs move into and through future seasons. (Taber, 2013, para. 30)

As I watched Seasons 2 and 3 of *OUAT*, I noted that the characters and plot did become more complex, although the program continued to reflect my findings as stated above. In the research discussed here, I continue my earlier analysis by focusing on pedagogies of gender in *OUAT* as relates to how the discourses of true and familial love function in relation to romance, representations of family, and intersections between fantasy, reality, childhood, and adulthood.

Romance

The discourse of true love is such a prevalent aspect of *OUAT* that it could almost be considered a character in itself. Even the evil Rumplestiltskin recognizes that true love is the "most powerful magic in the world" (Kitsis, Horowitz, & White, 2012a, "A Land Without Magic," Episode 122). In the series, true love is represented in two different ways, with respect to romantic love (discussed here) and to familial love (discussed below). Romantic love continues to be portrayed in heteronormative ways that are directly connected to strength and weakness, good and evil (Baker-Sperry, 2007; Zipes, 1979/2002a, 2002b). True romantic love functions as a discourse due to its embeddedness in the social relationships of the characters, as well as the ways in which their identities are wrapped-up in their love. Women are powerful in *OUAT*, but they are restricted by the ways in which true love plays out in their lives.

In the first season of *OUAT*, Snow White is a strong character in Fairy Tale Land flashbacks. She lives on her own in the woods, uses a bow and arrow to hunt and defend herself, and rebels against the Evil Queen. Much of the flashbacks tell the story of how she and Prince Charming met and fell in love, repeatedly saving each other from danger. When Prince Charming is forced to marry another, Snow White loses her self-sufficiency, moves in with the Seven Dwarfs, and obtains a potion that will make her forget everything (Kitsis, Horowitz, Thomsen, & Hemecker, 2012, "7:15am," Episode 110). In Storybrooke, Snow White/Mary Margaret is separated from Prince Charming/David due to the curse. She is not in true love, is a rather simpering weak character, and pines away for David. At the end of Season 1, when the curse is lifted, Mary Margaret and David remember their lives and love for each other (Kitsis, Horowitz, & White, 2012a, "A Land Without Magic," Episode 122). It is only then that Snow White is again represented as a strong character, in Fairy Tale Land and in Storybrooke.[3]

In flashbacks, viewers learn that Regina, the Evil Queen, was not always so evil. She herself was in true love with her stable boy fiancé, Daniel. Snow White inadvertently tells Regina's mother, Cora, about her love. Cora then kills Daniel, so Regina could marry the King (Princess Snow White's father) instead. Regina is devastated, vows revenge against Snow White, and begins her path to becoming the Evil Queen (Kitsis, Horowitz, & White, 2012b, "The Stable Boy," Episode 118). In Seasons 2 and 3, Regina finds herself at various places on a continuum of good and evil, depending on her relationships with others. Regina, Snow White, and Emma come to a somewhat of a truce. However, when her new true love, Robin Hood, is reunited with his Marion (rescued by Emma), leaving Regina supplanted as his lover, there are indications that she will again begin her vendetta of revenge, this time with Emma. Regina is furious, saying to Emma, "You. You did this? ... You're just like your mother. Never thinking of consequences" (Kitsis, Horowitz, & Hemecker, 2014, "There's No Place Like Home," Episode 322).

In the Beauty and the Beast flashback, as Belle and Rumplestiltskin fall in love, the Beast becomes more humane (Espenson & Cheylov, 2012, "Skin Deep," Episode 112). In Storybrooke, when Belle forgets her love for Rumplestiltskin, she becomes Lacey, a drunk barfly. Lacey brings out the worst of Rumplestiltskin (Kitsis, Horowitz, & Cheylov, 2013, "Lacey," Episode 219); it is only when she remembers herself and her love that Belle helps Rumple, as she calls him, find goodness (Kitsis, Horowitz, & White, 2013, "And Straight on 'Til Morning," Episode 222). Their story, as explained by Emilie de Ravin, who plays Belle, is about the "transformative power of her true love" (Titan Books, 2013, p. 118).

All romantic love relationships are between men and women. Heteronormativity continues to pervade mainstream versions of fairy tales (Neal, 2007). There is however, a hint that one of the characters, Mulan, is gay (Espenson & Zakrzewski, 2013, "Quite a Common Fairy,"[4] Episode 303). While this could be considered progressive for Disney, the way that ABC characterizes this plot is troubling. The website description[5] for "Broken" (Kitsis, Horowitz, & Hemecker, 2012, Episode 201), in which Mulan is first introduced, states that "Mulan denies" (para. 19) that she is in love with Prince Phillip; however, the companion guide plot description (published a year after Episode 201 aired) states that Mulan "also loves the handsome prince" (Titan Books, 2013, p. 158). In the website description for "Quite a Common Fairy," Mulan's feelings are also occluded; Mulan "is moved by Neal's declaration that if you love someone, you need to tell them" (para. 8) and "heads back to share her feelings with Aurora" (para. 9). Mulan leaves her feelings unvoiced when Princess Aurora tells her that she and Phillip are having a baby, and reconsiders joining Robin Hood's Merry Men. This storyline then drops, reaffirming the centrality of true romantic love, between a man and a woman meant to live happily-ever-after.

As Josh Dallas, who plays Prince Charming, explains, his character "will always find her [Snow White] because that's the way true love works, even if it's a struggle" (Titan Books, 2013, p. 90). Heteronormative ideals in fairy tales are once again cemented (Baker-Sperry, 2007; Baker-Sperry & Grauerholz, 2003; Zipes, 1979/2002a, 2002b); those without true love are consigned to evil or despair. Interestingly, however, with one exception (Rumplestiltskin), all the characters, whether good or evil, in love or not, are beautiful. The characters' appearances do not mirror the traditional evil ugly old crone witch (Baker-Sperry & Grauerholz, 2003), perhaps due to the medium of television, wherein women are overwhelmingly represented as conforming to beauty ideals (Walsh, Fürsich, & Jefferson, 2008). The program overall promotes a discourse of true love that reifies romantic relationships as between a beautiful woman and handsome man who are fated to be together.

Representations of Family

The discourse of familial love recognizes that families come in many forms, but centres on the idea that mothers must have ideal relationships with their children, else they are absent, indifferent, or evil. It is only when close relatives find each other that they become whole people, identifying as loving family members.

Family, as a crucial element of *OUAT*, therefore drives multiple plots revolving around the relationships between parents and their children. The Snow White family is the most complicated: Snow White and Prince Charming are similar in age (due to the curse that stopped time in Storybrooke) to their adult daughter, Emma, who was orphaned at birth. Henry, also orphaned at birth, is biologically the son of Emma and Baelfire, who is the lost son of Rumplestiltskin. Rumplestiltskin is the abandoned son of the ever-youthful evil Peter Pan. Henry is adopted by the Evil Queen, who is a single mother. The Evil Queen is the Wicked Witch of the West's half-sister (who was abandoned as a baby) and Snow White's step-mother. As such, *good* and *evil* characters intermingle in this unique blended family, which is characterized by hate and love, separation and reunion, betrayal and forgiveness.

There are no representations of nuclear families in the programs as family members are separated due to death, curses, and abandonment. While it is beneficial to view various family forms, it is unfortunate that the lack of stereotypical forms is blamed for calamity. The "advantages and the dangers of non-normative family forms" (Burr & Jarvis, 2007, p. 265) are explored in *OUAT*, but dangers are more prominent. Emma and Baelfire become thieves as a way to survive after being orphaned (Boylan, Espenson, & Barrett, 2012, "Tallahassee," Episode 206), the Evil Queen is bent on revenge for losing her chance at marriage (Kitsis, Horowitz, & White, 2012b, "The Stable Boy," Episode 118; Kitsis, Horowitz, & Hemecker, 2014, "There's No Place Like Home," Episode 322), the Wicked Witch of the West's insane jealousy of Regina's relationship with their mother turns her green (Chambliss & van Peebles, 2014, "It's Not Easy Being Green," Episode 316), and Peter Pan's manipulation of abandoned children turns them into malevolent lost boys (Goodman, Hull, & Boyd, 2013, "Nasty Habits," Episode 304).

Children's relationships with their parents are troubled; when they are resolved, it is through sacrifice and true love. Emma and Regina are initially portrayed as *bad* mothers; the former because she gave her child up for adoption, the latter because she is an evil queen. The dichotomy of *good* and *bad* mothers obscures the multiple ways in which mothering can be practiced (O'Reilly, 2006); Emma and Regina are only represented as *good* mothers when their familial love for Henry becomes true, giving them each the ability to bring him back to life with a kiss. In Season 1, Emma saves Henry with "true love's kiss" (Kitsis, Horowitz, & White, 2012a, "A Land without Magic," Episode 122). In Season 3, Regina saves him, again with "true love's kiss," which is directly linked to "light magic" (Vazquez, Chambliss, & Horder-Payton, 2014, "Kansas," Episode 320).

Indeed, Jennifer Morrison, the actor who plays Emma, explains that the "linchpin in Season 1 was really having Emma's heart thaw towards Henry" (Titan Books, 2013, p. 30). Lana Parrilla, who plays the Evil Queen, makes a similar statement: "It was in losing him [Henry] she realized he filled that hole in her heart. Now in the second season, she's on the road to redemption" (p. 51). Despite this stereotypical orientation to mothering, virtually none of the mothers in *OUAT* are domesticated; they are working mothers (Emma is a bail-bonds person, sheriff, and saviour of Fairy Tale Land; Regina is mayor and Evil Queen; Snow White is a bandit, Princess, teacher, and Queen) who are only seldom depicted doing any sort of chores. These representations go against the common trend for mothers to be portrayed as either mothers or workers in popular culture (Dillaway & Paré, 2008). The characters prove, as the series progresses, that mothers can be engaged in important work while raising children.

Emma, however remains estranged with her parents until she and Hook travel to the past in the Season 3 finale (Kitsis, Horowitz, & Hemecker, 2014, "There's No Place Like Home," Episode 322). Emma watches her parents fall in love, realizes her place is with them, and discovers Storybrooke is her true home. She tells Snow White and Prince Charming, "This is where we belong. This is where our family is." Rumplestitlskin sacrifices his own life to resolve his problems with his son (Kitsis, Horowitz, & Hemecker, 2013, "The Miller's Daughter," Episode 216). Baelfire later does the same, stating, "Thank you, Papa [Rumplestiltsin]. For showing me what it is to make a true sacrifice" (Vazquez & Egilsson, 2014, "Quiet Minds," Episode 315). Familial love will conquer all, as long as family members are willing to sacrifice everything. As it is explained in the companion guide, "the heart of the show stems from a brave little boy who just wants to find his *true* family" (Titan Books, 2013, p. 103, italics added). The discourse of a familial love in a true family is connected to that of true love. If one is not in true love, one is not in a family nor a relationship. Furthermore, one must be in love to be good (or, in Rumplestitlskin's case, less bad). Season 3 ends with Emma nestled in a booth at Granny's Diner with Henry, Snow White, Prince Charming, and her new brother, Prince Neal. Regina walks in with Robin and his son, the three of them holding hands, and Beauty and the Beast marry (with Belle's father giving her away). Everyone is welcomed into a family – it is only when Marion returns that Regina's happy ending is destroyed, and Elsa appears on the outskirts of Storybrooke, presumably the antagonist for Season 4: "Well, you just better hope to hell you didn't bring anything else back" (Regina in Kitsis, Horowitz, & Hemecker, 2014, "There's No Place Like Home," Episode 322).

Intersections between Fantasy, Reality, Childhood, and Adulthood

Discourses of true romantic and familial love circulate in the ways in which childhood, adulthood, fantasy, and reality intersect in *OUAT*. Romance and family are at the heart of Emma's difficulty reconciling reality and fantasy. They are also implicated in the actors' professed pleasure at bringing childhood stories to life as adults.

OUAT roots a portion of its stories in reality and explores complications that arise when magic is introduced. As Christine Boylan (writer and supervising producer/producer of *OUAT*), explains, "Seeing real life through the lens of metaphor is, for me, the best way to get to truth" (Titan Books, 2013, p. 21). The use of fantastical situations can open creative space for alternative societal representations (Atwood, 2011). It is not only the characters who negotiate the boundaries of reality and fantasy. Viewers are pulled in as they watch Emma struggle with the intersections of non-magical and magical worlds. Emma's ambivalence is wrapped up with her growing love for her son, culminating in the season finale (Kitsis, Horowitz, & White, 2012a, "A Land without Magic," Episode 122).

Mid-way through Season 3 of *OUAT*, Emma begins to question her and Henry's place with respect to magical worlds. In "New York City Serenade" (Kitsis, Horowitz, & Gierhart, 2014, Episode 312), Emma and Henry are living in New York with no memories of Storybrooke, Fairy Tale Land, and Neverland. When Emma drinks a potion to remember, given to her by Hook, she is faced with two choices: return to Storybrooke to help her family fight against an unnamed danger (which turns out to be the Wicked Witch of the West) or accept her boyfriend's proposal of marriage. She chooses the latter, but hides the fact that fairy tales are true from Henry. For the rest of the season, Emma debates her choice, believing the best thing for Henry is to return to New York and pretend magic does not exist. It is not until she finds her home, as discussed above, that Emma reconciles reality and fantasy.

The programs also examine the ease with which children can accept fantastical situations as well as the lure of fairy tales for adults (Zipes, 1979/2002a). Edward Kitsis describes how he and Adam Horowitz (Executive Producers of *OUAT*) "got the basic idea for the show" when they "were sitting around and talking about fairy tales, and how they're important to us [as adults], because they were the first stories we'd ever heard as children" (Titan Books, 2013, p. 6). In Season 1, Henry's main aim is to help Emma believe that the fairy tales she first encountered as a child are true. He uses a storybook as his evidence, reading it to Emma, telling her "it's more than just a book" (Kitsis, Horowitz, & Mylod, 2011, "Pilot," Episode 101). Instead of the adult teaching the child, the child teaches the adult; furthermore, the storybook crosses genres, from fantastical fiction to historical non-fiction. As Emma meets the citizens of Storybrooke, the book bridges realms, telling their fairy tale backstories. The book itself is a testament to the power of true love, with stories of romance between Snow White and Prince Charming, Beauty and the Beast, Ariel and Prince Eric, Cinderella and Prince Thomas, and Aurora and Prince Philip.

The cast and crew of the programs participate in plots that are based in a "juxtaposition between the modern world and the Enchanted Forest" (Horowitz, Executive Producer, in Titan Books, 2013, p. 10). In the *OUAT* companion guide, which is a cross-marketing tool for the program specifically and Disney generally, there are frequent references to a childhood love of fairy tales. Gennifer Godwin (actor who plays Snow White), explains that, as a child, she "was a Disneyphile" who "became an acolyte to Walt [Disney] and how he told stories" (Titan Books, p. 14). Mark Lane (set decorator) states, "It's just this feeling you're in the middle of a Disney ride and that makes you feel like a kid again" (Titan Books, 2013, p. 85). Colin O'Donoghue (Hook), discusses how "this is like stuff [being a pirate] you dreamed of doing as a child. It's absolutely brilliant to get the opportunity to do it" (Titan Books, p. 143).

These comments "acknowledge the connection between what a child experiences and the adult that child becomes (Neal, 2007, p. 58). Furthermore, the actors' identification with Disney movies in particular, as opposed to fairy tales in general, demonstrates how their perspectives are "disneyfied" (Dong, 2006), whether authentically or in order to market the program (or a mixture of the two). Disney movies invariably end with a prince marrying a princess and living as a happily-ever-after family, cementing discourses of true and familial love.

Those involved with *OUAT* also interact with fans. Several of the female actors discuss the importance of strong female characters in television: Ginnifer Goodwin (Snow White) explains that she enjoys being on a program that "treats its princesses as proactive role models who aren't waiting to be saved by their male counterparts" (Titan Books, 2013, p. 19). Jennifer Morrison (Emma) is drawn to the fact that her character is "a very full, deep, complicated woman'" (Titan Books, p. 30). Lana Parilla does not speak specifically about gender, although discusses how she enjoys playing "such a complex character ... [who] is multi-layered and multi-colorful" (Titan Books, p. 46). Emilie de Ravin explains how she has "girls come up to me and tell me they love how strong Belle is and that she's an influence on their life to be strong, so that's a very cool thing. It's amazing. It goes a lot further than just being a great acting job" (Titan Books, p. 123). Disturbingly, the *OUAT* romantic love storyline of Beauty in the Beast continues in the tradition of the Disney movie (see Olson, 2013, for a discussion of the romanticization of partner violence) and of television programs that feature lovely smart women married to unattractive overweight men (Walsh, Fürsich, & Jefferson, 2008), with Belle literally and figuratively trapped in her love for Rumplestiltskin. De Ravin's remark delineates how *OUAT*, through its convergence of magical and non-magical worlds, can influence viewers' realities, demonstrating the importance of critiquing popular culture.

CONCLUSION

The program discussed here is an example of how, "as they retell the fairy tales we all know, contemporary writers fill in gaps, reverse traditional situations, and imagine ways the stories could have been otherwise. As they contemplate the cultural forms older version reflect, they see what needs to be seen again and seen afresh – and show it to us" (Harries, 2001, p. 163). Certainly, Robert Hull (writer, supervising producer, and producer of *OUAT*) reflects this idea in his explanation of how he enjoys "getting to explore these iconic characters that I grew up with and then trying to find something new" (Titan Books, 2013, p. 155).

Certainly, there is room for critique, as my argument in this chapter demonstrates, but it must be acknowledged that *OUAT* goes beyond traditional Disney fairy tale stereotypes. The characters of Snow White, Emma, and the Evil Queen are complex protagonists. They are strong, adventurous, self-sufficient, assertive, and capable; moreover, they are not demonized for their strength. The provision of backstories allows the characters to develop, blurring lines between good and evil. As such, the programs are primed for viewer engagement and analysis. In his critique of Disney, Zipes (1994) once wrote that "the diversion of the Disney fairy tale is geared toward nonreflective viewing. Everything is on the surface, one-dimensional, and we are to delight in one-dimensional portrayal and thinking, for it is adorable, easy, and comforting in its simplicity" (p. 95). I would argue that this is still the case, when one looks at Disney as a whole. However, *OUAT* is an interesting exception. It is three-dimensional and multifaceted, portraying complex pedagogies of gender, with women saving men and evil characters garnering understanding.

Nonetheless, just as viewers do not passively accept stereotypical representations of gender and romance (Jarvis, 1999), they do not necessarily accept non-stereotypical ones. In previous research, I collaborated in a study that engaged female college students in discussions of the film, *Snow White and the Huntsman* (Taber, Woloshyn, Munn, & Lane, 2013). We had chosen this film because it portrays Snow White as a much stronger character than in the Disney original. As well, it does not end in a wedding, but in the coronation of Snow White as (an unmarried and unpartnered) Queen. Despite critiquing the general idea of true love and happily-ever-after endings, the participants craved an enduring relationship between the lead characters of Snow White and the Huntsman. In ways similar to Davies' (2003) findings in her research with children and the story, *The Paperbag Princess*, the participants reinscribed traditional gender roles upon non-traditional characters and plots.

Fairy tales are "produced and consumed to accomplish a variety of social functions in multiple contexts and in more or less explicitly ideological ways" (Bacchilega, 1997, p. 3). A non-traditional fairy tale in itself may not be enough to push back against the more stereotypical versions which are embedded in western society. It is therefore important for viewers to deconstruct this program's representations, using adult education, as well as a recognize learning that occurs in interaction with popular culture, in ways that can transform societal understandings of gender (Jarvis & Burr, 2011; Wright & Sandlin, 2009b). Feminist discourse analysis, as an analytic research methodology, can assist in identifying and critiquing gendered discourses that circulate in popular culture.

NOTES

1. Titles are grouped according to fairy tale and listed in general order of prominance in the program. Names for characters with different names in fantasy and reality are indicated as: Fairy Tale Land name/Storybrooke name. Characters not from fairy tales are Emma, Henry, and Balefire/Neal.
2. This NBC television program is loosely based on fairy tales of the Grimm Brothers.
3. At the end of Season 3, a pregnant Snow White is portrayed as increasingly vulnerable. Although the actor playing Snow White, Ginnifer Goodwin, was pregnant, which could account for her decreased prominence, even the style of her clothes becomes more conservative.
4. This seems to be an ironic title, considering "fairy" is often used as a pejorative term for those who do not identify as straight. However, the title is more likely intended to refer to the plotline about Tinker Bell trying to get her magic back.
5. All online summaries taken from http://abc.go.com/shows/once-upon-a-time/episode-guide

REFERENCES

Atwood, M. (2011). *In other worlds: SF and the human imagination*. Toronto, ON: McClelland & Stewart Ltd.

Bacchilega, C. (1997). *Postmodern fairy tales: Gender and narrative strategies*. Philadelphia, PA: University of Pennsylvania Press.

Baker-Sperry, L. (2007). The production of meaning through peer interaction: Children and Walt Disney's Cinderella. *Sex Roles, 56*(11/12), 717–727. doi:10.1007/s11199-007-9236-y

Baker-Sperry, L., & Grauerholz, L. (2003). The pervasiveness and persistence of the feminine beauty ideal in children's fairy tales. *Gender & Society, 15*(5), 711–726. doi:10.1177/0891243203255605

Beane, O. (2013). *A once upon a time tale: Reawakened*. New York, NY: Hyperion.

Boylan, C., Espenson, J. (Writers), & Barrett, D. (Director). (2012). Tallahassee [Television series episode]. In E. Kitsis & A. Horowtiz (Creators), *Once upon a time*. Los Angeles, CA: ABC Studios.

Burr, V., & Jarvis, C. (2007). Imagining the family: Representations of alternative lifestyles in Buffy the Vampire Slayer. *Qualitative Social Work, 6*(3), 263–280. doi:10.1177/1473325007080401

Chambliss, A. (Writer), & van Peebles, M. (Director). (2014). It's not easy being green [Television series episode]. In E. Kitsis & A. Horowtiz (Creators), *Once upon a time*. Los Angeles, CA: ABC Studios.

Davies, B. (2003). *Frogs and snails and feminist tales: Preschool children and gender* (Rev. ed.). Creskill, NJ: Hampton Press, Inc.

Dillaway, H., & Paré, E. (2008). Locating mothers: How cultural debates about stay-at-home versus working mothers define women and home. *Journal of Family Issues, 29*(4), 437–464. doi:10.1177/ 0192513X07310309

Dong, L. (2006). Writing Chinese American into words and images: Storytelling and retelling of The Song of Mu Lan. *The Lion and the Unicorn, 30*(2), 218–233.

England, D. D., Descartes, L., & Collier-Meek, M. A. (2011). Gender role portrayal and the Disney princess. *Sex Roles, 64*(7/8), 555–567. doi:10.1007/s11199-011-9930-7

Espenson, J. (Writer), & Cheylov, M. (Director). (2012). Skin deep [Television series episode]. In E. Kitsis & A. Horowtiz (Creators), *Once upon a time*. Los Angeles, CA: ABC Studios.

Espenson, J. (Writer), & Zakrzewski, A. (Director). (2013). Quite a common fairy [Television series episode]. In E. Kitsis & A. Horowtiz (Creators), *Once upon a time*. Los Angeles, CA: ABC Studios.

Fouts, G., Callan, M., Piasentin, K., & Lawson, A. (2006). Demonizing in children's television cartoons and Disney animated films. *Child Psychiatry and Human Development, 37*(1), 15–23. doi:10.1007/ s10578-006-0016-7

Giroux, H., & Pollock, G. (2010). *The mouse that roared: Disney and the end of innocence* (2nd ed.). Plymouth, England: Rowman & Littlefield Publishers, Inc.

Goodman, H., Hull, R. (Writers), & Boyd, D. (Director). (2013). Nasty habits [Television series episode]. In E. Kitsis & A. Horowtiz (Creators), *Once upon a time*. Los Angeles, CA: ABC Studios.

Harries, E. W. (2001). *Twice upon a time: Women writers and the history of the fairy tale*. Princeton, NJ: Princeton University Press.

Jarvis, C. (1999). Love changes everything: The transformative potential of romantic fiction. *Studies in the Education of Adults, 31*(2), 109–122.

Jarvis, C., & Burr, V. (2011). The transformative potential of popular television: The case of *Buffy the Vampire Slayer*. *Journal of Transformative Education, 9*(3), 165–182. doi:10.1177/1541344612436814

Kitsis, E., Horowitz, A. (Writers), & Mylod, M. (Director). (2011). Pilot [Television series episode]. In E. Kitsis & A. Horowtiz (Creators), *Once upon a time*. Los Angeles, CA: ABC Studios.

Kitsis, E., Horowitz, A. (Writers), Thomsen, D. (Writer), & Hemecker, R. (Director). (2012a). 7:15 a.m. [Television series episode]. In E. Kitsis & A. Horowtiz (Creators), *Once upon a time*. Los Angeles, CA: ABC Studios.

Kitsis, E., Horowitz, A. (Writers), & White, D. (Director). (2012b). A land without magic [Television series episode]. In E. Kitsis & A. Horowtiz (Creators), *Once upon a time*. Los Angeles, CA: ABC Studios.

Kitsis, E., Horowitz, A. (Writers), & Hemecker, R. (Director). (2012c). Broken [Television series episode]. In E. Kitsis & A. Horowtiz (Creators), *Once upon a time*. Los Angeles, CA: ABC Studios.

Kitsis, E., Horowitz, A. (Writers), & White, D. (Director). (2012d). The stable boy [Television series episode]. In E. Kitsis & A. Horowtiz (Creators), *Once upon a time*. Los Angeles, CA: ABC Studios.

Kitsis, E., Horowitz, A. (Writers), & White, D. (Director). (2013a). And straight on 'til morning' [Television series episode]. In E. Kitsis & A. Horowtiz (Creators), *Once upon a time*. Los Angeles, CA: ABC Studios.

Kitsis, E., Horowitz, A. (Writers), & Cheylov, M. (Director). (2013b). Lacey [Television series episode]. In E. Kitsis & A. Horowtiz (Creators), *Once upon a time*. Los Angeles, CA: ABC Studios.

Kitsis, E., Horowitz, A. (Writers), & Hemecker, R. (Director). (2013c). The miller's daughter [Television series episode]. In E. Kitsis & A. Horowtiz (Creators), *Once upon a time*. Los Angeles, CA: ABC Studios.

Kitsis, E., Horowitz, A. (Writers) & Gierhart, B. (Director). (2014a). New York City serenade [Television series episode]. In E. Kitsis & A. Horowtiz (Creators), *Once upon a time*. Los Angeles, CA: ABC Studios.

Kitsis, E., Horowitz, A. (Writers), & Hemecker, R. (Director). (2014b). There's no place like home [Television series episode]. In E. Kitsis & A. Horowtiz (Creators), *Once upon a time*. Los Angeles, CA: ABC Studios.

Lazar, M. M. (2005). Politicizing gender in discourse: Feminist critical discourse analysis as political perspective and praxis. In M. M. Lazar (Ed.), *Feminist critical discourse analysis: Gender, power, and ideology in discourse* (pp. 1–28). New York, NY: Palgrave Macmillan.

Maguire, G. (2007). *Wicked: The life and times of the Wicked Witch of the West*. New York, NY: HarperCollins Publishers.

Neal, L. A. (2007). (Un)happily ever after: Fairy tale morals, moralities, and heterosexism in children's texts. *Journal of Gay & Lesbian Issues in Education, 4*(2), 55–74. doi:10.1300/J367v04n02_05

Olson, K. M. (2013). An epideictic dimension of symbolic violence in Disney's *Beauty and the Beast*: Inter-generational lessons in romanticizing and tolerating intimate partner violence. *Quarterly Journal of Speech, 99*(4), 448–480. doi:10.1080/00335630.2013.835491

O'Reilly, A. (2006). *Rocking the cradle: Thoughts on motherhood, feminism and the possibility of empowered mothering*. Toronto, ON: Demeter Press.

Taber, N. (2013). Detectives, bail bond "persons," and fairy tales: A feminist antimilitarist analysis of gender in *Grimm* and *Once Upon a Time*. *Gender Forum: An Internet Journal for Gender Studies, 44*, Art. 2, http://www.genderforum.org/index.php?id=731

Taber, N., Woloshyn, V., Munn, C., & Lane, L. (2013). Exploring fairy tales in a college women's media group: Stereotypes, changing representations of Snow White, and happy endings. *Canadian Association for the Study of Adult Education (CASAE) 2013 conference*. Victoria, BC: University of Victoria.

Thomsen, D. T., & Bechko, C. (2013). *Once upon a time: Shadow of the queen*. New York, NY: Marvel Worldwide Inc.

Tisdell, E. J. (2007). Popular culture and critical media literacy in adult education: Theory and practice. *New Directions for Adult and Continuing Education, 115*, 5–13. doi:10.1002/ace.262

Tisdell, E. J. (2008). Critical media literacy and transformative learning: Drawing on pop culture and entertainment media in teaching for diversity in adult higher education. *Journal of Transformative Education, 6*(1), 48–67. doi:10.1177/1541344608318970

Titan Books. (2013). *Once upon a time: Behind the magic.* London, England: Author.

Vazquez, K. (Writer) & Egilsson, E. (Director). (2014). Quiet minds [Television series episode]. In E. Kitsis & A. Horowtiz (Creators), *Once upon a time.* Los Angeles, CA: ABC Studios.

Vazquez, K., Chambliss, A. (Writers), & Horder-Payton, G. (Director). (2014). Kansas [Television series episode]. In E. Kitsis & A. Horowtiz (Creators), *Once upon a time.* Los Angeles, CA: ABC Studios.

Walker, B. (1996). *Feminist fairy tales.* New York, NY: HarperOne.

Walsh, K. R., Fürsich, E., & Jefferson, B. S. (2008). Beauty and the patriarchal beast: Gender role portrayals in sitcoms featuring mismatched couples. *Journal of Popular Film and Television, 36*(3), 123–132.

Wasko, J. (2001). *Understanding Disney: The manufacture of fantasy.* Cambridge, MA: Polity Press.

Wright, R. R., & Sandlin, J. A. (2009a). Cult TV, hip hop, shape-shifters, and vampire slayers: A review of the literature at the intersection of adult education and popular culture. *Adult Education Quarterly, 59*(2), 118–141. doi:10.1177/0741713608327368

Wright, R. R., & Sandlin, J. A. (2009b). Popular culture, public pedagogy and perspective transformation: The Avengers and adult learning in living rooms. *International Journal of Lifelong Education, 28*(4), 533–551. doi:10.1080/02601370903031389

Zipes, J. (1989). *Don't bet on the prince: Contemporary feminist fairy tales in North America and England.* New York, NY: Routledge.

Zipes, J. (1994). *Fairy tale as myth/myth as fairy tale.* Lexington, KY: University Press of Kentucky.

Zipes, J. (2002a). *Breaking the magic spell: Radical theories of folk & fairy tales* (Rev. and Expanded ed.). Lexington, KY: The University Press of Kentucky. (Original work published 1979)

Zipes, J. (2002b). *Sticks and stones: The troublesome success of children's literature from Slovenly Peter to Harry Potter.* New York, NY: Routledge.

Zipes, J. (Ed.). (2003). *The complete fairy tales of the Brothers Grimm* (3rd ed.). New York, NY: Bantam Books.

Nancy Taber
Faculty of Education
Brock University

CHRISTINE JARVIS

9. HOW TO BE A WOMAN

Models of Masochism and Sacrifice in Young Adult Fiction

Buffy, Bella, Veronica, Katniss, Clary, Tris and Saba:[1] For two decades post-feminist heroines have faced life-threatening trials as part of their progress to womanhood. In this chapter I consider how young adult popular fictions operate as forms of pedagogy for young women by offering them particular models of maturity and womanhood. I explore the recurrence and reformulation of a persistent pattern of behaviour in which heroines engage in risky and/or masochistic behaviours for which they are often emotionally rewarded.

These recurrences function as a form of vicarious experiential learning in which readers and viewers learn that emotional gratification and adult status can be conferred through self-harm and self-sacrifice. Popular culture is not a monolithic form and young adult fictions are no exception. An analysis of fictional examples of this behaviour pattern challenges the idea that heroines today are empowered agents as a result of the legacy of feminism. At the same time, the analysis belies any notion that fictions are universally hegemonic and oppressive – fictions can and do disrupt and interrogate this pattern of emotional masochism. Scholars of public pedagogy have explored the complexities, contradictions and subtleties of the pedagogical process. Sandlin O'Malley and Burdick (2011) in their review of public pedagogy literature acknowledge that some scholarship has demonstrated how "the teaching and learning inherent within daily life can be both oppressive and resistant" (p. 144). Jubas and Knutson (2012) also see public pedagogy as an arena where contradictions and tensions are in play. They argue that we can see "new examples of dialectic or tensions … between the authority of the producer and the consumer; between traditional structures which ground identities and help people make sense of cultural texts, and personal agency which frees people to choose and invent identities and meanings" (p. 86). This analysis aims to contribute to understandings of the complexities of public pedagogy by showing how fictions aimed primarily at young women both resist and accommodate patriarchy.

The analysis focuses primarily on Stephenie Meyer's *Twilight Saga* (book and film versions), particularly *Breaking Dawn* (Meyer, 2008; Wyck, Rosenfelt, Meyer, & Condon, 2011, 2012) and the episodes "Anne" (Whedon, 1998) and "Dead Man's Party" (Noxon & Whitmore, 1998) from the television series *Buffy the Vampire Slayer* (*BTVS*), created by Joss Whedon, as these offer contrasting treatments of this theme of self-harm/self-sacrifice, reflecting the complexity of public pedagogy generally, and young adult fiction in particular. I aim to demonstrate that Whedon and Noxon's work, in line with the avowedly feminist intentions of the series, resists rewarding its heroine for her self-inflicted suffering, presenting mature womanhood instead in terms of responsibility and leadership. Meyer, by contrast, creates a heroine who matures only through self-inflicted suffering in which all her agency and determination is directed towards self-abnegation.

ROMANCE AND THE RUNAWAY HEROINE

Cawelti (1976) wrote influentially about repetition compulsion in popular fictions, arguing that their popularity was predicated on the existence of unresolved psychic conflicts, which drive readers back, repeatedly, to texts that offer fantasy resolutions to these problems. This idea was taken up in the 1980s and 1990s by critics of popular romance such as Radway (1984), who argued that women read romances in order to get the perfect parenting they long for – the hero provides the nurturing attention they crave in real life, and Modleski (1982), who discussed heroines' predilection for running away and falling into danger as forms of childish revenge, executed by women who feel powerless to get the love and attention they deserve in a male-dominated society. Heroes, she argues, are made to suffer for not loving, or not showing their love, by facing the possible loss of the heroine.

The romance genre is responsive to changes in women's position in society and can be inventive and subversive (Regis, 2011; Tapper, 2014; Wendell & Tan, 2009) and contemporary romance features fewer subservient heroines who need to force all powerful heroes into admissions of undying devotion by risking their lives than was the case in the 1960s and 1970s fiction examined by earlier critics. Nevertheless, the theme of female self-endangerment leading to male nurturing persists widely in young adult fiction, but is continuously remodelled and can accommodate aspects of feminism which overtly endorse female independence, choice and courage. This reflects the contradictory nature of a society in which girls and young women are told that male attention is not the object of their existence, whilst actually rewarding them highly for conformity to fashion and beauty ideals and for success in attracting male admiration. It is perhaps not surprising, given the compelling analyses of girls and young women's lives offered by cultural studies scholars such as McRobbie (2009, 2013), that elements of this passive aggressive approach to seeking (particularly male) attention continue to feature strongly in young adult fiction. In addition to the analyses of the texts mentioned above, I refer briefly to variations of this coercive self-harming across a range of contemporary young adult fiction to reinforce the point that this is a widespread and endlessly transforming characteristic of the genre.

TEXTS, AUTHORS AND ANALYSIS

Some of the excitement for me in analysing texts as public pedagogies lies in marrying different theoretical traditions, moving between educational theory, communications theory and literary theory, and holding these in tension. The analyses in this chapter are predicated on a synthesis of theoretical approaches to texts. They take from New Historicism (Veeser, 1989) in so far as they recognise that texts are situated in historical moments, and as such can illuminate and be illuminated by the historical and social context. This underpins my belief that popular fictions give insights into tensions and contradictions relating to social values, attitudes towards gender, and more specifically, what it means to be a young woman in Western society. I am mindful, for example, of the work of writers such as Baker (2010), Harris (2004), Pomerantz, Raby, and Stefank (2013), and McRobbie (2009, 2013), who resist arguments that suggest that feminism is no longer relevant to young women and problematize the idea of choice and agency. The analyses seek to demonstrate that mass media popular fictions continue to be sites where the concept of womanhood is created, resisted, and interrogated.

The chapter also assumes that the analysis of texts is a valid activity in itself. The existence of mass popular culture suggests that texts have what Hall (1980) called preferred or dominant meanings; there will be some widely shared responses and experiences when certain television or films are viewed, or books are read. That is not to say that there are no resistant meanings or alternative readings, or that people will not filter texts through their own frames of reference.

I also want to consider the resurrection of the author, or at least the resurrection of creative teams. Barthes (1977) in *Death of the Author* argued that authors' intentions were not relevant. Whilst I agree that interpretations cannot be confined to those intended by authors, I would still argue that creators of popular fictions can be positioned as pedagogues engaged in a deliberate process of communication. Some set out to influence and change perspectives. This certainly applies to the two authors whose work is considered in this chapter. Meyer, who studied at Brigham Young University, states in her interview on Amazon's *Twilight* page, "The book with the most significant impact on my life is the *Book of Mormon*" (Meyer, n.d.). She says that she "put a lot of (my) beliefs into the story, free agency is a big theme, as is sacrifice" (Morris, 2005). It is clear that the books reflect her Mormon values, something Dietz (2011) has carefully delineated. Meyer recalls, for example, refusing to include pre-marital sex in the story (Morris, 2005).

Whedon is an outspoken communicator with a huge, well-informed fan following. He joins in on-line discussions and gives regular interviews in which he makes it clear that he is focused on telling powerful stories but also on using them to present his political and social perspectives (see the edited collection of interviews by Lavery & Burkhead, 2011 or the biography by Pascale, 2014, for some examples). One of the best known is his speech to the international human rights organisation, Equality Now, in which he provided a series of answers to the repeated question, "Why do you always write such strong women characters?" In answering that question, he stated, "Because equality is not a concept....Equality is like gravity – we need it to stand on this Earth as men and women, and the misogyny that is in every culture is not a true part of the human condition" (Pascale, 2014, p. 274). Putting this all together then, creators of popular fictions actively seek to offer us certain perspectives on the world. In doing so they produce works designed to be read in particular ways by the communities and groups they target. Close examination of their work will give us some indication of what is being taught, how those ideas are being conveyed, and how they relate to historical and contemporary debates.

The work began with a moment of recognition. I was familiar with the phenomenon of the runaway/self-harming heroine as a result of my earlier studies in popular romantic fiction, including young adult or "YA" popular fiction. I was also conscious of the prevalence of strong, powerful heroines in recent decades, particularly Buffy the Vampire Slayer herself. When I encountered the *Twilight* books and films, the behaviour of Bella seemed to exemplify, even exaggerate the runaway heroine motif and the popularity of this kind of masochism puzzled me. It occurred to me that Buffy also ran away very dramatically, and I began systematic readings of both texts to consider how they represented these acts. I viewed the television series and the films and read the books repeatedly. I took a critical feminist approach; my analysis was concerned with the representation of womanhood and with questions of power and identity in gender relations. In line with the theoretical discussion above, I assumed that it was possible to identify preferred readings and to offer *a* textual analysis without undertaking audience research. Through a process of iterative engagement with these texts I noted how superficial similarities (running away, putting oneself into danger) were used as parts of stories that were very different in the models of mature womanhood they conveyed.

Both texts I discuss here were immensely popular. *Twilight,* four novels and five films, was a phenomenon, topping best-seller lists and box office receipts (Box Officemojo, n.d.). The TV series *Buffy the Vampire Slayer* (*BtVS*) ran for seven seasons (from 1997 until 2003 in the US), acquired cult status and has probably had more academic attention than any other television series in history (Lametti, Harris, Geiling, & Matthews-Ramo, 2012). Eleven years after its conclusion, articles and books continue to be published.

My discussion considers the way that the heroines' apparently masochistic acts are interrogated or endorsed by the context and emotional tenor of these texts. There are obvious parallels between them. Bella, the heroine of *Twilight* has just turned 18, Buffy is 17, both are still at school, initially (Bella has left by the time *Breaking Dawn* begins), and both have as their first, intense love, powerful vampires, who appear to be young men, but who are actually over a hundred years old, and have dark and murderous pasts. My analyses suggest that Bella's risky behaviour is rewarded and even applauded in the *Twilight* saga whereas *BtVS* presents a critique of Buffy's decision to run away in response to anger and disappointment. Readers learn very different things about the effectiveness of this kind of masochistic revenge/emotional blackmail. Bella learns that the more she suffers, the more she will be rewarded with love, attention and protection, and that she can bypass normal requirements of growing up and move straight to their material and social rewards, provided by a wealthy and powerful male, if she makes him sufficiently worried she might hurt herself. Buffy learns that emotional blackmail can backfire and learns to keep fulfilling her public responsibilities to wider society, even when she feels unhappy and rejected personally.

BELLA

My discussion of Bella in this chapter concentrates primarily on her pregnancy as a form of self-endangerment and self-sacrifice. I have discussed elsewhere Bella's deliberate risk taking and its relationship to the complexities of contemporary girlhood (Jarvis, 2013). As Edwards (2009) says, "Everyone wants Bella, to own, to love, to protect, to hurt" (p. 29). She is constantly rewarded for risking her life, which makes her the focus of attention and concern, particularly the concern of her vampire lover, Edward. Her ultimate reward comes when she is estranged from him in *New Moon* (Meyer, 2006). Following a series of misunderstandings, Edward believes Bella is dead, so tries to kill himself. They are re-united and he makes vows of undying fidelity and love. She gets what she wants – Edward's declaration – by hurting herself. Bella and Edward marry in Breaking Dawn. A conventional romance might end here, but the trauma and heightened emotion continues. Meyer uses what is for many an ordinary part of womanhood, pregnancy and motherhood, to continue to present a story about Bella being at extreme risk and Edward being terribly worried about her.

Though superficially indicative of maturity (the move into motherhood), pregnancy enables Bella to evade the more obvious maturing process that had been expected of her (going to college to take her degree, becoming an independent young woman). She promised Edward she would go to college, but made it clear she really wanted to become a vampire and live with his (very patriarchal) family. Becoming pregnant on her honeymoon enables her to get her way. Whitton's (2011) superb analysis of motherhood in the *Twilight Saga* argues that, in line with Meyer's Mormon beliefs, it is shown to be "the only role in which they (women) can find true fulfilment" (p. 125), but that the mother is always secondary to the father. She argues that *Twilight* valorises a form of motherhood that "is intrinsically masochistic" and ultimately, "the only good mother is a dead mother" (p. 127). Wilson (2011) also notes the Twilight Saga conveys the message that "woman does (or at least should) equal womb" (p. 79).

The half vampire child grows unnaturally quickly, kicking in the first few days and making Bella very ill. The book relates the story in the first person at this early stage in the pregnancy, so that the reader can share Bella's frenzy of emotion, including her overwhelming response to the prospect having "a tiny Edward in my arms" (Meyer, 2008, p. 116), and her tortured anxieties. The film also shows this stage, predominantly from Bella's perspective, when she watches Edward's reactions as he looks at her body for signs of pregnancy. Because the reader/viewer is inside her head at this stage, he or she experiences her behaviour as entirely altruistic; its manipulative effect is disguised. Hearing everything from Bella's perspective helps to suggest that, once again, Bella is in danger through no direct "fault" of her own – no-one believed a vampire could impregnate a human. She expresses concern for Edward, but also describes him as "an angry tornado" made almost crazy by his worry for her. The reader shares the pleasure of seeing this intense love and concern, without bearing responsibility for causing it. Edward rushes Bella home so that his surgeon "father" can, in Edward's words "get that thing out before it can hurt any part of you" (Meyer, 2008, p. 120). Rather than replace the first person narrative with dialogue, the film relies on long silences and the telling expressions of the actors to convey Bella's astonishment, her protectiveness towards the baby, and Edward's horror and guilt at the pregnancy. She stares at her stomach in the mirror with wonder in her eyes and watches Edward as he moves with frantic and supernatural haste around the house preparing for their departure. We see his set jaw and anguished expression as he prepares to leave. The film also intensifies the emphasis on the wealth and power of the Cullens; this wealth and power is now at Bella's service and is mobilised to protect her as soon as the pregnancy puts her in danger. The private island, belonging to Edward's mother on which they honeymoon is visually stunning. In the book Edward rings the airport to arrange a speedy departure; in the film they take a private jet.

Bella is adamant from the moment of conception that she will persist with this pregnancy. It is particularly important from a pedagogical point of view that the narrator switches from Bella to her friend and suitor Jacob once she arrives back at the Cullen house and her condition worsens. It would be difficult for Bella to discuss her extreme pain and the misery it causes, and to revel in the attention she gets, without appearing perverse and egocentric. Through Jacob's eyes, the reader/viewer sees Bella in the best possible light. The film also shows events predominantly as he sees them, although it occasionally switches to show us Bella as observed by Edward or another member of her family. The perspective moves between images of adoration and suffering. Jacob gives an excellent description of her power over everyone else. He himself is obsessed with her and her pain: "I heard Bella's voice, cracked and rough and I couldn't think of anything else" (Meyer, 2008, p. 156). The first thing he sees is "six vampires standing in a group by the white sofa" (p. 157) – the entire Cullen family is looking at and looking after Bella. Rosalie, the sister-in-law who had been highly critical of Bella is now, "hovering in a strange protective way" (p. 158). The film emphasises this by only offering Jacob and the viewer glimpses of Bella initially, because she is hidden/protected by Rosalie, who blocks Jacob's access and has to be instructed by Bella to let Jacob come to her. The film charts the progress of the pregnancy through shot after shot of Bella reclining on a sofa while one or more of the family looks on with concern, and in the case of Edward, anguish and guilt. Becoming pregnant and dangerously ill makes Bella the most important member of this family.

Jacob's descriptions show us her danger and the suffering it causes Edward. He describes her grotesque appearance in considerable detail, her dark circled eyes, emaciated face, fingers and hands and the swollen torso, "ballooning out in a strange sick way ... like the big bulge had grown out of what is sucked from her" (Meyer, 2008, p. 160). The camera zooms in on her discoloured abdomen, before she pulls her top down to cover it. It focuses on her lifeless hair, gaunt face and on the dark circles under her eyes that look almost bruised. She is dying slowly from lack of nourishment as the child absorbs her body. Edward's expression is "beyond agony"; his eyes are "all tortured looking" (p. 158). Just in case we miss the point Jacob tells us, "This is the face a man would have if he were burning at the stake" (p. 162). Jacob, hating Edward as he does, is able to represent Bella's concern for Edward as indicative of her selflessness; "she was beating herself up about hurting his feelings; the girl was a classic martyr" (p. 172). Robert Pattinson, who plays Edward in the film, perfected the art of the tortured expression – the downward turn of the lips, the tightening of the jaw and the large, haunted eyes. Kristen Stewart, playing Bella, combines wincing and gasping to show her pain, with little martyred smiles and a soulful expression.

As the pregnancy progresses, Jacob narrates, in great detail, increases in Bella's suffering. He finds watching this unbearable, but Bella keeps him there. She says, "It's just not whole unless you're here" – even though she rejected him for Edward, she expects his love and attention. In a rare moment of insight he says, "How about, Jacob, I get a kick out of your pain" (Meyer, 2008, p. 273). By suffering she manages to maintain the love triangle that fuelled the first three books, even after marriage and throughout a disfiguring pregnancy. The film, though primarily shown from Jacob's perspective at this stage, is able to incorporate additional scenes; at one point Bella looks at herself in the mirror, slipping the robe she is wearing from her shoulders, so we can see how emaciated her limbs are – Edward comes up behind her and shows his dismay as she hurriedly shrugs the gown back on. The pregnancy culminates in a ghastly, graphically described birth. Jake hears

> the strangest, muffled, ripping sound from the center of her body [and then sees her go] totally limp, slumping towards the floor....Bella screamed ... a blood curdling scream of agony. The horrifying sound cut off with a gurgle, and her eyes rolled back in her head. Her body twitched, arched in Rosalie's arms, and then Bella vomited a fountain of blood. (Meyer, 2008, pp. 318–319)

This goes on, and includes cutting her open with a scalpel before any anaesthetic has taken hold, a "shattering crack" as the baby breaks her spine (p. 323), followed by death, CPR, recovery, Edward tearing the womb open with his teeth and Bella dying again.

The film faithfully reflects this gory horror, although it has to be mindful of its wish to retain a 12 certificate.[2] There is no fountain of blood, but Bella collapses in an unnatural way, suggesting her back is broken at this stage rather than later, and we hear a tearing sound as the placenta detaches. She twitches and shakes horribly and screams as the knife goes in and the baby is extracted. Edward's mouth is covered in blood as he rips open the womb. Several lingering shots are taken from above the scene once Bella is dead, showing a deep womb-shaped blood stain and blood covering the whole of the underside of the bed on which she lies.

Metaphorically and symbolically a lot seems to be going on here that relates to contemporary concerns about domestic abuse and teenage pregnancy. Although the story makes it clear that Edward is not responsible for Bella's suffering, patterns of behaviour characteristic of domestic abuse can be seen throughout the films in the way Edward repeatedly hurts Bella, directly or indirectly, including during their sexual encounters, suffers for this, is exonerated, and comforts her for her suffering. He does not want to have sex with her in case he hurts her; but he does, and is devastated by her bruises. He does not want to impregnate her, or to continue with a pregnancy that will kill her. Nevertheless, he repeatedly hurts her, then comforts her. She has to re-assure him that he has not hurt her too much. It appears to encourage the reader/viewer to take pleasure from the love and guilt an abuser expresses, and to endorse a form of gratification in relationships based on "hurt/comfort."

This graphic description of childbirth might be expected to deter young women readers from procreation. The monstrous growth of the child mirrors the often suppressed feeling women may have that the child they carry is a kind of parasite, draining their life. Wilson (2011) links it to the idea of foetus "as cannibal" (p. 79). Its parasitic, life-draining qualities, and the fact that Bella is resurrected with a different identity – that of a new born vampire – also reflect anxiety that a woman may lose her identity as a result of becoming a mother. There is no doubt that becoming a mother is presented as a major sacrifice. However, the shifting narrative viewpoint and the focus on the intensity of Edward and Jacob's love for Bella, her presentation as a martyr, caring about everyone, and sacrificing herself for the baby, actually create a tremendous degree of masochistic gratification for the reader. The story suggests that women's fears about pregnancy and childbirth are entirely justified, but that by enduring and embracing this suffering and loss of self, the woman will be rewarded with obsessive love, and it enables the reader to live vicariously through that reward. Her persistence also sends a conservative anti-choice message; even if being pregnant will kill her, a real woman will want to protect the baby at any cost. It suggests that a young woman's life is less valuable than that of a newly conceived foetus, but gives great narrative pleasure by allowing the reader to experience how adored and important Bella becomes as a result of making this ultimate sacrifice.

The story also resonates with debates about deliberate teenage pregnancy. Politicians and popular media have expressed concern that deliberate pregnancy reflects lack of aspiration and a lack of alternative opportunities for young women (Goodchild & Owen, 2006). Researchers have challenged the stereotype of teenage pregnancy as a negative experience for young women. They report that young women use this as a rite of passage to adulthood which gives them status and responsibility (Kreager, Matsueda, & Erosheva, 2010). Bute and Russell (2012) analyse discourses surrounding teenage pregnancy, noting that it is presented as a "disruption to the social ordering of time" (p. 719), as well as a choice young women have a right to make, and as a way of taking responsibility and acting like an adult. Twilight endorses the idea of motherhood as a route to instant importance, making the teenage mother the centre of concern and attention. Bella certainly disrupts "the social ordering of time" by evading some generally accepted elements of growing up. She does not have to get her degree(s), establish herself in a career, or prove that she can earn a living. Her status as an adult is conferred instantly through motherhood.

Other critics have read Bella's behaviour as indicative of female choice and agency. Coker (2011) and Moruzi (2012) describe Bella's choices, including the decision to embrace young motherhood, as forms of post-feminist agency. Meyer herself focuses on Bella's choosing the role of wife and mother above all others, as indicative of her independence. I have interpreted her behaviour instead as a manipulative response to the exigencies of patriarchy. Her choices confine her to a permanent state of adolescent dependence on male concern. Her situation seems indicative of "the way in which everyday forms of power are organised, and function to both create the illusion of equality and the idea of activity, and the idea of choice and the idea of empowerment" (McRobbie, 2013, p. 3). The Saga constitutes part of the raft of what Pomerantz, Raby, and Stefank (2013) call "celebratory postfeminist narratives, such as Girl Power and Successful Girls" which "produce a view of girlhood that is beyond the need for help politics or a language of opposition with which to name gender injustice" (p. 202). Bella is indeed successful and exerts her will to get her own way. She chooses to suffer. I would argue that the texts present an exaggerated and horrific description of the pain and sacrifices associated with pregnancy and early childbirth, but counter this with a narrative that makes the girl/woman doing the sacrificing actually the most important person in the world, and that doing this teaches girls an important paradox: In order to have the love and attention they seek, that might validate their sense of their own identity and importance, they have to sacrifice themselves to the continuance of the patriarchal family.

BUFFY

Buffy's misery is not so well rewarded. She runs away from home after a verbal fight with her mother and a physical fight with her lover. Her vampire lover, Angel, fought with Buffy against the "forces of darkness" that the Slayer traditionally battles, until he lost his soul and switched sides. He rejects her brutally and humiliatingly at this point. He plans to end the world by awakening the demon, Acathla, who will suck the world into a demon dimension through a mystical vortex. Some of her friends feel her relationship with Angel was a bad choice and are not as sympathetic and supportive as she would like. In the midst of this crisis she has to reveal to her mother, Joyce, that she is a vampire slayer. Joyce wants Buffy to give up this role, and delivers an ultimatum as Buffy prepares to leave to stop Angel: If she leaves the house again she need not return. Buffy leaves anyway. Angel awakens the demon and the vortex begins to open. The only way Buffy can avert the end of the world is to kill Angel and push him into the vortex. Just before she does so, Angel's soul is restored to him and Buffy has to kill him knowing this. Devastated by these experiences, and feeling misunderstood and rejected by everyone, she leaves Sunnydale for Los Angeles. At this point the episode has very much the feel of the runaway trope Modleski (1982) discusses: The heroine runs away both as a reflection of her own misery and self-loathing and (subconsciously) to punish others for not caring enough. In the episode, "Anne" (Whedon, 1998) at the beginning of Season 3 we find her working as a waitress in LA, having given up her old role and her old life. She uses her middle name, "Anne," something Wilcox (2006) suggests reflects "her wish to hide within herself and lose her pain" (p. 62). She runs away from being Buffy, making no contact with those who love her and fear for her safety.

She meets other runaways. This begins to undermine the psychological pleasure offered by the runaway motif. The runaways are presented as sad, deluded creatures; neither Buffy nor the viewer who identifies with her can take satisfaction in being counted amongst them. She discovers that these vulnerable individuals are being exploited by a cult which purports to love them but uses them as slave labour. The episode's critique of certain aspects of religion also contributes to undermining the psychological pleasures of self-abnegation. The cult echoes concepts central to the mystical formulations of various religions, which teach that only through complete abnegation of self can the soul find its true identity through absorption into a divine consciousness. The runaways, like Buffy, have already abandoned their old identities. The cult insists they abandon *all* sense of self. They are asked, "Who are you?" and have to reply, "I am nothing, I am no-one" (Whedon, 1998). If they say their name they are beaten. This episode suggests that self-denial, far from leading to a fuller life, leads to enslavement. Its purpose is to ensure that the devotees have no will and no resistance, so can be used as slave labour. Once stripped of their identity, they are made to work until they are prematurely aged and ready to die. They are ripe for exploitation by those who appear to offer them the love and attention they crave. The pedagogy here does not suggest that Buffy will find happiness or love by abandoning her identity and responsibilities.

And indeed she reclaims her identity. She sees the exploitation, investigates the cult and is captured. In spite of running away from her relationships, as a result of the misery and anger they caused her, her identity as a relational human being re-asserts itself when others are endangered. When the cult captors ask Buffy, "Who are you?" instead of giving the expected reply, "I am no one" or even "I am Anne," she claims her name and her role: "I'm Buffy. The Vampire Slayer. And you are?" (Whedon, 1998). She defeats her captors and frees their prisoners. Wilcox (2004) notes that the series "repeatedly equates naming with existentialist choice" (p. 63). This may appear paradoxical at first. Buffy did not determine her own name; rather, she was given it. She did not decide to be a slayer; she was chosen. At various points in the series, however, Buffy owns this role and this identity. She exercises agency, not by running away from the responsibilities that have been given her, but by embracing them. The choice she faces here, between surrendering herself to a higher authority or fighting for her fellows and her identity, is characteristic of the way

Whedon portrays what Richardson and Rabb (2007) call his "radical existentialist ethics" in which "nothing relieves you of your responsibility for your choices" (pp. 69–70 of 3065). Having constantly to make the choice to be the Slayer is an "authentic existential choice" (p. 291 of 3065). Her self-worth, however damaged by Angel's rejection and by the lack of understanding from friends and family, is not dependent on stimulating their anxiety and love, but on her role as a leader with responsibilities to others, and growing up is defined by making moral choices that focus on responsibilities to others.

The following episode, "Dead Man's Party" (Noxon & Whitmore, 1998), begins with her return home and tackles the idea that the runaway wanted to draw attention to her suffering – perhaps even to punish friends and family, albeit unconsciously. Conventionally, the runaway heroine (and the reader identifying with her) would be rewarded by the outpouring of love from those who had been anxious about her absence. The episode offers little scope for allowing Buffy to experience any satisfaction in her friends' pleasure at her return or distress at her absence. It shows that relationships are more complex than this. Her friends and her mother are relieved to see her, but the underlying aggression and selfishness of the running away and her self-destructive behaviour is foregrounded when they express their anger as well as their pleasure at her return. And of course there is no hero to embrace her. Her friend, Xander, does not reassure her when she worries that her Watcher, who is responsible for overseeing her work as a Slayer, might be "mad" she left, but says, "Mad? Just because you ran away and abandoned your post and your friends and your mom and made him lay awake every night worrying about you?" (Noxon & Whitmore, 1998).

She has hurt everyone, and cannot simply pick up where she left off. They have begun to move on and are trying to fulfil some of the obligations she walked out on; they have even taken on some of her Slayer duties. They did not put their lives on hold. Later, she feels like an outsider at a party in her own home, where her friends are concerned with their complex relationships with each other, rather than their relationships with her. Her friend Willow puts this neatly when she explains that she had needed Buffy, at a time when her (Willow's) life was difficult; she felt let down when Buffy left. Far from feeling guilty that Buffy is suffering, she is angry with her. Buffy's mother, Joyce, also engages with Buffy in a way that challenges self-obsession. At the party, Buffy overhears Joyce explaining how difficult she finds the relationship with Buffy. Buffy's reaction to this, and to her friends' pre-occupation with their own affairs, is to start to pack to run away again, until discovered by Willow, who is furious. When Buffy tells Joyce she ran away because of her reaction to finding out she was a slayer, Joyce is not apologetic:

Joyce: Buffy! You didn't give me any time. You just dumped this, this thing on me and expected me to get it. Well – guess what? Mom's not perfect. I handled it badly. But that doesn't give you the right to punish me by running away –

Buffy: Punish you? I didn't do this to punish you –

Xander: Well you did. You should have seen what it did to her....

Xander: Maybe you don't want to hear it, Buffy. But taking off like that was selfish and stupid. (Noxon & Whitmore, 1998)

Xander and Joyce home in on the idea that running away was an aggressive act. The series will not allow this heroine to position herself and her concerns as the centre of the Universe. It shows that anger with her mother and friends forms part of the impetus for running away. Some of the psychology of the masochistic heroine is there, but Buffy, and the viewers going through the experience with her, do not get the big emotional pay-off for her self-destructive behaviour. It is precisely this lack of pay-off that gives the episode its pedagogical impetus. The viewer goes through this experience with Buffy as she learns to think about the world in a less egocentric way. As Willow says, "It's not all about you" (Noxon & Whitmore, 1998). This is a very different moral perspective from that delivered through *Twilight*. Buffy and her friends learn, throughout the series, that adulthood is about a different kind of sacrifice – not masochistic, attention seeking suffering, but the sacrifice involved in keeping going, even when you do not want to. As Reiss (2004) puts it, "on Buffy the real pain ... is often simply to live in the world" and to do so out of "compassion for others" (p. 13).

IN CONCLUSION: BELLA, BUFFY, AND SOME OF THE OTHERS

These analyses of *BtVS* and *Twilight* suggest it is possible to read them as representations of very different models of becoming an adult woman. *Twilight* presents womanhood as a masochistic state in which women are rewarded for suffering with love and comfort. It appears to exonerate forms of childish behaviour in which women gain attention through self-harm, and presents motherhood as a rite of passage in which a woman's life is presented as secondary to the requirement to reproduce. *BtVS*, however, demonstrates that the heroine grows up by rejecting patterns of manipulative self-harm. Running away damages her relationships and does not result in comfort or positive attention. Buffy is expected to face up to life's challenges and her responsibilities, even when she feels hurt or rejected. Respect comes from strength in standing up to oppression, alone if necessary, as shown in "Anne."

Patterns of behaviour whereby love and attention are secured by putting the heroine in danger are frequently found in young adult fiction that focuses on young women's transition to adulthood. Veronica Mars, the lead character of a novel, TV series and film, has plenty of reasons to adopt the kinds of masochistic revenge strategies beloved of romantic heroines (see Silver, Thomas, Ruggiero, Gwartz, & Stokdyk, 2004). She is misjudged, ostracised and publicly humiliated on a regular basis. Her boyfriends cheat on her and her friends betray her – but she generally settles for straightforward revenge and a stoic facing down of her enemies. In series three, following an attempted rape by a rapist haunting the campus, she appears on her couch, the object of her boyfriend and father's deep concern. She enjoys this momentarily, but the story goes on to show how stifling a relationship grounded in female vulnerability and male comfort and protection can be. She finds her boyfriend's continued protectiveness restrictive and demeaning and they break up.

But there are still many fictions for young adults that offer readers and viewers gratification based on causing suffering to others through self-sacrifice. This psychological manipulation can be found even in texts that feature strong self-willed heroines. Katniss, the heroine of *The Hunger Games* (Collins, 2008; Jacobsen, Kilik, Ross, & Lawrence, 2012), is a brave, self-reliant young woman who provides for her family. Although she endangers herself by volunteering for, what for most of the participants will be a suicide mission, hers is a heroic act, not something she does in response to feeling unloved or rejected. She volunteers to put herself in danger by taking her younger sister's place in the Hunger Games, a fight to the death between champions from different districts of the dystopian country of Panem. She is far removed from the weak and helpless Bella Swan. However, some of the narrative gratifications that accompany the self-harming heroine are evident in this story. Self-sacrifice is what brings attention to her. She is immediately loved and respected by her whole community, even securing the attention of her mother, who had been almost catatonically uninterested in her since her father died. Moreover, although she, like Bella, overtly rejects, even mocks, the trappings of femininity (e.g. fashion, hair styles, make-up), she has spectacular make-overs, and her newly beautiful self is paraded on television and much admired. She becomes the object of a love triangle, and the darling of the masses. She does not endanger herself in order to gain adoration and attention, but that is what the risk achieves. So, although the narrative endorses female strength, intelligence, resourcefulness, independence and courage, the heroine still receives (and more significantly, the young female reader receives) considerable gratification from the admiration and attention she gets because she is beautiful and people fear for her safety.

In yet another text, Tris, from Roth's *Divergent* trilogy (Roth, 2011; Wick, Fisher, Shabazian, & Burger, 2014), a world in which everyone lives in one of five factions, reflecting their character, would seem to be a good example of a heroine rejecting a sacrificial role for women. She leaves Abnegation, the faction whose over-riding characteristic is selflessness and sacrifice, and joins Dauntless, the faction that values courage. Yet even here, there are contradictions. She attracts love and attention by risking or harming herself. Although the hero admires her strength, it is her risky behaviour that keeps forcing him to show his feelings for her. At one point she runs away from the compound when he appears to reject her, causing him great concern; he says, "Sometimes I forget that I can hurt you. That you are capable of being hurt" (Roth, 2011, p. 366). Tris (and the reader/viewer) take pleasure from the reminder and the emotions he is forced to display.

As this entire discussion illustrates, young adult fiction is a dynamic form. There are many televisual and filmic texts in which young women who are transitioning into adulthood are shown models of courage, intelligence, assertiveness and independence. These texts reflect the multiplicity of roles and opportunities available to girls today. At the same time, there is a high prevalence of stories in which many of the narrative pleasures result from a kind of masochism, in which young women are rewarded with love and affection not for their courage or their achievements, but for suffering, sacrifice and pain.

I think a consideration of these texts has two implications for adult educators. First, it indicates how complex and contradictory teachings about adulthood, maturation and gender operate outside educational institutions, as part of the everyday experiences of reading a book, watching television or visiting the cinema. Those interested in the study of adult education are concerned with how adult education operates outside as well as inside the classroom. Second, it suggests the potential for working with adults to develop the skills and knowledge that will enable them to interrogate these texts and evaluate their significance. For example, adult educators teaching those who work with young adults (such as teachers or youth workers) may find it useful to explore these texts as ways of helping these professionals consider questions of gender, adulthood, and identity, and the interface between these and media representations of young womanhood. Such professionals may well want to go on and use these texts themselves as the basis for discussion with the young adults with whom they work. Adult educators may also find these texts to be a rich source of material for introducing and discussing a range of challenging concepts, such as motherhood, domestic abuse, self-harm, gender and power, and the relationship between agency and sacrifice.

NOTES

[1] Buffy from the TV series, Buffy the Vampire Slayer, Veronica from the TV series Veronica Mars, Katniss from the films and books The Hunger Games, Tris from the films and books, the Divergent trilogy and Saba from the Dustlands trilogy (optioned for movie production).
[2] This refers to the rating by the British Board of Film Classification that allows admission to children and youth aged 12 or older without an accompanying adult.

REFERENCES

Baker, J. (2010). Great expectations and post-feminist accountability: Young women living up to the "successful girls" discourse. *Gender & Education, 22*(1), 1–15. doi:10.1080/09540250802612696

Barthes, R. (1977). The death of the author. In R. Barthes (Ed.), *Image, music, text* (pp. 142–149). London, England: Fontana.

Box Office Mojo. (n.d.). *Marvel's The Avengers*. Retrieved from http://boxofficemojo.com/movies/?id=avengers11.htm

Bute, J., & Russell, L. (2012). Public discourses about teenage pregnancy. *Health Communication, 27*(7), 712–722. doi:10.1080/10410236.2011.636479

Cawelti, J. (1976). *Adventure, mystery, romance*. Chicago, IL: University of Chicago Press.

Collins, S. (2008). *The hunger games*. New York, NY: Scholastic Press.

Coker, C. (2011). That girl: Bella, Buffy, and the feminist ethics of choice in *Twilight* and *Buffy the Vampire Slayer*. *Slayageonline, 8.4*(32). Retrieved from http://slayageonline.com/essays/slayage32/Coker.pdf

Dietz, T. (2011). Wake up Bella! A personal essay on twilight, mormonism, feminism and happiness. In G. Anatol (Ed.), *Bringing light to Twilight* (pp. 99–113). New York, NY: Palgrave MacMillan.

Edwards, K. (2009). Good looks and sex symbols: The power of the gaze and the displacement of the erotic in Twilight. *Screen Education, 53*, 26–32.

Goodchild, S., & Owen, J. (2006, July 16). Teenage mothers see pregnancy as a "career move." *The Independent*. Retrieved from http://www.independent.co.uk/news/uk/this-britain/teenage-mothers-see-pregnancy-as-a-career-move-408186.html

Hall, S. (1980). Encoding/decoding. In S. Hall, D. Hobson, A. Lowe, & P. Willis (Eds.), *Culture, media, language: Working papers in cultural studies, 1972–1979* (pp. 128–139). Abingdon, England: Routledge.

Harris, A. (Ed.) 2004. *All about the girl: Culture, power, and identity*. New York, NY: Routledge.

Jacobson, N., Kilik, J. (Producers), & Ross, G., & Lawrence, F. (Directors). (2012). *The hunger games* [Motion picture]. United States: Lionsgate.

Jarvis, C. (2013). The twilight of feminism? Stephenie Meyer's saga and the contradictions of contemporary girlhood. *Children's Literature in Education, 45*, 101–115. doi:10.1007/s10583-013-9212-9

Jubas, K., & Knutson, P. (2012). Seeing and be(liev)ing: How nursing and medical students understand representations of their professions. *Studies in the Education of Adults, 44*(1), 85–100.

Kreager, D., Matsueda, R., & Eerosheva, E. (2010). Motherhood and criminal desistance in disadvantaged neighborhoods. *Criminology, 48*(1), 221–258. doi:10.1111/j.1745-9125.2010.00184.x

Lametti, D., Harris, A., Geiling, N., & Matthews-Ramo, N. (2012, June 11). Which pop culture property do academics study the most? *Slate*. Retrieved from http://www.slate.com/blogs/browbeat/2012/06/11/pop_culture_studies_why_do_academics_study_buffy_the_vampire_slayer_more_than_the_wire_the_matrix_alien_and_the_simpsons_.html

Lavery, D., & Burkhead, C. (2011). *Joss Whedon: Conversations*. Jackson, MS: University Press of Mississippi.

McRobbie, A. (2009). *The aftermath of feminism: Gender, culture and social change*. London, England: SAGE Publications.

McRobbie, A. (2013). Angela McRobbie on the illusion of equality for women. *Social Science Bites*. Retrieved from http://www.socialsciencespace.com/wp-content/uploads/Angela-McRobbie.pdf

Meyer, S. (n.d.). *10 second interview: A few words with Stephenie Meyer*. Retrieved from http://www.amazon.com/exec/obidos/tg/detail/-/0316160172/ref=ase_stepheniemeye-20/104-0160833-2386318?v=glance&s=books

Meyer, S. (2006). *New moon*. London, England: Atom.

Meyer, S. (2008). *Breaking dawn*. London, England: Atom.

Modleski, T. (1982). *Loving with a vengeance: Mass produced fantasies for women*. Hamden, CT: Archon Books.

Morris, W. (2005). Interview: Twilight author Stephenie Meyer. *A motley vision: Mormon literature and culture*. Retrieved from http://www.motleyvision.org/2005/interview-twilight-author-stephenie-meyer/

Moruzi, K. (2012). Post-feminist fantasies: Sexuality and femininity in Stephenie Meyer's Twilight Series. In A. Morey (Ed.), *Genre, reception, and adaptation in the Twilight series* (pp. 47–65). Surrey, BC: Ashgate.

Noxon, M. (Writer), & Whitmore, A. (Director). (1998). Dead man's party [Television series episode]. In J. Whedon, D. Greenwalt, M. Noxon, F. Rubel Kuzui, & K. Kuzui (Executive Producers), *Buffy the vampire slayer*. Los Angeles, CA: Twentieth Century Fox.

Pascale, A. (2014). *Joss Whedon: Geek king of the universe*. London, England: Aurum Press.

Pomerantz, S., Raby, R., & Stefank, A. (2013). Girls run the world? Caught between sexism and postfeminism in school. *Gender and Society, 27*(2) 185–207. doi:10.1177/0891243212473199

Radway, J. (1984). *Reading the romance: Women, patriarchy and popular fiction*. Chapel Hill, NC: University of North Carolina Press.

Regis, P. (2011).What do critics owe the romance? *Journal of Popular Romance Studies, 2*(1), 1–16.

Reiss, J. (2004). *What would Buffy do?* San Franciso, CA: Jossey-Bass.

Richardson, M., & Rabb, D. (2007). *The existential Joss Whedon* [Kindle DX version]. Jefferson, NC: McFarland.

Roth, V. (2011). *Divergent*. New York, NY: Harper Collins.

Sandlin, J., O'Malley, M., & Burdick, J. (2011). Mapping the complexity of public pedagogy scholarship, 1894–2010. *Review of Educational Research, 8*(3), 338–375. doi:10.3102/ 0034654311413395

Silver, J., Thomas, R., Ruggiero, D., Gwartz, J., & Stokdyk, D. (Producers). *Veronica Mars* [Television series]. Los Angeles, CA: Warner Bros, TV.

Tapper, O. (2014). Romance and innovation in twenty-first century publishing. *Publishing Research Quarterly, 30*(2), 249–259. doi:10.1007/s12109-014-9363-6

Veeser, A. (Ed.). (1989). *The new historicism*. London, England: Routledge

Wendell, S., & Tan, C. (2009). *Beyond heaving bosoms: The smart bitches guide to romance novels*. New York, NY: Simon and Schuster.

Whedon, J. (Writer & Director). (1998). Anne [Television series episode]. In J. Whedon (Producer), *Buffy the vampire slayer*. Los Angeles, CA: Twentieth Century Fox.

Whitton, M. (2011). Motherhood and masochism in Twilight. In G. Anatol (Ed.), *Bringing light to Twilight* (pp. 125–139). New York, NY: Palgrave Macmillan.

Wick, D., Fisher, L., & Shabazian, P. (Producers), & Burger, N. (Director). (2014). *Divergent* [Motion picture]. United States: Lionsgate.

Wilcox, R. (2006). *Why Buffy matters: The art of Buffy the vampire slayer*. London & New York, NY: IB Tauris.

Wilson, N. (2011). *Seduced by Twilight*. Jefferson, NS: Macfarland.

Wyck, G., Rosenfelt, K., & Meyer, S. (Producers), & Condon, B. (Director). (2011). *Breaking dawn part 1* [Motion picture]. United States: Summit Entertainment.

Wyck, G., Rosenfelt, K., & Meyer, S. (Producers), & Condon, B. (Director). (2012). *Breaking dawn part 2* [Motion picture]. United States: Summit Entertainment.

Christine Jarvis
Pro Vice-chancellor for Teaching and Learning
University of Huddersfield

CONTRIBUTORS

Tony Brown recently joined the University of Canberra, Australia after previously coordinating the University of Technology Sydney post-graduate programs in adult and organizational learning, and popular education. His key research interests have been the political economy of adult education and work, informal and formal learning within civil society organisations, and the use of film and narrative in critical pedagogy. He has been a senior government program manager in adult and vocational education, union researcher, Executive Director of the peak body Adult Learning Australia, and a University academic. Since 2013, Tony has been the Editor of the *Australian Journal of Adult Learning*. He can be reached at tony.brown@canberra.edu.au.

Christine Jarvis is Pro Vice-chancellor for Teaching and Learning at the University of Huddersfield, in England. She began her career by working for 12 years in community, further, and adult education. She is interested in the transformative potential of literature and fictions and this has been the main focus of her research. She has written about popular romance, the fictional representation of education and educators, young adult fiction and the work of Joss Whedon. She recently completed, with Professor Patricia Gouthro, a review of the literature on arts-based professional education, published in *Studies in the Education of Adults*. She can be reached at c.a.jarvis@hud.ac.uk.

Kaela Jubas is an Associate Professor in Adult Learning at the Werklund School of Education, University of Calgary in Canada, where she teaches courses connecting adult education and learning to community, work, and leadership. She completed a PhD in Educational Studies at the University of British Columbia, where she studied critical shopping as a source of adult learning about identity, globalization, and social justice. Her book *The Politics of Shopping* (Left Coast) is an adaptation of her award-winning dissertation. Since joining the faculty in Calgary in 2008, she has focused her research on public pedagogy, particularly the influence of medical shows on nursing and medical students' learning about themselves and their professions, and on how the border-crossing of these sorts of shows informs Canadians' understandings of health care policy debates. She can be reached at kjubas@ucalgary.ca.

Elissa Odgren taught high school students on a small island in the Caribbean after earning her BEd from Nipissing University in Ontario, Canada. Upon her return to Canada, she taught in adult education for the Near North District School Board, and then was hired to teach upgrading students at Canadore College. She has just completed her MEd from the University of Calgary, where she focused her studies on adult, community, and higher education. She is currently employed as a biology

Instructor in the Career and Academic Preparation program at Red Deer College in Alberta, Canada. Her research interests include environmental literacy, consumption, and popular culture. She can be reached at elissa.odgren@rdc.ab.ca.

Theresa J. Schindel is Clinical Associate Professor at the Faculty of Pharmacy and Pharmaceutical Sciences at the University of Alberta. Her educational background includes a Bachelor of Science in Pharmacy from the University of Saskatchewan and a Master's of Continuing Education from the University of Calgary. She is a PhD candidate in an interprofessional doctoral program at the University of Alberta in the Department of Educational Policy Studies and School of Library and Information Studies. Her research focuses on professional learning, development, and change. She can be reached at Terri.Schindel@ualberta.ca.

Nancy Taber is an Associate Professor in the Faculty of Education at Brock University, Canada. She teaches critical adult education, focusing on learning gender in a militarized world. Nancy's research explores gendered militarism as relates to military mothers, higher education, fiction, and popular culture. She recently edited the book *Gendered Militarism in Canada: Learning Conformity and Resistance*, co-edited *Building on Critical Traditions: Adult Education and Learning in Canada*, and guest edited a special issue on the state of feminism in Canadian adult education for the *Canadian Journal for the Study of Adult Education*. Nancy also collaborates in research about the experiences of girls and women in media discussion clubs that engage in a societal gendered analysis. She has published in leading educational studies, research methodology, women's, and gender studies journals. Nancy is currently using the genre of short fiction to explore the complexities of women's lives. She can be reached at ntaber@brocku.ca.

Pamela Timanson is a PhD candidate in the Educational Administration and Leadership stream of the Department of Educational Policy Studies at the University of Alberta. She completed her BEd and MEd (Workplace and Adult Learning) through the University of Calgary. Her doctoral research is focused on the examination of how teachers are learning informally within the knowledge culture of their workplace. She can be reached at ptimanso@ualberta.ca.

Astrid Treffry-Goatley is an ethnomusicologist who is based at the Africa Centre for Health and Population Studies at the University of KwaZulu-Natal, South Africa. She is involved in public engagement research at this facility and has led four public engagement projects since 2010. In 2007, she was awarded the Andrew W. Mellon Research Fellowship to do a PhD at the Centre for Film and Media Studies at the University of Cape Town. Her research interests include new media, digital storytelling, narrative inquiry, indigenous music, film and the use of creative methodologies to support and evaluate public engagement with and learning about HIV research. She can be reached at astridtg@gmail.com.

Gary L. Wright is a Lecturer of Mathematics at Penn State, Harrisburg. He earned a PhD in Curriculum & Instruction from Texas A&M University, and a BS and MS in mathematics from the University of Tennessee. In addition to mathematics, his teaching experience and interests include science and mathematics education, curriculum and instruction, teacher training, developmental education, and adult learning. His research interests include uncovering the motivating and transforming potential of popular culture, especially music, comic books, and film, for adult learners. He can be contacted at glw16@psu.edu.

Robin Redmon Wright is an Assistant Professor of Adult Education at Penn State, Harrisburg. She earned a PhD in adult education from Texas A&M University, and a BA and MA in English literature from the University of Tennessee. An award-winning researcher and teacher, her work is framed by critical and feminist theories and focuses on systemic, normalized inequalities, and the ways those discriminatory systems are, or are not, supported and reproduced through popular culture and the creative arts. She also researches issues of identity, socioeconomic class, gender, and education through autoethnography. She can be contacted at rrw12@psu.edu.

NAME INDEX

A
Armstrong, P., 5, 86, 91, 98

B
Barthes, R., 56, 57, 137
Baumgartner, L., 69, 79
Billett, S., 68, 73, 78, 84, 86
Brookfield, S. D., 18, 22, 26, 32, 33, 36, 41, 42, 45, 67, 80
Brown, T., 1, 3, 7, 49, 54, 87, 88, 104, 110, 115, 151
Bruner, J., 50
Burr, V., 1, 18, 67, 70, 88, 119, 126, 130

C
Caffarrella, R. S., 69, 79
Clifford, J., 106
Colley, H., 69, 83, 84, 86, 98

D
Dirkx, J., 35, 84

G
Gauntlett, D., 15
Gee, J. P., 88, 89
Geertz, C., 50
Giroux, H. A., 1, 14, 32, 33, 37, 42, 53, 61, 104–106, 120
Gramsci, A., 86, 87
Guy, T. C., 1, 37, 40, 41

H
Habermas, J., 22
Hall, S., 56, 137
Hartley, J., 11, 18
Hodkinson, P., 39, 69, 83, 84, 86, 98
hooks, b., 49

J
Jarvis, C. A., 1, 2, 7, 8, 18, 35, 36, 43, 67, 86–88, 93, 98, 99, 119, 126, 130, 135, 139, 151
Jarvis, P., 38, 40
Jenkins, H., 25
Jubas, K., 1, 2, 6–8, 32, 40, 46, 67, 69, 80, 83, 85, 98, 135, 151

K
Kilgore, D. W., 46

L
Lave, J., 39, 69, 79
Lazar, M., 121
Luke, C., 1, 86

M
Malcolm, J., 69, 83, 84, 86, 98
Marcus, K., 78
Marcuse, H., 26
Marsick, V. J., 32, 38, 69, 73, 75, 76, 79, 83
McKee, A., 17, 27, 31
McLaren, P., 13
McRobbie, A., 84, 85, 97, 136, 137, 143
Merriam, S. B., 68, 69, 79
Mezirow, J., 35, 78, 98
Meyer, S., 135–137, 139–141, 143
Miller, T., 12, 15, 31, 44, 52, 123, 127

NAME INDEX

N
Naples, N., 88
Nerland, M., 69, 70, 73, 74, 78, 79

O
Obama, B., 61
Ogden, E.,

P
Potter, J., 41, 67, 70

S
Sandlin, J. A., 1, 2, 4, 8, 26, 32, 33, 35, 36, 42, 45, 87, 89, 104, 115, 119, 130, 135
Schindel, T., 7, 67, 152
Stake, R. E., 18, 88, 141

T
Taber, N., 1–3, 7, 8, 119, 122, 124, 130, 152
Timanson, P., 7, 67, 80, 152

Tisdell, E. J., 1, 2, 4, 32, 35, 44, 45, 88, 98, 105, 119, 120
Treffry-Goatley, A., 7, 103, 104, 106, 115, 152

V
Ventura, P., 13

W
Watkins, K. E., 16, 32, 38, 69, 73, 75, 76, 79, 83
Wenger, E., 38–40, 69, 79
Wetherell, M., 67, 70
Whedon, J., 135–137, 144, 145, 151
Williams, R., 1, 16, 22, 50, 52, 60
Wright, G. L., 6, 11
Wright, R. R., 1, 2, 4, 6, 11, 14, 15, 18, 20, 26, 32, 33, 35, 37, 45, 67, 86, 87, 93, 119, 130, 153

Y
Yin, R. K., 104, 106

SUBJECT INDEX

A
Adulthood, 119, 120, 122, 124, 128 142, 146–148
Adult education, 1–4, 6, 8, 12, 16, 32, 33, 35, 64, 68, 83, 84, 88, 97–99, 105, 113, 120, 130, 148, 151–153
African-American, 53, 60
Animation, 8, 36, 43
(Post-)Apartheid, 7, 104–106, 111, 114–116

B
Backlash, 49, 50, 54–56, 58, 60, 63
BBC, 12, 13, 16, 25
Beat the Drum, 105, 111–114
Beauty, 46, 90, 108–110, 113, 114, 119, 120, 125–129, 123, 136
Buffy the Vampire Slayer, 138

C
Capitalism/Capitalist, 6, 13, 15–17, 22, 33, 35, 42, 44, 46
Case study, 6, 83, 88, 104–107, 115
Charter schools, 55, 61, 62
Childhood, 119, 120, 122, 124, 128, 129
Citizenship, 2, 8 12, 27, 32, 34, 35, 40–42, 44
Class (Note: this refers to socioeconomic status, not the classroom), 3, 7, 8, 14, 15, 17, 18, 26, 51–54, 56, 59, 63, 64, 70, 84–86, 89, 90, 92, 95, 106, 153
Classroom, 2, 3, 16, 18, 22, 32, 33, 45, 53, 54, 56, 61, 84, 86–88, 98, 148

Communities of practice/CoP, 6, 32–35, 37–42, 44
Constructionism (social), 70
Constructivism/Constructivist (includes social constructivism), 50, 36
Consumer(ism), 14, 15, 17, 19, 22, 31, 37, 40, 44, 49, 135
Content analysis, 11, 18
Corporate media power, 15
Corporatization, 6, 33
Critical pedagogy, 3, 11, 45, 44, 151
Critical theory, 18, 26, 88
Cultural consumption, 4, 7, 32, 86, 87, 98, 99, 104, 115
Cultural studies, 1, 4, 6, 14, 17, 84, 99, 136
Culture, 1–8, 12, 15, 16, 18, 20, 27, 31–33, 36, 37, 42, 44, 45, 50, 59, 63, 69–71, 73–76, 78–80, 84, 85, 87–89, 94, 96–99, 103, 104, 115, 116, 119–121, 135, 137, 152, 153
Curriculum, 14, 16, 25, 50, 61, 63, 153

D
Democracy, 18, 20, 37, 40–42, 103, 106, 108
Discourse analysis, 6, 7, 67, 68, 70, 88
 Critical discourse analysis, 88
 Feminist discourse analysis, 88, 120, 121, 130
Disney, 7, 62, 119–122, 125, 129, 130
Doctor Who, 6, 8, 11–13, 15–18, 23, 25–27, 112
Documentary, 8, 55, 57, 72, 73, 105, 108

SUBJECT INDEX

E

Education, 1–4, 6–8, 12, 15, 16, 20, 32, 33, 35, 45, 49–64, 68, 80, 83, 84, 88, 97–99, 104, 105, 109, 110, 113, 114, 116, 120, 130, 148, 151–153
   Public education, 49, 50, 54–58, 60–64
Edutainment, 8
Entertainment-education, 104
Evil, 34, 121–122, 124–127, 130

F

Fairy tales, 3, 7, 119–121, 125, 128–131
Family, 20, 57, 62, 77, 90, 92, 95, 109, 112, 116, 120–122, 124, 126–129, 139, 140, 143, 145, 147
Fan(dom), 6, 11, 16, 17, 25, 26
Fantasy, 8, 15, 120–122, 124, 128, 131, 136
Feminism, 84–86, 97, 135–137, 152
   Post-feminism, 84, 85, 97
Focus groups, 89

G

(Anti-)Gay, 62
Gender(ed), 2, 3, 6–8, 14, 17, 32, 43, 45, 54, 83–87, 90–93, 95–99, 115, 119–122, 124, 129, 130, 137, 138, 143, 148, 152, 153
   Female, 7, 8, 12, 17, 34, 43, 64, 83, 86, 89, 91, 92, 95–98, 106, 112, 119, 122, 129, 130, 136, 143, 147
   Feminine/Femininity/Feminization, 43, 83, 86, 92, 94–96, 120, 121, 147
   Masculine/Masculinity, 86, 90–92, 95, 96, 120–122
Globalization, 2, 5–8, 151
Good, 7, 22, 23, 27, 37, 40, 43, 53, 55, 63, 74, 75, 77, 86, 89, 107, 116, 120–122, 123–127, 130, 139, 147

Gramsci/an, 86, 87, 99
Grey's Anatomy, 2, 7, 8, 83–85, 88–91, 93, 94, 96–98, 151
Grimm, 119, 120, 122, 131

H

Health, 6–8, 17, 51, 55, 83, 89, 90, 93–97, 99, 103, 104, 110, 151, 152
Health care, 7, 83, 89, 90, 93–97, 99, 151
Hegemony, 15
Hero(ine), 12, 52–55, 112, 136, 138, 144–147
Heteronormative/Heteronormativity, 7, 124, 125
HIV/AIDS, 112

I

Ideology/Ideological, 3, 12–14, 17–19, 26, 32, 33, 41, 62, 63, 87, 99, 106, 108, 121, 130
Identity, 2, 6–8, 18, 26, 33, 38, 42, 49, 59, 83–86, 88, 90, 92, 95, 97, 98, 138, 142–144, 148, 151, 153
Industrialisation/Industrialization, 51
International relations, 17
Interpretive ethnography, 50
Interviews, 89, 105, 137

L

Learning, 2–4, 6–8, 16, 18, 20, 26, 31–33, 35, 36, 38–42, 44–46, 49, 51, 53, 54, 63, 67 80, 83 91, 93, 95–99, 103, 104, 113, 115, 119, 120, 130, 135, 151–153
   Adult learning, 2, 4, 32, 35, 36, 44, 45, 71, 79, 83, 84, 87, 97, 104, 115, 119, 120
   Informal learning, 69, 70, 79, 83, 84, 86, 98, 113
   Transformative learning, 6, 32, 33, 35, 36, 45, 69, 78, 98

SUBJECT INDEX

Workplace learning, 7, 67–69, 71, 73, 79, 80
Work-related learning, 7, 83, 96
Lego Movie, The, 32–37, 40, 44–46
Life, Above All, 105, 112–114
Love, 15, 24, 27, 52, 53, 64, 93, 114, 120–122, 124–130, 136, 138–148

M

Magic, 121–122, 124, 127, 128, 131
Marketisation, 60
Marxist, 11, 17
Masochism, 7, 135, 138, 148
Medical drama, 8, 67
Medicine, 71, 91, 92, 94, 95, 97
Meritocracy, 84, 96, 97
Minority Feisty, the, 43
Mother, 56, 90, 108, 111–114, 117, 123–126, 139, 140, 142, 143, 145–147

N

Narrative, 1, 3, 13, 37, 40, 49–51, 54, 58, 59, 63, 109, 112, 114, 116, 140, 142, 143, 147, 148, 151, 152
Neoliberal/ism, 6, 7, 13–15, 20, 22, 40, 42, 84, 96, 104, 106, 115, 116
New Historicism, 137
Nurse Jackie, 7, 8, 67, 68, 70, 71, 77, 79, 99
Nurses/Nursing, 7, 8, 67, 68, 71, 73–75, 83, 89, 91–98, 114, 151
Nursing students, 7, 8, 68, 83, 89, 94, 96–98

O

Once upon a Time, 2, 7, 8, 119–122

P

Parent Trigger Laws, 57, 60
Patriarchy, 95, 135, 143

Pedagogical, 6, 7,11, 14, 16, 17, 26, 32, 33, 36, 45, 49, 83, 87, 89, 98, 99, 104, 110, 115, 135, 140, 146
Pedagogy, 1–4, 6, 8, 11, 14, 32, 33, 36, 44, 45, 49, 58, 61, 63, 80, 86, 88, 97, 103–106, 115, 116, 135, 144, 151
Politics, 4, 15, 17, 18, 27, 31, 45, 54, 60, 106, 143, 151
Popular culture, 1–5, 7, 8, 15, 18, 20, 26, 27, 32, 33, 35, 36, 44, 45, 50, 58, 67, 80, 85, 89, 99, 103, 104, 115, 116, 119–121, 127, 129, 130, 135, 137, 152, 153
Postmodernism, 88
Poststructuralism, 88
Poverty, 7, 90, 109, 115
Privatisation/Privatization, 3, 62
Professional, 7, 8, 15, 57, 58, 67–71, 73, 74, 76, 80, 83–85, 88, 90–92, 95–98, 108, 111, 151, 152
Public pedagogy, 1, 2, 4, 6, 8, 11, 32, 33, 36, 45, 49, 103–106, 115, 116, 135, 151

R

Racial, 8, 14, 17, 54, 59, 90, 106, 112, 115
Research, 1, 2, 4, 6, 8, 12–14, 18, 32, 45, 67–69, 79, 80, 50, 88, 89, 99, 104, 106, 121, 122, 124, 130, 138, 151–153
Romance, 51, 122, 124, 128, 130, 136, 139, 151

S

Sacrifice, 7, 8, 126, 127, 135, 137, 139, 142, 143, 146–148
Schooling, 51, 54, 58, 61–64
Science fiction, 8, 12, 13, 15, 18, 27, 33

SUBJECT INDEX

Sexism/Sexist, 14, 22, 26, 43, 85, 96–98
Smurfette Principle, 43
Social media, 1, 4, 25, 32
Story/Storytelling, 1–3, 6, 8, 11, 14–16, 17, 22, 25–27, 31, 34, 40, 43, 45, 49, 50, 52–56, 58, 59, 72, 74, 76, 86, 88, 108, 109, 112, 113, 115, 117, 122, 124, 125, 130, 137, 139, 142, 147, 152
Student, 3, 57, 63, 64, 67, 68, 72, 73, 75, 77, 79, 83, 89, 94–97, 113, 116

T

Teacher/Teaching, 2–4, 7, 25, 49–61, 63, 64, 67, 79, 80, 83, 88, 89, 92, 105, 109, 110, 113, 114, 127, 128, 135, 148, 151, 153
Textual analysis, 6, 11, 12, 18, 27, 31, 44, 88, 90, 138
Transmedia, 6, 11, 25, 26
Twilight, 7, 8, 135, 137–139, 143, 146

U

Unions, 50, 58, 60

V

Voucher programs, 61

W

Waiting for "Superman", 55, 62
Women, 3, 6–8, 15, 24, 43, 56, 60, 83, 85, 86, 91, 92, 94–97, 109, 111, 113, 115, 120–122, 124–126, 129, 130, 135–137, 139, 142, 146–148, 152,
Won't Back Down, 8, 49, 50, 56–59, 62, 63

X

Xenophobic, 18

Y

Yesterday, 8, 105–116
Young adult, 7, 119, 135, 136, 138, 146, 147, 151
Youth, 25, 51, 52, 56, 123, 148

Printed in the United States
By Bookmasters